'BOXER SHORTS

an anthology

'Boxer Shorts
an anthology

All Rights Reserved © 2003

Published by Inkblot Books

Dayton, Ohio

www.inkblotbooks.com

ISBN 1-932461-00-0

Printed in the United States Of America

Cover image © 2003 Cherish M. Pageau
www.yellowgecko.net/cherish

To Wil
Wil Wheaton
Yes, that Wil Wheaton
TV's Wil Wheaton
Without whom we'd just be a bunch of aimless monkeys

Poetry

A Dilemma
Stephen Cote

Must I fight?
And which will win, my valor or mercy?
Will I pen a righteous page in history?
Bring fortune and fame to my family?
Embattled, my will, maims and kills
Embittered, my soul, must I grow old
Standing in the wake of tyranny?

When I do wrong
Will I be saved from the damned by my victories?
Or be cast from Eden for eternity?
What fruit have I tasted from the garden's tree?
It's all so unclear, am I far or near?
My sight is pure, then grows obscure
The sum of my decisions defines my destiny

Out, out of paradise - leave this garden, be cast to Hades
Burn in despair and the flames for eternity
So I fear should I misguide my destiny
Insipid, your heart, a cannonade rips apart
Vapid, your dreams, empty meaning
Realize life's delicacy and fragility.

Out Goes The Light
Stephen Cote

Out goes the light
Extinguished from sight
No feeling
Of transcended being

Ensconced by night
In my flight from life

Strength once within
Now eroded by wind
An ethereal breeze
Blows in me

Cautious steps into the unknown
A light that shines from the good lord
The faithful's awakening
Is happening

Reborn with angel wings
Fluttering swiftly, astoundingly free

Never time for prayer
Didn't care who was there
But pulled from the damned
By the good lord's hand

Don't know why he did it
I know I don't deserve it

Time has passed
Stars never last
The galactic truth

Wax the moon, sink the sun
A finite future for our daughters and sons

Out, out away from here
Yet somehow near
The promised land
For all women and men

Souls that have been liberated
Living in what a divine hand created
My nocturnal cloak
Now sun-soaked

And the angel wings
Are fluttering swiftly, astoundingly free

The corona in mind
And penumbra behind
Our thoughts of Earth

Wax the moon, sink the sun
It's a finite future for our daughters and sons

In the incandescent glow
Of what the light shows
Where will we go
Now that we know?

Taking flight into the unknown
Of a universe made by the good lord

My wings fluttering swiftly, astoundingly free

Aquamarine
Stephen Cote

Aquamarine silver dream
Invaders to the papacy
Of his sepulchral privacy
Cautious of the world

A communiqué by slight of hand
The creature reached out and then he ran
Deep into the dream machine
In which they'd arrived

He stumbled upon the secret plans
They planned to invade his home land
He stole out into the night
To warn the world they'd arrived

The heuristically-written alien scheme
Had infected his sanity
He blazed his way down a gravel road
To the safety of a neighboring home

Now, keep in mind, he spoke in code
He said "the commie-pinko faggots are down the road"
"Give me a shotgun and a magnum load"
"And I'll blast their Siberian ass."

Courage in his hand, bravery in a shell
He decided he'd blast the aliens to hell
He stole up on the ship
So close he couldn't miss

An aquamarine alien being
As friendly as could be
Was killed by some guy who never finished third grade
Because he didn't understand.

Falling Leaves
Stephen Cote

Memory, do not fail me;
A majestic oak's leaves
Tumbling and falling.
A precarious branch
Mourning its creased skein's blanch
Weeps spirals of methodical floating
Falling through a brisk wind pirouette
Upon an earthen collet,
The crumpled remains are fleeting.

Memory, do not forget me;
You, sir, have betrayed me.
Languishing in rivulets
Of pollen speckled rain,
Spattering the falling
Offspring moments of magnificence,
Are mere minutes of memories failing
To recall your pitch black heart.
Revel in those falling leaves.

Transposition
Stephen Cote

I speak of tongues long since lost
Of supple breasts splashed in exotic woodruff
For the virgins sacrificed on primeval altars
Whose steps are drenched in prepubescent red
And the self-proclaimed deity heralding
From above the servant's sun
A gospel of reveled maxims
Of events that transpired against us

My lips smack with the sulfuric residue
Left behind by a Conquistador's musket
His kiss for her ravaged temple of body and land
She exuded somnolence and melancholy spirits
Her humor drained of its black bile
Sucking in the dusty air
She whispered a dry and porous prayer
Of events that transpired against us

The Butterfly
Stargazer

The Butterfly is beautiful in its freedom.
Flying about in unbound Glory.
We love it for its beauty.
We want to be a part of it.
Lacking wings to fly with, we cannot though.
We want to possess it, own it.
So into the cage it goes.
Unable to fly, unable to be what it is, a beautiful butterfly.
Its wings will beat mercilessly against the bars looking for a way to
fly.
But still you see it as it was.
You only know that you own the butterfly.
Soon the cage is silenced.
The butterfly has lost its ability to fly.
Wings once full of color and life, now sit broken and bent at the
bottom of the cage.
The butterfly is dead inside.
It can't fly or be a butterfly.
Who would cage such a unique and beautiful creature?
Look around you, we are all Butterflies.
Some of us just can't fly anymore.

They Laugh
Samantha Lee

The clown makes them laugh.

They Laugh.

He gets out of his car.

They Laugh.

He walked to the doors.

They Laugh.

He looks sad to see her.

They Laugh.

She's all cut up.

They Laugh.

He vows to get the man.

They Laugh.

His blood is shed.

They Laugh.

He lays in a coffin.

They Laugh.

Four poems
Ionicus

Symposiast's Song

At three in the morning
The other less moderate drinkers
Are deep in conversation
On weighty matters of
    Morals
    Politics
    Religion.

You and I sit a little apart
Sharing a more leisurely bottle
And as we silently mock them
With glances we discuss
    Love,
    Without
    A word.

A new Astyanax

He hears the rifle's crack resound,
    He sees the bullet spinning, spinning.
He tumbles to the dusty ground,
    Where his wooden top is spinning, spinning.

The Tyrant

From his mouth they dangle,
These newly worked letters.
They resemble a beard.

His words are our fetters;
Their power can strangle.
They are why he is feared.

Suburban Haiku

Birds leaving the trees.
As a cat begins hunting,
A feather descends.

Butterfly
Miranda Hall

How could you do this to me?
You pin me down;
I am your butterfly –
Such a pretty little
Dead thing.
You touched my wings
And tried to hold me,
But only
For a moment
As you watched me
Die.

Rainbow Boy
Miranda Hall

You woke up in a brand new skin
Lick that grin
Off your lips
You've no idea what you're in for

Attitude will get you nowhere
You're already there
After all
We know you're invincible
Right?

It's not so easy
Rainbow boy
It's not just purple roses

What do you think you've become?
Following the Sun
Chasing Moon
We know all your secrets now

It's not that easy
Rainbow boy
Even purple roses die

Are you ready for the pain?
You're nothing
Without rain
Faded spectrum
Lost behind
The shadow of the Sun

An Angel's Peace
Miranda Hall

A starless sky,
A soundless night —
A chalice, full,
A blade beside...
A velvet shroud,
A satin bed —
A pounding heart,
A dizzy head...
A hopeless soul,
A crystal tear —
A searing pain,
A nameless fear...
A flash of steel,
A sip of wine —
A taste of blood,
A light, divine...
A final prayer,
A muffled cry —
A fading flame,
A whispered sigh...
A lifeless stare,
A sweet release;
A demon's death,
An angel's peace.

i begin
Miranda Hall

i want to cry
i want to die
i want religion
And i don't know why
i want to look in the mirror
And see right through me
i want to know why
i keep doing this to me

Is that really so much to ask?
i want to go deeper
But not too fast

i want to be
i want to see
i want to stop feeling
So fucking scared of me
i want to stand up to myself
And look me in the eye
i want to tell myself
It's time to say goodbye

Is that really the way it ends?
i want to be finished
But where do i begin?

Goddess
Miranda Hall

Her chin rests, soft,
Upon her hand,
A smile plays on her lips,
Her eyes cast down –
In dreamy gaze –
Her gown falls round her hips,
Her bosom, full,
And stomach, round,
Sparkle in the light –
Glow brighter than
The moon itself
On clearest autumn night.
Her hair falls free
Past graceful neck
And shoulders, white as cream –
Her beauty, pure,
Untouched by time –
An alabaster dream.

kiss
Miranda Hall

"I've never felt so warm,"
she sighed,
rolled back her eyes
and tried to hide
the shame and fear
and tears of bliss
and hid her mouth
inside my kiss.

cigarette
Miranda Hall

my cigarette is burning out
and the funny thing is that i don't smoke
but i've done nothing wrong
i have not sinned
and i'd die from something anyway
more than just the promises i broke
if i'm not careful
i'll burn myself
that would leave a scar
but i've got those already
and i'm not one to play it safe
at least i haven't so far
the fire is red and angry
and the moon is gray tonight
it could be ashes
it could be everything i've exhaled
i guess it could be just the clouds
but that would be too easy
and i'm just thinking out loud
i like the burn with every breath
no, that's not true
but then what is
or what isn't
and what's either or
i just like not feeling
everything else within
it's almost out now
and i'm almost ready
what am i waiting for?

Energy
Miranda Hall

In the darkness
I cannot see you
And our skin
Between us is too much

I can feel you
Within my soul's heart
And your heat
Is all that I can touch

You are a whisper
We are each other
I am the energy you feed me in each kiss
I do not exist
Until I feel your fingertips
You are all around me
Your energy surrounds me
And makes me real

Unfinished
Miranda Hall

I've nothing left to offer
I've reaped my soul of worth
And killed myself in trying;
I'm waiting for rebirth

I've stripped off all the layers
Cast off flesh and bone
Exposed now, I still cling to
A heart without a home

Never
Miranda Hall

He'll never know she loves him
She'll never feel his touch
He'll never kiss her tears away –
She's never hurt so much…

He'll never dream about her
She'll never see him cry
He'll never see inside her soul –
She'll never let him try…

He'll never get to hold her
She'll never let him go
He'll never know she loves him –
She'll never tell him so…

Phoenix
Miranda Hall

he is an angel
and he soars on gossamer wings
driven by fire
consumed by the flame
and i die just a little
each time he sheds a tear
but he will rise
from the ashes
and take to the sky once more
i am amazed at his strength
and touched by the weakness of his fear
and i die a little more
to know he holds me dear

Sorry Bin Laden there is only one Intimidator
Pamala Lauren Pacha

We've lost Dale Earnhardt.
Dale crashed and the crowd rose and cheered.
Damn right you don't mess with the Intimidator
He'll take your ass out we thought as we cheered.
This time he didn't get out of his car

No thumbs up and a smile from him this time.
The crowd went silent.
Jr. Sprinted to his dad's black car.
The world stopped turning for millions of fans
Who watched in horror as the medical workers cut Dale out of his car.

He would have turned 50 three months later
The Intimidator who was untouchable
A hero's watch stops ticking

He can't be healed
No robotic leg can fix him
No artificial limb will help him now

The dream catcher hangs over my bed
But can't stop the nightmare of his death
A friend, a dad and a hero died before our eyes

I cried more than ever
More than I did when Jammer died.
I want to get up and leave
Leave this unimaginable nightmare
Leave the pain and fly away
Maybe to Vegas

Monday the tribute songs begin
Kid Rock, Garth Brooks, and Tim McGraw
Any singer who knew this man, this hero

The music is made to soothe
It only causes more pain

The funeral service is on Thursday
Millions watch on TV crying
"The compass of this sport has lost its true north"

We were angry when we learned
His belt broke when he was hit
How could his belt break!
They aren't supposed to break.

The race went on the next Sunday
The men raced with heavy hearts
And Dale in their minds.

The angels cried for a loss of a hero
I cried during the race
The race wasn't right without him there

Race after race went by
With tributes to Dale every week
Reminding us of the loss
Reopening the wound in our hearts

Until that wonderful day in July
When Jr. took the checkered flag
Winning where his dad died

And we cried as he celebrated in the infield
We laughed when he surfed the crowed of people
We watched with Dale in our memories.

From there on we honored Dale through going on
Watching every race and not being down
But being glad Dale had been there
And his memory lives on through us

September 11ᵗʰ a new knife pierced our hearts
In honor of our nation we went on to race
One sign flew high
On it said: Sorry Bin Laden there is only one Intimidator
And it ain't you!

The Hand
Mark Carpenter

I wander the mist
of what is between
as I strain to glimpse
that which is unseen

the path before me
is narrow and tight
the air is thick
I carry no light

ghosts hover and dance
deep in that strange mist
shapes that frolic so
and cavort and twist

and a sound I hear
from out of the gloom
voices of laughter
of mirth and my doom

"What, ho!" I let shout
"would you have me for?"
and then ... silence
for they sing no more

no weapon on hand
and no charm nor spell
helpless against them
if they nay meant well

a sheen to my side
brighter than the rest
takes form of a man
in his courtly best

from behind his mask
he spies with one eye
the other is dead
shriveled and dry

he offers his hand
clad crimson and white
and all I can do
is nay run in fright

"A good draw, my friend."
he says with a grin
"With me at your hand,
you are sure to win."

and with that he does step
right off of the path
I follow meekly
for I fear his wrath

as the howls come
followed by their hosts
the knight does reply
with jabs and boasts

his arm sweeps a pass
through the forming hoard

leaving behind naught
but his gleaming sword

then out of the dark
steps the knight's own twin
not trimmed in scarlet
but obsidian

they clash with a roar
with thunder, with steel
neither can gain ground
in this even deal

"Low or high this hand,
I need you in play!"
the red knight did shout
as I saw him sway.

with courage unbidden
I leapt to his side
empty hands at best
bards could sing, "He tried..."

but the ruse paid well
as the twin did shift
he dubbed me a threat
let his swordpoint drift

before I can blink
the dark twin falls dead
the white of his cloth
turning a bright red

the knight points his sword
to a trail yonder
"Now take this way home.
Don't pause to ponder."

only a short jaunt
and now I am free
and see my dear home
standing before me

as I splash my face
beside a cool stream
I begin to doubt
was it naught but dream?

my eyes are drawn down
cards tucked in my belt
the Jack and the Ace
the hand I was dealt

In Search Of Marsha Larts

The Effects of The Martial Arts On The Spousal Lifestyle
-or-
How The MAs Have Changed My Life

Michael E. Thompson, A.A., B.S.N., M.S.N., C.R.N.A.

It began innocently enough; my son asked if he could "take Karate lessons." He was 8 years old and my wife and I thought it over, deciding that it would be good for him. Soon he was attending TaeKwonDo three times a week.

I was very surprised three months later when my wife announced that she was also going to train in TaeKwonDo. She said that it would be good exercise and that she would like to be able to defend herself if she ever needed to. At the time I thought it would be great for my wife and son to be able to do something together. Little did I realize that life as I knew it was about to change forever.

There have been many changes in my life over the last few years. After several months of class my wife announced that she was making changes in our family's diet. We would eat less fatty foods and eat more fruits and vegetables. I have nothing against a healthy diet... but I never realized that rice could be served 107 different ways.

My wife and son started going to tournaments. They have done remarkably well. I don't even mind going to seven or eight tournaments a month. I am very proud of all the awards and trophies they have won. However, having to build the extra room on the house to store all those awards and trophies was rather expensive.

My wife has gradually changed the decor of our home over the last two years. It started with a few little things, such as oriental prints on the wall, and a mural of Jackie Chan. We now eat sitting on the floor and sleep on futons. I am not allowed to wear shoes in the house and have had to learn to care for an assorted collection of Bonsai trees.

My wife's wardrobe has changed in the last two years. She used to wear jeans and t-shirts almost exclusively. Her attire now includes 17 different Doboks and 4 complete sets of sparring gear. I suppose I don't mind the new look too much... that black Ninja outfit she sleeps in is kind of kinky.

In the last two years she has amassed an impressive collection of martial arts paraphernalia. Our video collection includes the complete works of Bruce Lee, Jackie Chan, Samo Hung, and Jean Claude Van Damme. We have a large assortment of weapons, including 7 bo staffs, 6 pairs of nunchakus, 4 set of kamas, 6 katanas, a 3 sectional staff, 3 sets of sais, a steel whip, 16 shurikens, and 3 shinai. Next week I am to fly to China to purchase something known as a Nine Dragon Trident...

Our garage has become, in effect, a dojang. We have 2 heavy training bags, a headache bag, 2 wing chun dummies, and a Flexmaster III. I don't mind having to park my truck out on the street, but it is kind of hard to use my power tools in the attic.

Yes, the martial arts have definitely changed my life. I have even tried them myself on occasion. Sometimes my wife uses me as a sparring partner, especially when she is training for a tournament. I really don't mind too much. My ribs have healed nicely and I think the broken nose makes me look dignified. The doctors say I should get the use of my left hand back with only 8-12 months of physical therapy.

I need to end this now. I have to finish the laundry, clean the bathrooms, and get dinner on the table. My wife will be home soon and she tends to become angry when things are not done. She is not a whole lot of fun when angered, and I really don't like getting a boot to the head...

Ode To The Irish MA Tofu
The True Life Story Of A TKD Dork
K.A. Thompson

'Twas a month after New Years, and all through the Kwan
The students were shivering, though the heat was turned on.
Anticipation hung like a pall in the air
In hopes that the test results soon would be there.
The students were decked out in stiff brand new *gis*
(So it's a Korean art, forgive my slip, please)
And I in my red belt was feeling quite blue
For I was still no more than MA Tofu.
The test list would come, in spite of the fears
That some would leave smiling, and some leave in tears.
It mattered to me not, for I knew in my head
That my MA life would be spent left in red.
The test, it was boring, I survived in a trance
Stuck in the corner, left in horse stance
When what to my wondering eyes did I see
But a Black Belt pointing directly at me.
With a sharp little finger (he's short, name is Ben)
He beckoned to me, "Come join the class once again.
"You look mighty sad, and as nice as you are
"I thought perhaps that you might want to spar.
"Now, listen," he said, with respect and some glee
"This person you spar sure as heck won't be me."
He surveyed the students, looking at all
And he settled on Brett, who stood up by the wall.
As dry heaves before the lunch doth will fly
I met this Behemoth, toe to toe, eye to eye.
I put on my gear and adjusted my *gi*
(All right, it's a *dobok*, just have patience with me!)
And then in a flash, his kick it did come;
I resisted the urge to flee or to run.
As I drew back my fist, I was thinking I'd hit
And he grinned cause he knew I punched not worth spit.

He was cocky, I saw, sure he'd have me most beat
But had already forgotten what I once did with my feet.
My last test was awful, a board barely missed
And somebody's nose, with my foot it was kissed.
So I faked a wimpy punch and a front kick I did try
And it landed just so, and I thought he would cry.
His grim little mouth was drawn up in pain
And his attitude changed, yes his grin was in vain.
He shook off the pain, and then did he smile
My reputation with him up by a mile.
He nodded, respect, and then tried with new might
To make it a good one, make it a fight.
The Instructor, he watched, and he wanted to see
Had the horse stance and punching made a man out of me?
He watched as I bowed, and I shook Brett's big hand
Then pointed to me, where he thought I should stand.
No more corner for me, no more painful horse stance!
He noticed I cared, I was given a chance!
He turned to his box full of belts, and the test
Rewards for those rising, the best of the best.
The students were patient, no remarks made were snide
And new belts were worn with a keen sense of pride.
Then he stopped and he stared, and he pointed at me
He told me to turn, close my eyes, not to see.
My belt he took off, which he hung 'round my neck
And I wondered with fear, "What's he doing? What the heck?"
With a tug and a grunt a new belt he did tie
And it left me with more than a tear in my eye.
"You earned this," he said, "You never gave up.
And I felt you've become more than just one more *gup*."
He turned me around, with a slap on my back
And the belt, when I saw it—the belt, it was *black*!

MURPHY'S WORLD:
The Essays
Ian Murphy

Ian Murphy is a 4ᵗʰ degree black belt in TaeKwonDo and Freestyle Self Defense; these essays are excerpted from his monthly column Murphy's World, written for Martial Artists Wired.

Empowering Women

Women in martial arts are no longer a rarity. Walking into a martial arts school and encountering a large female student population is no longer as surprising as it was 15-20 years ago. Still, there are far fewer females than males entering the martial arts, and fewer still adult females willing to embrace the rigors of training.

Why?

In recent years the trend in psychology has been to examine unconscious motivations for behavior: why people do the things they do. Most of those explanations are too neat, feeble excuses that pass as reasoning to give credence to otherwise inexplicable actions. Drug use, bullying, promiscuity, and a host of other societal ills are brushed away by the wave of the psychological hand – your mother abandoned you, your father abused you, your friends teased you as a child; well of course you're afraid to trust and to love and to venture beyond your own doorstep.

Those explanations are too convenient. They lend a large and validating hand to people who have genuinely suffered in one form or another to adapting into and adopting the mold of a victim. They are not valid reasons for a person to mire themselves in continuing series of disappointment, trauma, and bad decisions. They are, at best, excuses.

I am not trying to be unkind, or refusing to understand the maladies of life that place stress on an individual psyche, or belittling true suffering. I am sympathetic to pain and disadvantage. I do, however, believe that life is a series of choices, and any single individual has the power to make those choices that will help bring himself above the circumstances that would otherwise label him as a "victim." This doesn't place blame at the foot of the victim; it simply acknowledges that anyone, regardless of circumstance, has the choice to rise above it all and move on.

I have a very close female friend; in most respects she has the right to lay claim to the title of victim. She would otherwise be able to rightly claim that life dealt her a dirty hand, and she would be able to justify turning inward to herself, to shy away from society and men in particular, to have become a promiscuous young adult and self abuser. The first time I met her over 25 years ago she sported a large, red, hand-shaped welt across her face. Over the next couple of years I witnessed innumerable bruises, broken bones, cuts requiring stitches—none for which she ever offered explanation, and at such a young age no one ever thought to ask. In hindsight I now know the cause; at 12 I could never have fathomed.

In mid-adolescence she encountered male brutality in the guise of a 19 year old male acquaintance who, after several beers, determined that the very act of accepting a date meant "yes," and no matter what, she would not return home as innocent as she had left.

As a young adult, a new mother, she witnessed the attempted abduction of her 2 month old infant; it was unsuccessful largely due to her own quick reaction time, but the attempt left the stamp of trauma. Anyone who has ever loved a child can understand the enormity of the act.

Under the accepted actions of today's notions of victimization, she could easily have embraced the accumulated baggage of her life and turned it into a series of bad choices, disappointments, and reckless behavior. Yet, she has not. Unpredictably, her emotional outlook is keen and optimistic; she harbors little fear other than a few odd personality quirks. Why has this person, to whom life has been determinably unjust, not fallen prey to the role of victim?

"Whatever I do, I am responsible for... the things that happened changed how I view the world, and changed me, but ultimately, whatever I do, in spite of anything else, is my own responsibility..." What she chose to do ultimately, was rise above and beyond the bad things in life to create the good.

A large part of that was the decision to never again allow herself to be in the position of physical abuse. "I've been there," she once told me, "I'll never be there again... and I have little patience with women who wrap themselves up in rape and use it as an excuse to keep the world out... All men didn't do it. One man did. That's all I need to remember."

This all brings me back to my original question of *why* more adult women don't seek practical, long term instruction in self defense. While the numbers of women in martial arts grows, so does the population of women with no training in the art of defending themselves. Women have made tremendous strides in all areas of life, a reckoning force in business, finance, management, government; they raise our children – some single handedly – run our homes and our lives and keep track of the infinite minute details that enable us all to live better. Women are increasingly present in facets of life that as little as 25 years ago were considered male-only domains.

Yet, still, in a male-dominated arena where women *should* be present in vast numbers, they are not. The demand of equality is being met with a stubborn resistance to empower.

It's a sad fact: women are often brutalized at the hands of men. Women can learn to protect themselves, yet in large numbers do not.

Is it because society in general frowns upon women engaging in combative activities? I need to ask why should women *care* what society (meaning men for the most part) thinks about the act of female survival. Women traditionally rise past the male-societal view of acceptable female activities; why is self-protection different?

In my own little world of ideals, our children would learn basic defense as a matter of course through our schools; our daughters would be armed early on with the knowledge and skills to protect themselves from the untoward of life. In Murphy's World women would comprise at least half of the martial arts community, making the choice to embrace self acceptance and defense of oneself over an ill-formed societal view. Women would buck the norm, shuck away the accepted notions of the acceptability of victimization.

If you empower a woman, she will never be a victim.

When It's Not "Can I?" But "Will I?"

You are undoubtedly the best student in your school. You have a flair for technique; you have speed, timing, and you have dexterity. Your practice of forms is enviable; while you work hard at it and deep down you know that what makes it seem effortless is hundreds of hours of careful attention to the basics, others watch in admiration, because you make it seem so easy. New students aspire to your level of expertise. Most students want to partner with you, or be there when you teach a class, because you know your art backwards and forwards, and you have an innate sense of how to teach. Your own instructor marvels at your dedication to the art and your willingness to pass on what you know. You are, in every sense of the word, excellent at what you do.

But—can you defend yourself?

The issue is often raised, whether or not proficiency in any given art will automatically give a practitioner the upper hand in an altercation; my experience with some very competent black belts over the last couple of years tells me that the training and the persistent quest for quality does not mean that one can adequately defend himself. Sometimes it's a matter of the way one was taught; their particular system might rely heavily on sport applications, or the school might take the road towards teaching a particular curriculum without regard for teaching the defense applications of those techniques in a manner that makes them immediately useful in a modern fight.

In the midst of all the different teaching methods available, and the drive to present a system which is more than adequate in terms of offering reliable self-protection and preservation of the fundamental roots of the art, there exist practitioners who excel at their art, who excel at teaching their art and making the information understandable, but who cannot use what they know for personal defense.

Over the years I have become acquainted with an individual who possesses incredible skill and has the ability to teach on levels I can only hope to attain. Technically her form is very good and her knowledge base sound, but when push comes to shove she will fold up into a tight little ball and start crying her eyes out. She *knows* how to defend herself, but her confidence, even through all her years of training, has been systematically eroded by an emotionally abusive father who methodically picked away at the layers of her self esteem and manipulated her into situations no child should ever face. The abuse is in her past, but she has not yet learned to accept herself and take as a part of her the confidence she has learned as a facade. In years of training, she has never felt worth defending, and has never given herself permission to defend.

With a good instructor, confidence comes with training; as you learn, you become more aware of your surroundings, you know that you have the tools to deal with situations as they arise, and the confidence builds on itself. Knowing you have that power, even though in all likelihood you will never have to use it, notches your self esteem up a few more points. It becomes not instinctive, not in the sense that a mother would die to protect her child, but reactive. A punch comes flying at your nose and you've blocked it without thinking. You don't need to think; you react.

There are some things that even those who are ready to defend themselves cannot bring themselves to do – like poking someone's eye out. It's gross. It's irreversible. It's not something many people want to learn. They don't want to know that they can have someone choking to death on their own blood within seconds. They want to defend themselves, but don't wish to hurt someone in the process. This is where a person has to give himself permission; a person must know, deep down, that they are worth it, that if someone else cares so little about them as to attempt to cause intentional harm, then they have right to react to protect, even if that means truly, deeply injuring another human being in some very despicable ways.

Other defense techniques, throwing techniques, leg locks, wrist locks, those are the easy things to learn because they don't come with much baggage; you can learn those because you know that when you go to bed at night, the worst you would be doing is breaking an arm or a leg, something that with time will heal. When you get right down to it and know that what you do can blind someone forever, or have them gasping for breath through a larynx crushed beyond repair, have them choking to death on their own blood, you have to make the decision: "Am I worth it? Do I deserve to live more than this scum who is attacking me?"

In this world exists a high number of advanced black belts who would have to honestly answer no; deep down they *don't* think that their lives are worth more. They can perform all the necessary techniques and teach them well, but they can't carry through, and not from lack of ability or desire. Because of their personal foundations, they cannot give themselves the permission necessary to use all means needed when an altercation arises.

When you decide that your life is just as valuable as anyone else's, your reactions will allow you to defend yourself, even in the most distasteful ways if necessary. There is not a single person out there whose life is not valuable; get the reactive response needed.

Give yourself permission to defend, and to live.

...

The Balance Of Life

Imagine, if from the very first moment that you took up a martial art and began training in earnest, that you never failed. Everything shown to you comes easily, as though it were already an integral part of your being, and it requires no effort to accomplish, only the sweat that comes with physically moving your body from point A to point B. You remember, subconsciously, all you are shown; if someone barks "*Chosan*" or "*Sam Il*" or "*Unsu*" you can perform the *poomse* or *kata* flawlessly. A static jump reverse double inside-outside crescent kick doesn't faze you in the least. The training requires such little effort that you breeze through from day one until your coveted black belt test in less than 2 years. You're nothing short of a prodigy.

So there you are, wearing a crisp, brand new black belt, left in charge of a room full of new students, and you're showing them how to get from the first technique in a form to the next, when some brave soul asks "Why? Why do we do that?" and you don't really know. *You* do it because it's what you were shown to do. It's what you are able to do without much conscious thought. The block precedes the punch which precedes the kick—what more do you need to know?

No one particularly likes it when bad things happen to them. Most people would rather go through life without being touched by illness or death; we would all prefer that those marriage vows we took in good faith remain as strong as was the intent behind them, no one wants to lose a job or fail an exam, there isn't a soul amongst us who would enjoy being told "I just don't love you, so goodbye."

The human instinct is to find the things that make life pleasant. We gravitate towards the things that interest us, that make our lives more peaceful and more pleasant. We avoid the pitfalls along the way, and strive to be as happy as we possibly can. Some of us subconsciously venture out onto paths that are inevitably contrary to our happiness and well being, but the shadows that lurk there aren't so obvious from the outset. The goal is evident: don't worry, be happy.

Still, if you have never failed, how do you measure your success? If you have never felt ill, where does your yardstick to measure your health begin? If you have never felt sad, how do you know if you're happy?

Several years ago, after 10 years of marriage, my first wife decided that for whatever reason (there were several, to be sure) it just wasn't working, and it was time to end the relationship as we knew it. This wasn't easy; we had been a couple since the very beginnings of puberty. I was content in the relationship, at least I thought I was. I never harbored any thoughts of leaving, or seeking out other women. I made the commitment and I intended to stick by it. My wife, on the other hand, saw what I did not: long, frequent business trips, restlessness, weekends buried in paperwork that could have waited, bickering over stupid things. She made the painful decision. She left. She took a chance for both of us and changed forever what had been intended to be a life long union.

Yes, it was painful. And I was angry for a time, mostly at myself for failing to recognize the truth. Yet not too long afterwards someone else entered my life, and changed my perceptions entirely. My sense of self soared; I realized then that contentment and happiness are not one and the same. You can be utterly content with spaghetti for dinner every night, but it's not necessarily healthy. By stepping outside the confinements of what I thought was happiness, I found the real thing. It was worth the pain, and it was worth the confusion of letting go of things in the past (and for the nosey, yes, I remain friends with my ex-wife, and wish her nothing but happiness with her new husband and six stepkids).

Last year, at what I thought was the apex of good health, I crashed and burned. I had a heart attack. My perception of healthy changed drastically. I had low body fat, low cholesterol, none of the markers for potential cardiac problems. I ate well. I exercised.

Surprise, surprise.

Earlier this year, without any real prep time, or warning, and without the benefit of Time in Training that should not have been ignored, I entered a rank test and passed. Did it make me happy that I could advance quickly, or make me proud of the accomplishment?

Not in the least. Contrarily, it disappointed and upset me.

It lacked balance.

There exist real reasons for the stumbling blocks of life. Call it the yin and yang of personal existence. When a life ends, it is profoundly sad; when a life begins, it is profoundly joyous. When one relationship ends, it hurts; when a new one enters your life, it brings back the excitement of living, and when it clicks well, the feeling is intense. When the rank test you were sure was yours for just showing up doesn't yield the results you expect, it isn't a failure; it's an opportunity to glean from the experience the little things you missed the first time.

If everything in your training comes to you without effort, with such ease that you never have to question why –or you can't answer someone else's "why?", then it's time to pry the proverbial coin up off the floor and flip it over to get a really good look at the other side. Nothing worthwhile should come without a price, at least not without effort. If you breeze from point to point without any self doubts, or questions about efficiency of your art, or its applicability, then something is wrong. You can't have total success without a measure of at least doubt if not occasional failure.

The balance of life touches everything.

Step By Step

My youngest son learned to roll over this summer. He surprised himself, and the sudden realization that he was not staring down at his toy on the floor but looking up at the ceiling made him cry. His brother laughed, his sister rubbed his tummy and told him he was all right. They proceeded to show him they could also roll, and spent the afternoon rolling around the living room, with a wide eyed infant staring at them like they were positively nuts.

My newest student learned to punch this summer. He surprised his parents, who were positive he would never look up from the floor, never think of striking out at anything, whether another person or inanimate object. His father puffed with pride, his mother cried. The boy uncurled himself, straightening his shoulders and standing tall, and punched again, a room full of fellow students watching without knowing the effort this young boy made to simply look them in the eye.

My youngest son learned to lift himself up to his hands and knees, and to rock back and forth. He knows, on some level, that if he can figure out how to make those hands and legs move, he'll be able to get from where he's at to where he wants to be. If he can just get them to work in tandem, the world as he knows it will be his.

My newest student learned to say "no" and to walk away. He knows, deep down, that if he can walk away from a bully, not cave in to the fear, he'll be able to pull himself up from the darkness of being the class punching bag to the relative safety of being just like all the other kids. If he can just convince himself he is just as good and just as valuable as everyone else, the world will be his.

My youngest son learned to sit up, and to eat from a spoon. He knows the pure delight that the food that should be nourishing him feels just as good all over his face, squashed into his hair, and thrown at the dog, as it does in his mouth. Without knowing, he understands that the things we have to do don't have to be boring; he can take something as simple as eating or bathing and turn it into the most wondrous thing he has ever done. He marvels at the feel of rice cereal between his fingers. He squeals with joy when water is poured over his bare belly. The very basic things of life are sheer pleasure.

My newest student learned to jump, and to kick. He knows the satisfaction of a form done right, and that the simple gold belt form he has finally memorized the moves to is just as much fun for him as learning an advanced form is to a brown belt. No one has told him that he is working hard, that he sweats because the physical effort is as demanding as the mental effort. He smiles broadly when told he's doing well, he laughs when he falls because he knows he has another chance to do it right. He's having fun. The very basics of the art he's learning are sheer fun.

Those first few months of life are so filled with change and rapid learning that it's easy to lose sight of the joy to be found in the very small things that are so important to learn before we can go on. Learning to roll, learning to rock back and forth on our hands and knees, smashing cereal into our hair and peeing in the bathtub are essential learning blocks; without them, sooner or later we'll meet something we can't figure out, can't get past. For the baby just going through those milestones, the process is nothing but fun, especially when the people around him giggle right along, aren't afraid to act silly, and don't rush the process.

The first few months of training are filled with as just as much rapid change and learning—and it's very easy, with so many students in need of our time and attention, to lose sight of the importance of those critical first steps, getting the foundation of each technique, and the joy it brings our students to not only learn them, but to be praised for the effort as well as the success. Teaching and learning in a martial art don't have to be deadly serious all the time; we enjoyed the learning process as infants, we can enjoy the learning process – as well as the teaching process – in our arts.

No matter what you've endeavored to do, it starts with those first small steps. If you skip them, sooner or later you'll trip. If we allow our infants to enjoy the process of growth, we wind up with happy, healthy children, and hopefully later on, well rounded adults. If we allow our students to enjoy the process of learning their art, we wind up with happy, well trained students, and hopefully later on, well rounded instructors. It all begins with that first little step, and the thousand to follow.

Between Bullets and Tears

" *...so what happens is that some boys can't cry tears. They cry bullets." – William Pollack, author of <u>Real Boys: Rescuing Our Sons From The Myths Of Boyhood.</u>*

Big boys don't cry.
Act your age – be a man.
Don't be a sissy, fight back.
Just don't *cry!*

One of the rules for underbelt sparring in our dojang is that no face contact is allowed. At red belt, adults may engage in light face contact by mutual consent; kids, however, are encouraged to avoid making contact with their sparring partner's face. The risks of permanent damage outweigh any training benefit derived from making face contact, so in the interest of our students' long term health and well being, it becomes one of the first rules they learn.

A few nights ago I watched two young students, one 7 years old, the other 9, both beginners, square off in the ring. Both boys, both free of fear, both eager to strut their stuff and show just how good they were, how tough and unbeatable. A little over a minute into the match, which wasn't much more than two wildmen swinging at air, the younger of the two made solid contact with the other boy's nose. It was a sickening dull thud that stopped them both in their tracks. The older boy immediately covered his nose with his hand and stared in total astonishment. The younger boy burst into tears.

It only took an instant to soak in the reactions of the students present;

males in their teens and early twenties grimaced, but made a determined effort to not watch the young boy crying distraught tears over having hurt someone. They obviously felt a certain amount of empathy for the young man holding his bruised nose in hand, but the look was clear: whatever you do, don't cry. And he knew his lesson well, he shook it off and was ready to resume fighting.

I ended the match and sent him off the floor to get an ice bag from the freezer; my wife drew the younger boy aside to console him and explain that no one was seriously hurt, nothing that a good apology couldn't fix.

It occurs to me now that in 2 more years, perhaps 3, the younger of the two boys will have developed that wall that most males do, and he'll be able to hold back the emotion, choke off the tears, and blow the whole thing off with a machismo-laden "you're ok, let's keep going."

My son will be 3 years old in September. He's a very determined creature, free-spirited, and unencumbered by what he will eventually perceive as the expectations of society. He has a caring soul, loves openly and without hesitation or reservation, and cries if he's hurt. He cries just as hard when someone else is hurt. His baby sister, only 18 months old, bumped her head on the bottom of the table; he raced to hug her, kiss the owie, and used the situation to sucker Mom for cookies for the both of them. He has no notion that his gentleness and freedom to express his emotions will someday be seen as less than masculine. He expresses what he feels when he feels it.

In time, he will learn to hide his feelings. He'll adopt the mask of masculinity, he'll toughen himself against the things that hurt him, he'll learn to choke back tears, to swallow them, until they no longer flow easily. He'll become the 9 year old in the ring, astonished at sudden pain, but unwilling to display any outward appearance of it.

And that saddens me.

I'm not an advocate of Tears in Training. I see no useful purpose in actively encouraging students of either gender to cry when it hurts; it *is* going to hurt, and it will hurt often. But the shame I saw drawn in the faces of other males present almost astonished me. I had forgotten The Code; I had let slip the details of growing into manhood, the unwritten rules that say you must not cry, you swallow it whole, but you do not cry.

Part of being male is aggression; testosterone alone makes men more aggressive than women. Part of aggression is anger—and part of training is learning to control anger before it controls you, before it clouds your mind and turns a situation where you may need to defend yourself or someone you care about into a situation of uncontrolled confusion. There's still that part inside that no matter the training, in spite of years of sweating to gain control of yourself, that refuses to let go. We let the dictates of society determine how we express ourselves—and when you can't express sorrow in tears, or joy, or tears of abject astonishment, it has to go somewhere. For some it becomes rage that feeds upon itself.

These are the boys who cry bullets instead of tears. The boys who, without any other direction or understanding of how to channel their feelings, harden that mask of masculinity and turn to violence. They are no longer capable of venting sorrow or frustration the way they did when they were small. No one has ever given them any other options. The message has been pounded into them through every available avenue: be tough, be strong, don't wimp out, don't let anyone step on you, and don't cry.

How many pre-adolescent and teenage males in your schools are encroaching into the gray area between understanding their feelings, how to express them, when to hold them back, and when it's ok to show them?

I had the opportunity to make a small dent in the testosterone armor and I did not take it.

Hindsight tells me now that I very easily could have been the one to step into the ring and comfort both boys; though only one was crying, I know well enough to realize the older boy was only practicing what he had learned would serve him well. I instead relied on stereotype: I let a woman address the tears, and I sent off a 9 year old to stoically handle his own pain. It's what's expected.

It's not what is right.

Like it or not, we are role models for our students; male instructors have the golden opportunity to be for their young male students an example of what a man can be. We don't always have to be tough, we don't always have to hide behind the masks we learned to wear so well as children. We can be gentle, we can scoop up a crying child and comfort; we can, through our own example, let them see that real men can be tender, real men do have feelings, and real men display them without being wimps.

It's a major task to cut through the stereotypes we've woven around ourselves throughout life; in a place intended to train people to fight, and to fight hard, tenderness is very nearly an anomaly. This is a chance, however, for our male students to witness something they may never get elsewhere, to learn something very subtly they cannot get from the myriad of action movies and cable TV they watch; they can learn that this toughness is only a small part of who we are. No matter how skilled and tough in the ring, how well we can fight, they can learn from us the skills to cope with the emotions they've fought to bite down on.

Sometimes big boys *do* cry.

Gutting It Out

Thirteen people stand on the workout floor, ready to test. Several are physically gifted students who should be able to sail through the test without much difficulty. Two are students with well defined problems, one of them has never been able get more than two inches off the ground, and she probably never will; the other has physical disabilities which make many techniques impossible. All know the techniques and forms on which the test will be based; if not, they would not have been issued the invitation to test in the first place.

I've heard it whispered in moans in the locker room that testing is a waste of time; if we already know the students who are testing know the material, both mentally and physically, why don't we just give them the belt and move on? It can't be for the money—we don't charge for testing.

There's the *Power Of The Deadline*. It can push a student to work harder, break beyond any barriers they feel they have—some real, some imagined. It's tangible proof that the hard work pays off, that a prolonged moment of stress can be met with success. When you know something will not just be handed to you, but it must be earned, you'll work at it if you really want it.

In the effort, there lies the success.

All of our testings are open; students and family are free to come and observe. That doesn't mean, however, that observing previous tests will indicate to a student what he should expect. Testing protocol can change to suit the needs of the day; where one test might have seemed relatively easy, another may not. While watching students warm up, we are still formulating this particular test.

So here we are, with thirteen students eager to start, and to get it over with. Most of them undoubtedly feel they have nothing to prove; they've done it all in class over and over. They've sparred, they've sweated through forms, they've done their time on the mat, throwing and being thrown, they've each demonstrated a measurable knowledge of self defense; when presented with a series of attacks, each is capable of offering more than one defense tactic as response. Some are better than others. Still, there is the possibility that more than one will leave the test disappointed; in spite of their abilities proven in class, they may not find success in this test.

Since this is an advanced rank test, all were cautioned to set aside a good portion of their day. Previous tests were merely a rehashing of curriculum, two hours at most, with the physical exertion required comparable to that of a good conditioning class. None had any reason to expect anything different when the test began; when the warm up ended nearly an hour later (which were not the familiar exercises they expected, but more of an aerobic class format), more than twice as long as the class norm, most began to suspect this would not be the cake walk they had hoped for; some began to expect it was the torture they had feared.

The grumbling began at the water fountain. "What does this have to do with the test? If I wanted to prance around I'd join a gym."

The grumbling continued in the weight room, angry hushed groans of bewilderment; what in the world did weight training have to do with testing for a red belt or a brown belt?

While conspicuously ignoring those comments, we focused instead on the few who were not questioning motive, but doing everything asked of them, with the best effort they could put forth.

Nearly two hours later, when most expected this test to be over, it finally began in earnest. Tired and exhausted, they assembled back on the floor for forms. While some may have assumed that after all the previous sweating, we would require only the advanced forms, we began at day one, white belt basics. When taken through to the final form, our black belt form, all were offered the chance to step aside if they were unfamiliar with it; most chose the opportunity to rest, to catch their breath. Only five took the chance to try it, even though they had only seen it a few times and had been through it in class two or three times at most.

There were five different versions of the same form going on at the same time; the student who cannot get off the floor modified the form on the spot to suit her limitations and removed several jump kicks. The others simply did what they remembered and formulated the rest on their own. In spite of what was, by then, sheer exhaustion coming at them from every angle, and muscles burning with use, none of those five gave up. While they may not have known the form, the success was in the effort.

After the last sweat drenched punch, the remaining students lined up, fully expecting this was the end; hope, at least, was evident in their faces. Instead we dragged out the mats for defense drills. We attacked, they responded. We attacked harder; some put forth benign efforts that clearly said "I don't want to do this anymore." Some gave their best efforts, which, because of fatigue, were clearly less than their abilities—but their fire was not gone.

With the mats put away, the hope that this was over was obvious pleading in the eyes of most. I saw raw determination only in a few faces. In that determination, I also saw trust. These few knew that in spite of the torture, I would not push anyone to the real breaking point; I would not allow harm to come from this test.

I pulled out my sparring gear. Clear defeat blanketed several students when they realized that they would not be sparring with their equally fatigued testing partners, but that they would be sparring with me. Most of them ran around the ring, avoiding contact, avoiding looking at me directly. A few made obvious effort to fight back and defend. One, who knew I would not hit hard, made the attempt to distract me with cries of a sharp leg cramp; when I moved in to make sure she was all right, she kicked me square in the chest. Yes, I saw it coming. Yes, I could have blocked. Sometimes allowing the shot to come through is the right thing to do. She was not giving up. I could have kept her in that ring until she could no longer stand. She intended to fight until I said the fight was over. She deserved that shot.

No, she cannot jump. She cannot spin well. Her balance is not perfect and her speed is not always good enough to close the distance. She does, however, have a keen sense of what she is doing, she knows her technique, she knows her forms inside and out, and she can differentiate between practical and show, and she can defend herself—but most importantly *she does not quit.*

She had, at the onset of the test, hoped to leave as a first gup brown belt; she left as a black belt candidate. She may never possess the raw talent and sheer ability others have, but she has the tenacity of a black belt.

No one walked off the floor at any point and refused to continue; some put out more effort than others, but all did give what was, for them, a best effort. All passed, but some *shined*. They gutted it out past expectations, both their own and mine. The most physically talented student cannot match the gift of that determination. Most, I think, learned the value of the test that began with no martial arts meaning. What comes with ease is not always what is worth rewarding. What comes with effort and determination is.

Amazing Grace

The first time I saw Justin Simms he was three years old. He lived in a 4 bedroom house with 14 relatives, slept on a twin mattress on the floor of his cousins' bedroom, played contentedly in the kitchen, on the floor, which was located near the back of the house—the "safe place." He did not dare venture outside to play in the yard, could not fathom the idea of a swing set or sandbox, and the grass out front was only something the neighbor's untrained, ill-kept dog used as a waste repository.

Justin's world was inside that house; unlike many of the houses in his neighborhood—a place he rarely saw—his was a home. He lived without fear and was protected by a large family who dreamed mostly of Justin growing up and growing away from the neighborhood. They had, after all, managed to raise two young girls into womanhood, safe and unscathed by the turmoil around them, and had seen them both into college and one into a successful government career. With the same guidance, Justin could escape the grip of the city gangs.

I was an anomaly to Justin. His only vision of white people was through the television screen, and although only three, he was keenly aware that what he saw emanating from that box was not real; nothing there had a connection to his own reality. When I walked through the door, he had his first face-to-face contact with a white man; being three, he was not shy about exploring his curiosities.

It took him a very long time to believe that my skin was real skin; he lifted my shirt, studied my chest, looked at my back. He even lifted my pants legs and pulled down my socks, checking everything he could to see if this strange person was white all over. And when he was done, he just smiled and told me I was "funny lookin'." There was no judgment there, no preconceived notions about who I should be or how I should act. Justin was his own world of innocence and opinion, and as long as I was willing to get down on the floor and play with his cars with him, and as long as I did not mind reading the same story to him countless times, I could be his friend. I fell in love with this little boy, and if I could have, I would have taken him home with me then and there.

The next time I saw Justin Simms he was six and a half years old. He was quiet and unmoving, twisting the handle of a vinyl gym bag around his fingers, unwilling to look up and meet the eyes of anyone in the room. Still years away from adolescence, his face had the tired, worn look of someone old, and he carried himself with an air of distrust. He had not forgotten me; we spoke often on the phone, he remembered Christmas and birthday gifts that came without fail, and reminded me that I was still "funny lookin'." Still, he refused to approach me with the same abandon he had as a curious toddler.

He eyed the swing set in the side yard with suspicion; he sat at the edge of the sandbox in the front yard tensely, watching his younger cousins play, but held back from actual participation. He looked up occasionally to take in the surroundings of trees and blue sky, and watched with unbridled amazement as birds flocked to a feeder stand, and as a rabbit hopped confidently past the garden. What he did not do, something that should be as natural as breathing to a six year old, was play.

For the first time in his young life, he had his own room; his bed was not a mattress thrown on the floor, but a full bed. His room was ready for a boy to destroy in the way that kids do, a bookcase waiting to be filled, a toy box stocked with typical little boy cars and Legos, with room for whatever else his young heart would want. He touched none of it. Instead he sat close by as the adults talked, he absorbed every word, watched every nuance. There was no little boy there any longer, and I wanted to know what had happened to Justin Simms.

His uncle stated it simply and succinctly: "He went outside..."

Brad Simms has been, for all of his own childrens' lives, the force that kept the family together. While at questionable odds with the way he made a living to support them, he made sure his house was filled with love, rules, and more love. He pushed education as a value he would not permit to be belittled; he instilled in his family a deep abiding faith that if they did what was right, worked hard enough, and stayed away from those he had no choice but to deal with, they could rise above their own circumstances and be better than society wanted them to be.

His youngest nephew was no exception. He wanted for this boy the things his own children had been able to make for themselves: advanced education, careers, and families that did not have to hide in houses with barred windows. He wanted the child to have a life where the sound of a bang meant someone's car was backfiring, not that someone one street over was being shot. He was not, however, Justin's father, and when Justin was 5 years old, his mother moved from their house, and took her son along.

Justin went outside, and he was never the same.

I have never pressed Brad Simms for the details of his life in the neighborhood in which he raised his two daughters. It was always enough for me that he loved his children more than his own life, that he treated them with respect and honor, and that he wanted for life to be better for them than it had ever been for himself. When Justin's mother moved out, with the rest of his family old enough to make their own life decisions, Brad left his home and moved to be closer to his oldest daughter and his grandchildren. He kept contact with his sister and exerted as much influence as he could over his young nephew's life, but with the miles between them and the realities of life in an inner city neighborhood, his influence was diluted. When Justin's mother realized her little boy no longer felt safe, when he knew things that no child should ever know and had seen things most adults never will, she made the most painful decision of her own life: she packed up what few things he owned, and sent him to live with his uncle.

I wanted, though, to know what had happened to transform Justin from the curious, outgoing, happy toddler I first knew, to the quiet, seriously tense little boy who stared at this family of virtual strangers with suspicion and trepidation. His curiosity hadn't vanished, I could see that much from the occasional light that popped out when he watched the wild animals, or when he realized his baby cousin was doing something for the very first time. It was kept in check, reigned in tightly. He no longer felt free enough to explore.

After weeks of quiet adjustment to his new surroundings, Brad brought Justin to the dojang. Ostensibly, it was to show him where his older cousin, Brad's daughter, disappeared to every afternoon, but we all also wanted to see if it would spark some interest in him. He watched for a while, shrugged and said in no uncertain terms "I can do any of that. I don't need no lessons."

Let onto the floor with protective gear and the freedom to try, Justin came at me wildly, kicking and hitting, with a keen instinct for what would hurt the most. Had I been another six year old boy, I would have been seriously hurt. He fought as if he meant it, and yet he soaked in every detail about his surroundings. He stopped swinging long enough to ask about the flowers he'd seen in a vase in the lobby.

"Who died?" When assured no one had, he balked. "Flowers are for dead people. They get shot, they die, then you put flowers down on where they got shot." When asked if he had ever witnessed a shooting, he looked at me as if I had asked the most inane question possible. Everyone, he knows, has seen another person shot dead in the middle of the street. It's just the way it is. You don't even have to see it happen to know if the dead was young or old, male or female. All you need is to see what is there on the street the next day; flowers and ribbons, or teddy bears for the very young. Candles and crosses sometimes.

"You know," he tells me earnestly, without a trace of disgust, "when dead people lay there a long time, their bodies get hard."

Over the next few weeks, while summer slid by and Justin came to the dojang to "fight the old man" he began to relax and began to talk more. At six and a half he has seen more than anyone ever should. He can tell you what a prostitute is, where to go in his neighborhood to see the spot in the park where used condoms litter the ground; he knows that a magazine is not always something you read, but a clip in which bullets are loaded. He knows, too, that had he stayed with his mother, he would "be like everyone," and either die before he turns 21, or end up in jail.

Justin has lived through the stereotype of urban childhood, he is proof in the flesh that the world in which my wife grew up but does not speak of exists. He is a testament to my father-in-law's wisdom and courage in remaining in that environment to be a positive influence on youth. He is a young soul still able to grow the wings he will need to soar, he can rise above the brief time he spent surviving there. He is luckier than most: the boys with whom he plodded through kindergarten will not be so lucky. More than half will wind up in gangs. Some will die before they hit puberty. Most will live in poverty and will always suffer the slings of racism.

Every single one of the students who have come through our dojang door have done so for a reason, yet I would bet real money that none have seen the realities of Justin's life; in seeking to learn to protect themselves they are guided by the ghosts of media violence as seen on television, whispered stories they hear of what happened to someone else. Some have experienced real brutality and choose to prepare themselves for the possibility it may happen again. Yet none have lived it on a consistent, day to day basis, and none assume that bodies on the street are a simple fact of life, and that flowers are only for the dead.

There is a grace in surviving the horrors of life. When it means escaping the rings of violence, bypassing the lure of drugs and the easy money they bring, coming to understand that sex is something you share and not something you purchase, that there is a dignity of self that is a person's right and not something to be given or taken away, it is incredible. I can teach my students to defend themselves, I can teach them to avoid situations that present real physical danger, but I cannot teach them the things that a hard life can place at their feet. That a six year old can look into the bowels of life and not lose himself to disgust, but emerge intact and with more grace than most adults have in a lifetime, it is more than just impressive. It is amazing.

Bang Bang You're Dead....

I should make it clear up front that I own a gun. Several, in fact. I am licensed to carry a concealed weapon and if you plop me down on a target range and pop up a very small target I will probably hit the center of it 9 out of 10 times. I can hit moving targets, static targets, full body outlines or things smaller than a playing card zooming by at fairly high speeds. I have spent countless hours developing my skills, mostly out of necessity, partially out of ego. I am not anti-gun.

However, I will say this: if you use a gun as an offensive weapon, you are nothing more than a coward.

We all grew up playing cops and robbers, pointing our index fingers at each other and screaming "BANG! You're dead!" and we all took our turns at melodramatic death, clutching our chests and wailing loudly as we slowly dropped to the ground in a convulsive fit. It was funny, it was cool, it was nothing but play-acting, and it was a time in our young lives when death had not yet touched the fabric of our beings; the surrealism of play had nothing to do with the realities of life. We played a violent game with pacifistic hearts, we took our turns at being dead and we took our turns at pointing fingers and shooting our friends, but when dusk settled we all got up, said goodbye, and went home.

The chance that any of us had ever seen with our own young eyes a *real* gun was slim at best; my father was a police officer, and I vaguely recall catching a glimpse of his sidearm once, other than when it was holstered as part of his uniform, but other than that glimpse, it was kept well hidden from my curious eyes. Several of us owned bright shiny plastic replicas of cop guns, or if you were really cool, you had a metal cap gun that barely worked, but real guns were beyond our comprehension; we knew they existed and what they did, but we didn't think much about it, because those were for grownups and not for kids. They were for cops, and maybe hunters, although we were all sure hunters did not use handguns; they used rifles, and they came home with more stories than dead animals.

Today the average 5 year old knows what a gun is and that it is a weapon intended to kill people. Not that it's something a cop has, or maybe a hunter: it's a weapon for use in killing people. Bad guys have them and shoot people they don't like. Cops have them and shoot bad guys. Mom has one in case someone breaks in, and she says she'll kill anyone who comes near her.

It's as easy as being a patient soul to get a gun now. Go to the store, pay for it, wait 5 to 10 to 15 days depending on the state in which you live, and the gun is yours to take home. You don't have to have special training, you don't have to prove you know how to clean it without killing the kid in the next room, you just have to pay and wait. No one is required to tell you that if you intend to use this gun for self defense purposes, you're more likely to get killed with it because you choked and had it taken away from you, and then used on you. Just pay and wait.

My 11 year old nephew knows that somewhere in my house is a safe with at least 2 guns. He also knows that if I ever catch him purposely looking for it, he'll be banned from my house for a very long time. If I were to ever catch him with so much as a finger on my gun, or any other gun, I would probably do something I have never done to a child; I would probably whack him one. His older brothers also know that somewhere in the house my guns are locked away, but they've reached the age where they either don't care, or just plain know better. The difference between them, and the difference between me at their ages, is the loss of innocence. Not only are they acutely aware of weapons and functions, they have had more than a glimpse of the real thing. They have all held a gun, pointed a gun, and fired a gun. They know the smell of a spent shell, the power of recoil. The know that a hole blasted through a paper target equates a hole in a body. An injury. A potentially fatal wound.

They graduated from playground games of cobs and robbers, using their fingers as the weapon, to standing in a cold firing range with an uncle bent on making sure they learned the power of the gun, to handle one correctly, and that the weapon they hold in their hands is not the innocuous necessity their chosen entertainment venues make it out to be. You don't shoot someone and have them spring back to life in the sequel. You don't pull a weapon on someone and count on there being an empty chamber for the sake of drama. You can't shoot and then expect to put a quarter back in the slot and start all over. They need to know now, while their opinions are being formed by experience, that it is not a toy. It is real. And it can kill them.

There are no weapons in TaeKwonDo. It is an empty hand art; you fight with your hands, you fight with your feet; your opponents, on the other hand, might very well be armed with a weapon. I have heard from several students already that they see no value in learning to use a gun as part of their training; they came to me to learn to defend themselves with the weapons God graced them with, and nothing more.

Whatever God graced them with, it was not the innate knowledge of what to do when staring down the barrel of a gun, nor how that gun will react when the person holding it is kick, or grabbed. God didn't plant seeds of wisdom that will help even the most physically talented martial artist to keep from inadvertently redirecting the fire of that gun towards an innocent bystander. God may have given them all weapons in the guise of hands and feet and heads, but he also gave them brains.

I am not advocating that every person out there with aspirations in the martial arts rush out and join the NRA (for those politically oriented, no, I am not a member). I *do* strongly advocate that as part of defense training the very basics of handling and firing guns be learned from a trained professional. In a nation where the right to bear arms is constitutional law, more and more people are opting to do so – and many of them are the bad guys, the people who would seek out to cause you deliberate harm.

The times when we stood in our yards and pointed innocent fingers at one another, chanting "Bang bang, you're dead, fifty bullets in your head..." is long gone. The guns are real; the bullets are real. In our grown up world, so should be our education. It does not shortchange ones' martial arts training to admit that guns should be a part of it; that training can enhance it. Whether you ever choose to own a handgun or not, the odds favor you more if you know the full potential of a weapon.

Shorts and Not So Shorts

King Kong Memorial High
Alistair Coleman

If you leave London to the West, you soon leave the urban sprawl behind you, and with the temple of noise that is Heathrow Airport in your wake you eventually reach the green fields and small commuter towns and villages of Berkshire. That is precisely what my family did in the winter of 1972, with younger brother, older sister and parents leaving Fulham behind for a new place in Twyford, some thirty-five miles to the west.

My parents as medical students tired of the endless round of toga parties, rag weeks and toga parties and set off in search of the good life. We travelled the world: Ireland, Canada, the States, before grimy London drew us back like a magnet. Twyford was as far as we could get, with dad dragged back to the capital by train on a daily, soul destroying basis.

We grew up in a quiet cul-de-sac with the local swimming pool literally through the hedge at the end of the garden. We played, we learned to ride our bikes, we made friends, and of course, we went to school.

School was Polehampton Juniors, the village school to which the swimming pool belonged. It was literally squeeze through a hole in the hedge and I was there. Turn left for free swim, turn right for school.

I hooked up immediately with Geoff Cooke, who was asked to look after me on my nervous first day, becoming a lifelong friend in the process. His imagination was endless, he invented stuff, make life-threatening gadgets, tried get get us all killed experimenting with battery acid and spent playtimes planning even more dangerous things for us to do. His mum cooked the best egg and chips on the planet, and her 1937 classic Austin Seven car was the envy of the neighbourhood.

My brother Andy, on the other hand, fell in with Dave Mac, who enjoyed looking up girls' skirts by sitting under the climbing frame, and spent rather a lot of time outside the headteacher's office as a result.

When I reached eleven years old, it was time for Big School. No more jumping through hedges, it was up the big hill, down the other side and over a main road thundering with traffic before I even got close. I was allowed to make this trip on my bike, which just hiked the danger up several notches above and beyond what kids would be allowed to do these days. But I was not alone.

There were over a thousand kids at Piggott, which some genius built in the countryside slap bang between Twyford, Wargrave and Charvil. Even though it was miles from anywhere, going to school by car was virtually unheard of in the seventies. You were looked upon as a bit of a wimp if mummy dropped you off at the school gates. Laughing at the dangers of the Bath Road, hundreds of us swarmed to school on our bicycles.

The school was ruled with a rod of iron by Dougie Bull. When he wasn't headmastering, he was a magistrate and knew the law and all kinds of cruel and unusual punishments inside out. His catchphrase, used whenever indiscipline reared its ugly head, was "If this is the law of the jungle, then I'm King Kong". I could see the likeness.

When you're thirteen years old, you find all kinds of things funny. Most of these things happen to involve sex, nudity and bare genitalia in some form or another. It was hardly surprising that anything involving one or more of these combinations was certain to be a hit at our school. So on one spring afternoon, when all these things came good, our lives were changed forever. The Phantom Cock struck for the first time.

I remember that sunny day in 1979 like it was yesterday. School had finished and we headed to the cycle sheds to pick up our bikes. So many of us cycled to school that the bike sheds filled an entire tennis court. As I reached my bike, something was different. Wrong. There, chalked on my bike saddle was a crude picture of a man's cock. And I wasn't the only victim. There were half a dozen nobs scrawled across bike saddles in a frenzy of phallic graffiti.

The next day, our mystery artist struck again, only more so. At least twenty bikes had been graffiti-ised, including an eighteen inch member on the giant saddle of one lad's Raleigh Chopper. As the week went on, our school's answer to Picasso got braver and braver, and by Friday, the bike shed was a sea of chalky cocks. The villain became brazen in his excess. There, scrawled on the music block wall behind the bike shed were the words "The Phantom Cock Strikes Again." It wasn't big, and it wasn't clever. A hero was born.

By the following Monday, Cock Fever swept the school. Not a single piece of chalk could be found in any classroom, and the staff had to break out emergency supplies. "Puds," as they came to be known appeared anywhere where the perpetrator could spare a few seconds without being spotted. The playground was awash with them, as were walls, corridors, exercise books and the backs of lower school pupils who could be held down while a pud was chalked onto their jersey.

One genius got his gang to steal every single bag, satchel and lunchbox they could lay their hands on, and created a massive sixty foot long member on the school field as the masses cheered and the teachers watched in puzzlement.

It couldn't last. This was one craze that burned short and bright. The teachers had already gotten wind of the bike-puds after the Phantom Cock carelessly chalked up Mrs Clark's bike saddle, and a special watch was kept on the bike sheds. They didn't have long to wait, the Phantom Cock was unveiled as Rob - a kid from my class - who was allowed to go home for lunches and used the time he had in the bike shed to carry out his calling.

With our leader in the cooler, it was only a matter of time before the Pud Craze was brutally suppressed. And it came during morning assembly at the end of the second week. We'll never know who did it, but the deed had somehow been done. Rob, to this day, denies all knowledge and I believe him. It was made all the worse by the fact that we were a church school, and the local vicar insisted on preaching to us on a weekly basis. In short, we caught hell.

Someone managed to switch the slides on the overhead projector. We were supposed to see the words to "At the Name of Jesus" twelve feet high on the wall of the school hall. Instead, we got the biggest pud in the history of the world. With plums. And hair. And a fuck-off big purple helmet spurting jizz. As Mrs Clark on the piano launched into the hymn's intro in blessed ignorance of what was projected on the wall above her head, there was a moment of stunned silence, followed by roars of teen-age laughter.

I was utterly helpless, tears rolling down my cheeks, bent double with hysterics. And I wasn't alone. The cream of British youth was helpless at the sight of the world's biggest wang. Quite a few of the girls, too, one couldn't help but notice, not to mention one or two teachers.

Two people NOT laughing however were "King Kong" Bull and the vicar. It was Wrath of God time, which was to be visited upon us regularly over the next few weeks. We got the "King Kong" speech, followed by the cruel and unusual punishments. All graffiti on walls, books or other school and private property was banned. The bike sheds had a guard mounted, and all chalk supplies were strictly monitored. All the boys (but funnily enough, none of the girls) were made to spend breaks washing puds off walls, and the vicar came in even more often than usual to lecture us on good, healthy, clean living and the benefits of cold showers. It was hell on Earth.

If cycling to the place wasn't bad enough, we made it our life's work to make school as dangerous as possible for our fellow students. There were risks to be taken in the name of our art, but the teachers soon wised up to us. And there laid the problem. You may think you're a comedic genius with an outrageous plan to take over the school and then the world; but to the adults, you were just another teenager with an attitude problem. We were always caught. But that didn't stop us from trying.

School held few priveleges for us. We were routinely told by our teachers that we were "the worst behaved year we have ever had," and after the seventh fire alarm of the week I was inclined to believe them. That opinion was possibly something to do with the fact I was squeezing one out in the toilets in the Science Block at the time, and I was torn between finishing the job and running for my life. So, as the old saying goes, it was up to us to create our own entertainment.

And that came in geography class, held in freezing cold temporary classrooms separate from the rest of the school. The teacher, "Harry" Harrison was about ninety years old and was as deaf as a post. Because of this, he relied on the pupils to tell him when the school bell had gone for the end of the class, the poor trusting fool.

Jenny had an innocent face. "The bell's gone sir," she would say, fluttering her eyes rather too unnecessarily. And we were free.

With five or ten minutes to burn, we slouched up to the "old school" where our next lesson was. We hung around in the corridor, a fifty yard stretch of highly polished floor that became a race track as soon as the first-years were released from their French-lesson hell. We leant against the wall outside class one, our bags full of schoolbooks at our feet, chatting about girls, the latest bands and why Spurs were so crap.

Bell. A door at the far end literally thumped open, and the first formers exploded forth down the hall, idiot grins on their faces evidence of their escape.

Timing was critical. These kids may have been going like the clappers, but make your move too early and you'd be sussed out. Too late and it just becomes messy. As the first runner approached, Ernie nudged his bag out into the middle of the hallway, straight under the feet of the leading runner.

Invariably, there would be a moment of almost serene silence, followed by a cry of "Muuuuuum!" as the victim took off and landed somewhere in the cloakroom chin first, coming to a halt among the lost property. With exceptional timing, you could take down two or three of these idiots before the hall became too crowded, and we'd mark the end results out of ten. It never ceased to amaze us that this trick worked day after day, week after week without the fools wising up to us. But we had reckoned without Mr. Prince.

Prinny was our games teacher. He was a former boxer of some repute, even if he had a face that looked like every punch had got through. He was as hard as nails, and even if we weren't scared of him, he had our respect and a certain amount of hero-worship. He was also the king of the ironic punishment, as we were soon to find out.

Cut back to the Hall of Fear. First year number 387 flew through the air, wondering what the hell happened to his feet, and why the ground is coming up to meet him so quickly. Round the corner came Prinny just in time to see the victim to come screeching to a halt at his feet. He didn't even have to ask what the bloody hell was going on, we were caught like Treens in a disabled space-cruiser, our faces a tableau of guilt.

Time froze. He said nothing. We were silent, afraid to make the first move. The victim scuttled off, like scared townsfolk fleeing from a shoot-out in a western movie. An evil smile filled Prinny's face. He silently beckoned us towards him. We were doomed.

Prinny made us polish the school floors for a week, while he allowed the cleaners to sit back and offer us encouragement such as "You've missed a bit" and "Only thirty-seven classrooms to go."

Were we to be discouraged by such a set-back? Well, yes we were to tell you the truth. No more would we attempt the Flight of Doom in the Old School corridor, for we knew that Prince was watching us, some-how, somewhere.

One-legged Mike, however, was not to be defeated. One-legged Mike only had one leg, and had a false foot that was held on with buck-les. Instead of kicking a bag out at the racing first-years, he oh-so-subtly let his foot fall off in the face of the charging hoardes. There were hys-terical screams that shattered glass. One girl fainted, while another puked all over our freshly polished floors, and there was the faintest smell of urine which may or may not have been Filthy Pete going past. Even Prinny, not fooled by "Sorry sir, it just dropped off," couldn't think of an ironic punishment for that one.

So we all got detention, forever, followed by the "King Kong" speech from Bull. The guy had no imagination.

Things weren't any safer in the playground. It was all a big effort to impress the girls, you see. We were at that age when hormones were raging, and in the post-punk suburban apocalyptic nightmare that was the dawn of Thatcher's Britain, what they said in Smash Hits was law. Just as long as we didn't break the school rules. There were limited opportunities to dress the part what with us all wearing the same school uniform, so you had to act tough to survive in the shallow end of the gene pool.

The uniform sucked. All you could do was something with the tie, and that was at the whim of the fashion police. Sometimes the knot had to be as big as your fist, later that term the school fashion gurus decided that the knot had to be the size of a raisin. The particularly fashionable never took their ties off. Not because they didn't want to, but because the knot was so small that they couldn't actually get it undone without un-dergoing surgery. Trucker, ever the genius, got his mum to sew a bit of elastic in at the back and had his tie specially narrowed, and his knot so small you could hardly see it. Girls swooned at his feet, a complete waste of effort as he was almost always out of his head on Bostik.

The Law of the Playground is quite specific. "Games shall be as brutal as possible, and there shall be no snitching to the teachers if you get hurt." Are we absolutely clear? Good. Because break times at our school came with a public safety warning. It was tough out there.

Take the gentle game of "One Touch" for example. You've got to kick a ball against a wall. You've only got one touch of the ball to do it (hence the name) and if you fail, you're out. Last person left is the winner. Simple enough.

But at Piggott this pursuit mutated into "One Touch Dobbings." Nobody dared to miss the wall because not only were you out, but you had to make it to the edge of the pitch without receiving a kicking from the other players. The later into the game, the worse the dobbings got as the lads dealt out harsher and harsher punishments. A particularly good game of One Touch actually attracted non-participating spectators whose sole purpose in life was to dob the vanquished. The more the better, and one or two of the lads would resort to wearing protective clothing.

Woe betide you, however, if you played One Touch Dobbings with Jonah. His idea of a good dobbing was a steel-capped boot in the testicles. You only played One Touch Dobbings with Jonah once, usually minutes before you crawled into a quiet corner to die.

One Touch? Pah! Why play that wusses' game when you had Kingy. In America they've got Dodgeball. It's played with a huge great ball that is impossible to throw with any great force and nobody gets hurt. There's even an International Dodgeball Federation for crud's sake, leagues and twenty foot high trophies that you can only get in American minority sports. I bet its even got a TV deal somewhere.

Hell no. That won't do. We took the so-called game of Dodgeball and turned it into Kingy. We didn't have no truck those great big soft balls. We wanted action. We wanted power. We wanted pain. Being the maniacs that we were, we had tennis balls injected with water. For extra effect, they'd come straight out of the freezer in the chemistry lab. In skilled hands, they were deadly weapons, and some people actually preferred the risk of playing One Touch with Jonah over the painfest that was Kingy.

The rules were simple: One person was Kingy. He had the ball. He had to chase the other players round the playing area chucking the ball at them. If he scored a hit, the two then team up against the rest until everyone was hit. The last guy left was the winner and was Kingy for the next game.

And boy could you get some power with half a pound of water-filled tennis ball. A good hit left a bruise that stayed for weeks. I saw with my own eyes James taking a hit from close range right between the arse cheeks by a member of the school cricket team. The ball was travelling with such force that it actually got wedged in there and James just silently keeled over forwards, the ball still clenched up his arse. As far as I know, it's still there. We carried him from the field, face down, and dumped him outside the classroom door, ready for the next lesson. Unfortunately for him, it was physics, perched on rock-hard science lab stools, the poor kid.

Early on in the game, you were more likely to get a fluky hit that didn't hurt so much. The longer you lasted, the greater the odds against you and the bigger the chance of receiving a close-range whupping. And pain was the price you paid for being so bloody good at it. On the other hand I was about as rubbish as you could get and couldn't throw a ball to save my life. The one time I was Kingy, I only managed to hit the equally crap Cookie, and we spent three quarters of an hour throwing the ball like a pair of girls, only managing to hit a tree while the rest of the gang taunted us from several miles away.

But playing this wide-ranging game of chase and pain on the school field was not enough. We wanted more! One damp day, with the field closed off, we decided to play Kingy in the enclosed space between the maths block and the sports hall. Holy Mother of Donkey Poop. There was nowhere to hide. Rod the Mallet didn't even have any trees to run into. It was brutal.

A whole game, which normally lasted twenty minutes out in the field lasted maybe two or three. Bodies lay scattered across the playground nursing wounds or crawling to safety. If you were hit and went down, they hit you again "just to make sure," or resort to the time-honoured tradition of "Dobbings" in a horrific playground crossover that took the genre just a little too far. Breaktime, once a fun refuge from the rigours of the classroom soon became something to dread; and wary of breaking the Rule of the Playground and wimping out, we grimly got stuck into our brutal task.

However, the line was crossed and there was no going back. And like drug addicts, we wanted more. And Mad Jonah of the bollock-crushing boots provided it. "Screw the tennis ball," he said, "Look at what I've got."

It was a golf ball. One ounce of Slazenger's finest white plastic malevolance. Not only did it hurt, it had the ability to draw blood. And in the enlcosed maths block/sports hall space, the thing ricocheted around to catch you unawares, leaving you in a groaning, bleeding heap on the deck, just ripe for a dobbing prior to your trip to the emergency dentist.

One breaktime of that was more than enough. People were about to crack. To hell with the Playground Law, teachers would have to be told. Luckily, honour would be preserved. One breaktime of Golfball Kingy was all we got.

The trouble with golfballs on a hard surface is that they bounce. A lot. And once it's going, no bugger on Earth is going to try to stop it. So come lunch time, out came the Ball of Fear and off we went with another game. Jonah was Kingy and let fly with the Mother and Father of all misdirected throws. We watched with astonishment as our nemesis bounced once, twice, three times, right across the playground, younger kids diving out of the way, scattering in abject fear.

There was a sickening crash of glass as Jonah's Exocet missile scored a bulleye on the dining hall. Witnesses on the inside spoke of an explosion of glass, panic, outrage and a free meal to anyone who claimed they'd got glass in their food. And there, at the very epicentre, was Mrs Taylor, the fearsome dinner lady, who had taken the full force of a supersonic golf ball right in the left tit.

The shit hit the fan. Mrs Taylor's tit had to be avenged, and the head stormed out of his office like a big fat, sweaty angel of death. He collared the culprits and subject the terrified boys to the "King Kong" lecture. There are times when you have to say bollocks to Playground Law, and this was it.

Month upon month of Jonah's steel-capped boots in the nuts was enough for all of us, and his time had come. One day we might want to have children, or at the very least, See A Lady Naked. He was handed to the authorities on a plate, and our ordeal of Death Kingy was over. And thank God for that, we could get back to regular brutality. Cookie, ever the genius, had devised a version of Kingy with radio-controlled rockets. That was more like it.

If there's a moral to all this, it's that sometimes we have to bend the rules. Playground Honour is one thing. A boot in the nads is another.

Ah yes, the boot in the nads. If trying to biff the hell out of each other in the name of playground sports wasn't bad enough, some genius decided that the violence should be organised, and if we played it right, televised too.

If there was one thing our school was good at, that was fighting. You see, far from being middle-class suburbia defined, someone, some-where decided in the early 1970's to move "problem" families out of dark, dank inner-city London and out in the country, where the open spaces would, presumably turn them into better people, skipping through fields and being nice to fluffy animals.

What a load of goat-shagging bollocks. We ended up with a village full of psychos, crooks and close relations of the Kray Twins who'd cut your knackers off and rob you blind as soon as look at you. OK, I'll concede that some of them were lovely people, and I'm not just saying that because of the coffee table they nailed to my head. It was just the fact that their psychotic kids all went to my school.

No-one remembers how it started. There was probably a playground argument at some stage, or at the very least a whole host of bragging followed by someone fetching somebody else a damn good kicking. The upshot of it was that it was decided that all the fourth form boys would be "compelled" to fight for the honour of being The School's Hardest Fourth Year. Someone even had the idea of taking our school champ and facing him off against the champs of other local schools, but subsequent events meant we never quite got to that stage. But most importantly, girls would be impressed.

A secret For-God's-sake-don't-let-the-teachers-find-out committee was set up and the rules laid out. Fight until the other boy surrendered. No weapons except fist, boots and head. Non-triers would be ridiculed. Every boy's name (and one girl as well - Linda was a savage animal who cared not a jot if you were a boy or girl. She'd kill you anyway) was put in the hat and a draw was made for the first round. With an elaborate system of seedings based on whether you were deemed "hard as nails" or "a poof," the first round parings were made and the tourney started.

The secret committee were masters of their work. They scoured the playground at breaktimes and made sure the fights happened. Some boys were willing, some were not. The protagonists were taken (some kick-ing and screaming) to the Hallowed Place between the sports hall and the science block, where no school law held sway and teachers never went. Most of the time it was the fighters, their seconds and the referee, specially selected to ensure foul play. It was like a duel, only with Bovver Boots.

The early rounds went off relatively quickly, with the wimps tending to run away and hide when it was announced they would be fighting the likes of the second-seeded "Biffer." Like me, for example. I eventually gave in to official "persuasion," came out of the toilet stall and took on third seeded "Turnip" in a one-sided contest, which saw my limp body peeled up and posted back to my parents within thirty seconds of the start. Gaz refused to accept the meek surrender of little Kenny, who took tail and ran for his life. The chase was on and the school was treated to a Keystone Cops-style procession of competitors and "judges" round the playground as Gaz repeatedly kicked the retreating Ken up the arse until he reached the safety of the cloakrooms.

The competition itself lasted for a couple of weeks, a tribute to the skills of the Secret Committee as they managed to get fifty kids to beat crap out of each other over several rounds. The veneer of secrecy wore a little thin though, as teachers soon got to hear the classroom gossip as the event reached a climax. The first rule of School Fight Club was not to talk about School Fight Club. But we all did. All the time. The whole thing wasn't helped when Sean opened a book on the final outcome, and large quantities of lunch money began to change hands, mostly backing Psycho Phil, who'd been to Borstal for clocking some kid twice his size over the head with an iron bar. Phil was ace, the guy every kid wanted to be. It was rumoured that he'd even had (gasp) sex with a lady once, without having to pay, even. He scared the shit out of me.

However, as we reached the last four, bravado got the better of the competitors. The Law of the Hallowed Place was soon forgotten, and the American Paul vs Psycho Phil rumble went off right in the middle of the playground in front of an audience of hundreds. This was our undoing. I was in the second row, using best mate Cookie as a shield. Paul dived in with a haymaker of a punch, missed, and ended up on the floor. Phil kicked Paul in the head. Phil kicked Paul in the head again. And again. And again. And again. And again. And again. For several minutes.

There was blood everywhere The Headmaster stormed down from his office along with the entire school staff, whistles and cattle prods. The police were called. The entire school was kept indoors for a week.

There was no winner, but no-one was going to argue over Psycho Phil's victory by default. No-one had been so consistently maniacal throughout the entire tournament or spilt more blood as he single handedly destroyed the flower of Britain's youth. I'm pretty sure that the other two semi-finalists were secretly relieved that neither had to fight him, as by the law of averages, one of them would probably have ended up on a slab in the local hospital, or worse still, in trouble with their mum. Sean the official bookie, called all bets off and kept our money, wisely giving a generous cut to Phil to ensure his survival.

The event's passing was marked by a school assembly in which the local vicar was called in to lecture us on "declining moral standards in today's youth" while several of us sniggered at the back, comparing bruises.

Bull got up and made his famous if all-too-predictable "If this is the law of the jungle, then I'm King Kong" speech. The bloody liar, he wouldn't have got past the second round. We were off fighting by then anyway. Porn was the thing.

The wonders of pornography! As a gang of fourteen and fifteen year olds, we weren't terribly good with girls. They were strange, giggling creatures with weird sticky-out lumps that hypnotised us, toyed with us and spat us out the other end as objects of bruised and battered ridicule. If you were lucky you might get a slow dance and a quick squeeze at the school disco. Only Ernie managed to hold down a steady girlfriend. He was seen as the height of sophistication, and in our eyes, practically married. The rest of us, by comparison were doomed to a life of solitude and hairy palms. Cookie has a girlfriend once, who called me "carrot nose", sparking a life of weird vegetable fetishes and a hatred of Status Quo fans. Girls were a no-go area, and that's where the jazz came in.

But first, you must be made aware that there are some unshakable truths in the world which just cannot be changed. One: You can't vote, because the Government will get in. Two: Policeman are younger than they used to be. Three: You just can't get rid of pornography. And we were just about to discover how true rule three was.

Disposal of porn is like trying to get rid of chemical weapons or nuclear waste. No matter what you do with it, you're running the risk of discovery, humiliation, and worse still, contamination of an innocent population. Take a look at Adolf Hitler. Invaded Poland, had the peoples of Europe crushed beneath the jackboot of the Third Reich, but it was the sack of porn under his bed that was his downfall. Churchill found out, and the rest, as they say, is history.

It was early 1981. Thatcher had been in power for two years, unemployment was rampant, nuclear destruction seemed imminent, and Britain was rocking to the sound of Joe Dolce's "Shaddap You Face". In short, society was doomed. Not that this bunch of fifteen-year-old schoolkids cared while we kicked a soccer ball round Stanlake Meadows that evening. A misdirected punt ended up in the bushes and our lives changed forever. Well, for a month, tops.

Rob waded past the knee-length grass and into the bushes. There were shouts of excitement that had us all running and crowding round. There was Rob. There was the ball. And there was an old sports bag stuffed to the gills with pornographic magazines. Paydirt.

The football game was forgotten as the filth was passed round for "sampling". It wasn't particularly strong stuff by today's depraved standards, but for a bunch of pimply fifteen year olds from a village west of London, even page three of The Sun was seen as the acme of smut. With time getting on, a decision had to be made. What to do with it? Disposal, at this stage, was not an option. Someone had to look after it. Step forward Metal.

Metal was a bit special. We was rich for starters, and he got time off school because he was an actor. He was often booked to do commercials (who can forget the tour de force that was his Corn Flakes ad?), and once had a small speaking part ("Goodnight sir") in a BBC costume drama and had flicked cigarette butts into the Blue Peter Italian sunken garden. Because of this, he was a little bohemian in his tastes, claimed to have once "seen a lady naked," and already had a burgeoning collection of filth hidden in his bedroom. That was good enough for us. Metal had experience where it mattered most, and he promised on his dog's life to bring the spoils to school the next day.

So, come the morning, there was Metal at the school gates. The sports bag was now a sleek attache case. He dialled the combination (696969, the perve) and we all crowded round agog, like a scene from Pulp Fiction. The goods were there, glowing slightly, and one or two hands made a grab for the top copies. The lid snapped shut amid cries of pain.

"There'll be no touching until break time," explained Metal. "As you can see, I've taken the liberty of cataloguing the mags, and I've added one or two from my own collection." He produced a small school exercise book, where each mag had been meticulously catalogued with name, date and contents. There was also a column marked "Who."

"Who?" we asked.

"That's for who it's loaned to. Nobody's going to take stuff from MY jazz library without my knowing it."

Yeah, right.

And thus was born the Metal Porn Library. The bastard had stolen our stash, and only let the rest of us take them home one at a time on a system of tickets and record-keeping that would bring a tear to the eye of our school librarian. It was when he started charging kids outside our gang to see our filth and trousering the proceeds that we decided enough was enough. There could only be one punishment. The Tree.

It was simple. Lure the victim onto the school field. Overpower him and get him on his back. Some kids supported his body and arms, and two other groups took his legs. Then you ran at the tree. One leg to the left, the other to the right. End of punishment. Metal still persisted in his role of School Porn Baron, only now on a rather more democratic basis. The cash was split twelve ways. I got ten pence. It's amazing what crushed nads will do to your attitude.

The collection was mind-boggling in its variety, but most highly prized was a recent edition of Fiesta magazine, the Rolls-Royce of British top shelf publishing. There, across the centre pages was a shapely young lady called "Julia." You could see her nips, flanges and everything. The clincher was that we all knew Julia as "Miss Shagwell" (name changed to protect the innocent, but believe me, I didn't have to change it much), our biology teacher. She had taught us all about human reproduction, whilst sitting on the corner of her desk wearing a very tight, white dress that finished just above the knee. We hung on to every last word.

Getting hold of the Shagwell Edition was a nightmare. There was a waiting list as long as your arm, and a black market in crude photocopies which just weren't the same as the real thing. If you were lucky, you got a glimpse in the playground for half a second, but that was all. There were major arguments, and bribery to get up the waiting list was not out of the question. When Julian finally got his turn he kept it at home for a week, only bringing it back after repeated use of The Tree.

Alas, the arguments over possession of the Shagwell Edition did not go away, and spilled over into the classroom, and this was to be Metal's downfall. Metal had kept possession of the prize for rather longer than was absolutely healthy and Ernie really, really wanted his go on her. A whispered conversation in maths got louder and louder until it developed into a vicious tug-o-war over the attache case.

"What the hell is going on back there?" thundered Mr Wallace as the fight turned into an out-and-out brawl. Ernie let go, just as Metal gave one final, resounding tug. The case flew from his hands, soaring across the classroom in a low arc narrowly missing your narrator, to score a direct hit on Wallace's desk. Pens, pencils and exercise books were crushed under the assault, and the case burst open with slag mags exploding everywhere in a shower of tits, flange, arse and filth. And as if ordained by fate, the Shagwell Edition flopped open at Wallace's feet, those "Come to bed, big boy" eyes staring up at him.

"There had better be a damn good excuse for this," whispered Wallace, looking frighteningly like a volcano about to destroy several small Italian villages.

"Yes sir," said Metal in that annoying sing-song voice of this that you knew was going to get him a visit to the Headmaster, "It's our porn collection."

So it's OUR porn collection now, is it? Cheers, mate.

Metal was marched off to see the Head, where by all accounts a certain gorilla was mentioned, and Wallace being Wallace had the entire class working through break-times for a week. Except for the girls, who had spent the entire episode discussing the nocturnal merits of bananas.

Because of his special status as school TV star, Metal got off lightly. The porn was confiscated, and proving that You Just Can't Get Rid Of Porn, was fished out of the school bins and sold back to him within two days. However, the Shagwell Edition was missing. And so was Miss Shagwell. The school had known about her "photographic work" and had decided to brazen it out. As it had become common knowledge amongst pupils, she was transferred to another school fifteen miles away, who, I found out later, were very happy to have her. On a regular basis.

But that was not the end of it, by any stretch. Metal decided his library need a headquarters, somewhere he could work under the cover of legitimacy, rather like Capone's speakeasies in prohibition Chicago. And that headquarters was the school darkroom. Ironically, he hid the entire stash in the roof space above the staff toilets. By pretending to be an ardent photographer, he ran his little business empire with impunity.

This was all well and good, but it soon got on the nerves of the genuine photographers, myself and Cookie included, who found the constant comings and goings a bit of a nightmare when you were fiddling with your exposure. So we swiped the lot and decided that The Porn Had To Go. It was a kill-or-cure.

And thus, Cookie and I found we weren't the first, and certainly not the last to discover that You Just Can't Get Rid of Porn. God, we tried. The fear of discovery mortified us. Bins - at home or elsewhere - were out as somebody might find it. The thought of our mums finding a pile of jazz mags was just too much to bear. We considered dumping it in the hedge where we had first found it, but on our reckoning it had only been there about ten minutes before we discovered it, so that was out of the question too. Burning it, illogical as it sounded, was "a waste of good porn" and would just draw attention and, knowing our luck, the Fire Brigade. So we decided to bury it.

Later that evening, two figures were seen behind the allotments on the Hurst Road digging a bloody great hole and dropping in a bin-liner full of naked tarts and Reader's Wives. Within a week, drawn by the sound of Jumanji drums (not to mention a particularly tasty bribe which I never saw a penny of), a group of junior perverts from the year below us dug the lot up, and there was a new Porn Baron in town.

Not long afterwards, we found that belonging to the school camera club had its advantages, and not just by being in the room next to the school stock cupboard outside of school hours. One evening, going through the tangled mess that was the negative drawer, we found an entire roll of film shot by a sixth former the previous year, showing the voluptuous Miss Shagwell in various states of undress. We made a fortune.

Still, our schoolteachers and parents trusted us. The fools! Didn't they know what we were like? We couldn't be trusted out of anybody's sight without trying to kill each other, blow up the school or attempting to cause a military coup and overthrow the government. They were going to let us go one a school trip. Away from school. Were they mad?

In these litigious days, you can't send your children on a school trip without a taking out a full risk assessment, life cover insurance, third party insurance, legal insurance and let's-sue-the-teacher-anyway-if-the-kid-comes-back-with-so-much-as-a-dented-lunchbox insurance. Not that they go anywhere exciting anyhow. Exciting means dangerous, and dangerous means legal action. About the most exciting you get these days is a trip to the cotton wool factory across the road from the school, and that's not without its dangers.

We were accompanied by Mr Wilkinson. He was our hero. Wilkie was also our physics teacher, but to this group of fifteen year olds, he was also the coolest man on the planet. He used to work at Aldermaston making nuclear bombs, but had quit in disgust and become a CND activist. This guy knew about blowing things up, and for we fans of firey destruction, that was good enough for us. Mr Wilkinson also ran the Outdoor Activities Club, and anywhere that Wilkie went, we followed.

When he announced a trip to the frighteningly named Devil's Punchbowl somewhere in the south of England for a weekend of youth hosteling, walking and general larking about, we signed up in a shot. One minibus, two teachers, a dozen kids and the biggest stash of sweets, cigarettes and porn in the known universe. We planned the itinery for weeks, and the quantities of chocolate-flavoured trash were frightening indeed. We even brought some real food, presumably to bring us down from the sugar rush.

All the usual suspects signed up - Cookie, Ernie, Rob, Downsey, Enders, Mike and Harry, plus a whole bunch of girls in stripy jumpers and leg-warmers. Basically, we left the soft boys at home. What am I talking about? I was one of the soft boys. And I was trapped in the middle of nowhere with a bunch of teenage maniacs.

The Devil's Punchbowl was a funny old place. Just off the main London to Brighton road, you had to leave your transport up at the gates and walk about a mile down a wooded track to the Youth Hostel. It was literally hidden somewhere in a wooded glade, about halfway down the bowl, and at one stage I'd swear it was the home of some child-eating witch. It was old, it had a huge log-burning fire, and most important of all, there was a hole in the wall where you could see into the girls' dorm. They found out after about three seconds.

And so the weekend began. Stuff your face with sweets. Cook breakfast. More Chocolate. Nip out to the shed for a crafty smoke. Follow

Wilkie on a hike through the local army range with a rucksack full of chocolate snacks. It would be late afternoon and getting dark by the time we got back to the hostel.

"If you guys want a log fire," announced Wilkie, "You'd better get some wood together," and he went off for a crafty smoke and whatever with Miss Smith, who had a disturbing habit unbuttoning her blouse down to the navel with no other visible means of support.

At this point, our esteemed teachers had left a small group of fifteen year old kids buzzing about on a saccharin-induced high, only rivalled recently by the introduction of Sunny Delight, alone in the woods with a bow saw, several large axes and a two wheeled trolley-cum-wheelbarrow.

We treated our duties responsibly and with great attention to our personal safety. For about five minutes. We diligently found fallen trees and branches, cut them into logs and wheeled them up the hill in the barrow to the hostel. That lasted for about one trip, while Wilkie and Miss Smith sat with their feet up, shouting words of encouragement out of the door. It wasn't long before the slacking-off qualities of the barrow became apparant.

"Bollocksed if I'm walking all the way back down there," said Ernie, "I'm getting in the cart."

So he got in. And it was the Devil's own job getting the extra weight back down the hill without letting go, while Ernie sat like a king in his sedan chair, waving to his passing subjects. But teenage minds were already working towards greater things...

As we dumped another load at the top of the hill Downsey looked fear in the face and jumped in. God alone knows what I was thinking, but I jumped in behind him and yelled "Ride 'em cowboy!" as the cart slowly trundled down the ever-steepening path. The trouble was, we were expecting the rest of the lads to wheel us down the hill like we had done Ernie just minutes before.

When I looked round there was nobody there except the flare of a match illuminating Cookie's face as they stopped for another crafty smoke break. It it was just me, Downsey and Newton's Laws.

It took us about 1.2 seconds to realise that something was wrong. We were staring over the abyss and gaining speed rapidly as we rattled down the track. I distinctly remember Trudy pointing at us and saying

"Aren't you supposed to be..." before saving her own neck and diving out of the way. Nothing was going to stop us now. The wind was in our hair as we accelerated at 9.81 metres per second squared towards escape velocity. All those months of sitting in Wilkie's classroom learning physics weren't going to be wasted, I could tell you for nothing. Velocity, accelaration, angular motion, the gravitational constant, it was all coming back to me on a practical basis.

About halfway down, we hit a root, and for a couple of seconds we were flying. Really flying, without the aid of wings, engine or helpful flight attendants telling us to get into the crash position. It was also at that point that Downsey and I realised we might not actually survive the trip, and frantic thoughts spun through my head like "Will this hurt?", "I'm going to die a virgin," and "What are my parents going to think when they discover all my porn?" We clung on for dear life as we roared towards the bottom of the hill, axe-wielding schoolgirls scattering before us.

Newton's Laws of Motion finally caught up with us as we neared the bottom of the valley. Luckily, we only caught the tree a glancing blow. Someone, who turned out to be me, yelled out a bloodcurdling cry of "Fookenhell!" and Downsey and I were airborne once again, this time leaving the twisted wreckage of the cart behind us. I landed in a holly bush, scratching my face to buggery but otherwise escaping with my life and the correct number of limbs. Downsey, being at the front, flew a bit further and touched down with a spectacular belly-flop into the stream at the bottom of the hill, like one of those fighter planes missing their aircraft carrier at the Battle of Midway. Even in my prison of prickles I was impressed.

We both stood up, dazed. My face was a network of scratches and dirt. Downsey was a black spectre of water and mud. I puked my guts up as a sackful of chocolate and junk food came back to haunt me, and I slowly came round to the noise of my classmates cheering and applauding us. We were stupid. We nearly died. We were heroes.

"Shit man," said Downsey, "As soon as we get that trolley fixed up, I'm going again." So we did. And we had to wait bloody ages for our turn.

We did so many trips with that barrow up and down the hill, we virtually stripped the entire Punchbowl of trees; and the ensuing log fire nearly burned the hostel to the ground. Our teachers turned a blind eye as no-one got killed or too badly hurt, even after the axe fight. I could hardly imagine them reporting back to Bull with tales of death, destruction and stupidity. He probably had a special version of "King Kong" especially for the teaching staff, with extra bananas.

I spent five years in that school before exams, life, college and jobs broke the gang up. Most of the guys are still alive out there somewhere, and I still see Downsey at Reading Football Ground every now and then; a smile and a nod shows our lives forever entwined by our youthful brush with the Grim Reaper, who is waiting in the sidelines, taking notes.

Bull died a few years ago, atop a skyscraper, flailing away at fighter aircraft screaming one last, defiant "I am King Kong!" before plummeting to his doom. The school, somewhat against the odds and despite our best efforts in science club, is still there. And judging by the line of bottles fifty feet up on the school chimney as I drove past not long ago, it's rather pleasing to report that the old spirit still lives on with the Annual Lunatic Challenge. Tradition passed on from father to son. That's how it should be.

Naming Your Blade
Justin Azevedo

Too often do I hear about the importance of naming your sword. It seems that every stable boy and scullery maid under the age of thirty winters can't even push a broom without referring to it with some fluffy, theatric nickname. I suppose other swordmasters encourage their students to do this. They usually tell the pups that it helps them build a personal relationship with their weapon. If you ask me, what it really does is cause the poor and uneducated to aspire to being conscripted, just in case "Blackthorn" or "Deathfang" one day becomes the subject of a Bard's song.

I, obviously, do not require such measures. Oh, it certainly does help, I'll give them that much. Fighting with a sword requires a certain sort of intimacy. Unlike them, however, I do not think this is something every young soldier needs to do. Personalizing your weapon requires quite a bit of thought, and I think that leaving your blade nameless is acceptable, if you happen to have a very good reason. My own reason is not so good, perhaps, but maybe you'll find wisdom in it just the same.

The battle I'll tell you about took place a long time ago. As I recall, it was during one of the wars that took place some time before the Imperial bloodlines were merged into the Senatorial Houses. I honestly couldn't say which war. There were so many, I don't think it makes any difference, anyhow.

I was young back then. Too young to understand what being a soldier was all about, other than the facade of glory that accompanies every young man's fantasies of battle. I seem to remember that I had never had to face the reality of killing someone before that day. I suppose I could ramble on about the loss of my innocence and the horrors of warfare, but it would serve no real purpose. I knew exactly what I was to be prepared for, and that day was the culmination of all of my training. At least, that's what I was expecting that day to be.

It had rained for days before that morning, so it was almost surprising to see the sun finally creep over the jagged cerulean line of the mountains on the horizon. That's precisely why I still recall it. Sleepy orange light danced on the pools of standing water in the muddy grass around us. I remember that the air had a crisp, invigorating smell to it that all autumn mornings seem to have.

We had marched for hours before that. We were the vanguard unit of infantry, and our scouts directed us to the narrow, sodden valley amidst a range of foothills that stood right in the center of the hapless enemy's patrolling route. All that remained as the sun rose higher in the lazy sky was to wait for our adversaries to enter the valley. By the time we sprang upon them, the rest of our army would be there to bolster our charge with real power.

The unit commander inspected our formation almost obsessively as we stood in our ranks, weapons shuffling quietly and banners catching the stiff morning breeze. Now that I think about that, I suppose he might have been doing it just to keep busy, because it certainly was all I could do just to sit still. As he passed me, I shifted excitedly like a restless child. I couldn't seem to help myself.

The cold bite of the air slowly melted away as the sun continued to rise above the uneven horizon, its light shifting from a sleepy golden to a more unforgiving white glare. All of the activity among our ranks eventually stilled as the morning dragged on, our trembling energy turning inward in a strange sort of meditation. I watched, and waited.

I heard them long before I saw them. An imperceptible hum somewhere at the back of my senses became the rumbling cadence of feet marching along soggy ground. Snatches of sound reached my ears—the murmur of mixed voices, the rattle of sheathed weapons. My eyes remained fixed upon the foothills before us, waiting for my chance to uncoil, to strike.

Somewhere amidst the misty curves of the hills, a stray beam of sunlight reflected off of something. A helm, perhaps, or a shield. It was the only signal we needed. A deep-throated yell, one collective voice of rage and excitement, leapt from our throats as we surged forward. I drew my sword as I ran, and the blade felt as light as the wind itself in my hand. Time slowed, passing with each footstep, each breath.

The enemy had some time to prepare for our onslaught, but not nearly enough. They had just begun to fan out into something that re-sembled a proper defense when we broke headlong into them. I was one of the first to reach them. We rushed into the first straggling lines of their column, accompanied by screams and the cold ring of metal against metal. The two armies crashed against one another like a riptide, and the battle began in earnest.

Violence erupted around me in small pockets of sweat and blood. I lowered my head and raced through the chaos, intent on finding my first victim, my veins beginning to fill with the fire of battle and the rising panic of self-preservation.

Now, I am well aware of the romanticized version of a swordfight. Two duelists weaving, exchanging expert blows, fighting back and forth in a tidy little dance of finesse. Anyone who lives to see a true battle will have that version dispelled like the fanciful garbage it is. I was almost disap-pointed after my first skirmish, after I realized it had taken mere seconds.

I didn't have much time to think about it. Another enemy soldier rushed towards me, pressing my guard. I weaved through the violent morass, en-gaging and defending. Each melee was quick and ultimately unmemorable. It didn't take long for the enemy to blur together, becoming less like indi-viduals and more like different, faceless parts of a singular experience.

I made plenty of mistakes, too. Remember, this was my first real experience on the battlefield, and despite all of my training and arrogant self-assurance I certainly didn't know what I was doing. I never escaped a skirmish unscathed, taking a shallow cut on my arm here and a shield edge to the ribs there. Somehow, I managed to come out on top each time, ignoring the nagging pain from those wounds and turning my sword to yet another adversary.

I was nearly animalistic with the pound and roar of battle when my blade crossed hers. It took me a long moment to even realize that I was fighting a woman—her hair was cropped close about her chin, and her large eyes glared at me out of a round, tough-skinned face.

Even so, she radiated a harsh kind of femininity with each swing of her sword, each shifting of her weight, as we circled one another and sized each other up. She was mannish and homely compared to the "civi-lized" standards of beauty, but amidst the carnage around us, she seemed as lovely as any angel I had ever imagined.

She lunged underneath my guard, forcing me to jump backwards and parry clumsily. She repositioned herself, trying to slide around my side. Our eyes remained locked on one another's, wide, watching.

I could read my own scattering thoughts in her stare. Or, perhaps, my memory is making things up, convincing me that something else really happened that day near the foothills. But I could swear to every god in the heavens that as we traded feints and lunges, our minds were on something else entirely.

A drop of sweat slid off of her cinnamon eyelashes and into her eye, and I took the opportunity to swing my leg around and send the edge of my blade whistling towards her neck.

I know my memory is not fooling me in this. That swing should have killed her. It would have killed her, in any of the short-lived battles that I had trudged through before then.

I pulled back at the last possible instant, shifting my weight just slightly, unbalancing myself just enough to allow a brief, fleeting opening. She dropped to one knee, my sword arcing so close to her that it brushed the tips of her sweat-dampened hair. Her sword came up in response, forcing me to retreat once again, circling and searching for another opportunity.

I should have been furious with myself. Even at that young and stupid age, there wasn't a doubt in my mind that I was a lethally skilled soldier. I should have been cursing with rage at letting an easy victory slip through my fingers like so much sand. Instead, I was exhilarated. I don't know if it showed on my face. She, however, let a faint, somewhat disbelieving grin touch the corners of her mouth. She turned to the left, then broke back right and twisted her body at the waist, preparing to send a backhanded slash at me.

Our eyes again locked as her body turned. The pause was just enough. I ducked, and felt the sword whistle inches past the back of my head. We were no longer battling. We were playing with one another.

This was the battle that all of those ballads speak of. The swordfight that is one long draw, one near miss after another. Challenging, arrogant smiles now touched both of our lips as we danced, probing one another's guard. Our gazes never left one another. We continued to struggle, playfully stalemated, and suddenly I found my mind turning to things quite different than the meaningless border war around us.

I wondered, for just a split second, what could have been if our greed-blinded barons and kings weren't intent on destroying each other. I wondered what might have been if I had met this tough, mousy woman in a marketplace rather than on a battlefield. I was of an age back then that my interests in women tended towards the bestial, and amazingly, there I was in a sea of blood, screams, and metal contemplating growing old. Tending gardens. Holding children.

I circled back again, shifting my guard. They were things I couldn't afford to think about. Even if I really did see the same bizarre wonderment in her that I felt, it would only succeed in getting me killed. There was absolutely no conceivable way that I could make even a shadow of that split second a reality.

Besides, in a war, skirmishes didn't stay one to one for very long. And my people were outnumbered that day.

I told myself it was a side effect of the adrenaline. Between the battles, the sensory overload, and the pain of my various small wounds, I was had to have been irrational. I have believed that less and less as the years have passed. Her movements suddenly became more earnest, and a potentially lethal thrust slid dangerously past my ribs. It was as if she had come to same realization as I had.

My mind shut down again, sliding back into the chaos of battle frenzy. She swung again, aiming a slash at my gut, but even though our little game had turned into something a lot more genuine, I still saw a hint of something I couldn't quite identify in the set of her face.

My body was acting on instinct, by that point. It wasn't going to allow me to make a trivial mistake again. I swatted the blade aside, and riposted. The tip of my sword opened her throat as easily as if it were slicing unfettered through the air.

As soon as I saw the blood, my body seemed to lock up and grow cold. My bloodlust faded, congealed, and turned into doubt and horror as her eyes widened in pain.

I had done the only thing I could, and it was something that she most certainly would have done to me if I hadn't taken the initiative. At that moment, though, as her life drained slowly down the front of her leathers, it was hard to remember any of that. All of the sudden, I wasn't so sure I had done the right thing.

My body felt numb. I couldn't move, wracked by the horror of what I'd just done, and dumbstruck that I would have such a ridiculous thought while in the middle of a battle. I certainly hadn't spared so much as a thought for any of my other victims.

She took advantage of my indecision, doing the only thing she could do. Her sword lashed out as she stumbled forward, and the point buried itself deep into my side. I gasped, dropped my own sword, and crumpled alongside her.

I pressed my hand to the wound, trying the staunch the rush of my own blood as I felt it soak into my own paltry armor, and turned my head up. She had fallen onto her stomach, her face turned towards mine. To this day, I can remember how she looked as the awareness slowly left her eyes. Even now, my dreams are sometimes haunted by it.

My wound wasn't serious. Had I really wanted to, I could have pulled myself onto my feet, picked my sword up, and plunged back into the fray. Granted, I wouldn't have lasted very long after that. As it was, I simply laid my face back into the mud and grass. I had given up.

The battle was still new. Five, maybe ten minutes had passed. Early enough for some of my fellow soldiers to have the presence of mind to pull me away from the front, where our field surgeons could take care of me.

The stab healed, as all wounds do, though I carry the scar to this day. It did nothing to impede or cripple me, in the grand scheme of things. However, it was a long time before I could walk out onto a battlefield again. When I finally did, I was a different person. Changed. I can't explain why, or how. Maybe that's what the songs really are about.

And from then until now, I have never named my blade. This is because I never did learn that young woman's name.

You know, now that I have told it, I'm not so certain that story is really about swordplay. Every story has a reason for being told, though, I suppose. Perhaps swordsmanship really is more like other aspects of life than we realize. Or perhaps that's just the ridiculous platitude it's always sounded like to me.

Enough of an old man's blathering. Pick up your weapon. Your left-handed slash is still weak, and we have all afternoon.

The Autumn Engagement
Stephen W. Cote

FREEZE FRAMED FAILURE

A poorly rendered three-dimensional kaleidoscope of advertisements and spectators, colorfully dressed in the latest fashions, flickered and became very pixilated whenever the music started to play. During the worst moment, the inset speakers in the ceiling would rattle with a tinny-sounding rendition of the Andromeda Galaxy's premiere orchestra playing the Star Spangled Banner. The music sputtered, and the three kids sitting behind the dugout actually froze for a full second as the visiting team leapt to their feet, erupting in triumphant cheers. The World Historians Society had recorded every minute detail of the baseball game.

Moments prior, it had been the bottom of the ninth inning. The visiting British Willows were one run down, had a runner on second, and one of its premiere batters was facing the wicked arm of the Cascadia Chateau's prize pitcher.

Janus Franko still felt a twinge of excitement as the eight month-old game footage played in a sim-3D staccato on the worker class apartment walls. Perfect calm had controlled his movements on the mound, giving no visual indication that the ball might fly astray. However, moments after the ball left his hand, he knew it would sink too early.

Janus switched off the playback. He could still smell the ambrosia of champagne and salmon completing the affluent ambiance of the high-class suite he once occupied. The cornucopia-dream of fame, fantastic wealth and perfect love had been in his grasp and still he longed to savor its succulent flavors. While he had expected the triumvirate - fame, wealth, and love - to come hand-in-hand with success, he was not prepared for all three to be stripped away within the hour following the Chateau's loss.

At his worst, he nearly managed to believe that his love for Priscilla was only a ruse, and that his lost fortune didn't matter as much as the lump in his chest told him it did. But he could not bring himself to forget the parties that came with excessive wealth, fame, and perfect love. Gazing at the chalky apartment walls, he wished he had ordered a copy of the Winter Festival from two years prior. His companionship with Priscilla had been at its best that evening. Gowned in a radiant near-translucent gown, she had acted as though she was with him for his company, not his success.

He mused on the irony of three-dimensional video technology: he could only freeze-frame his failures.

And without a crystal clear reminder of his successes, he could only replay his failure. Between replaying the episode of his errant pitch and the climactic finale of his accounts being drained and Priscilla walking out on him, he simply frittered away his time. Baseball had been his life, his vitality, and the vindication of his existence.

Lately, he had turned to writing down cuss words on bits of paper, wadding them up, and studying the trajectory as he flicked them at Priscilla's picture. His spine would tingle and his lips would curl in the vague outline of a sneer whenever the more exotic cusses made contact with her mouth. In such moments of miniscule success, he fancied she had just spoken that particular word and committed a grave faux pas.

Mid-flick, Janus' attention turned to the brochure resting on the molded plastic end table next to his couch. He knew what it was without reading it, and having had no interest in its content, had let the brochure soak in his misery rather than reading it or tearing it up and using it for ammunition. Printed mail was very unusual and generally preserved for the wealthy. And the brochure was from nothing less. Now, he picked it up and followed the rich lettering with slightly blurred vision: Summer Festival. Although he was no longer a part of the elite social class, he still received invitations from one family.

After his last game, all contact with the socialites had ceased, except from the Welch family. Though he would have preferred to discard it as he had done with the others, the timing of the party, especially the invitation, was uncanny.

The Chateau lost more than a game because of his errant pitch. At stake had been fourteen of the most productive diamond mines on the Luxemburg flats of Mars. Diamonds had become a valuable commodity since the recent introduction of diamond-carbide bonding, a technique used to manufacture synthetic brains and super computer processors. As with any game dealing in extraterrestrial property, especially one of such lucrative value, a period of reckoning was required before the exchange became final.

The date of the party marked the last day before the transfer became final.

Janus contemplated the date of the party and felt a growing sense of dread. He was forced to admit his failure in forgetting his lost life, and this date. The party was in two days, and on the following day, his failure would be sealed.

He tried to push the fantastic thoughts of recovering his status from his mind by shaking his head. Getting invited to a party was not the only step required for attendance. A large contribution to a political or non-profit organization was typically requested, or, in this particularly eccentric engagement, a particular type of date was required; a synthetic. Therefore, he rationalized he could not attend and could return to the tedious task of wallowing in his failure.

On his return trip into the depths of his angst, his phone chimed and interrupted his thoughts. He touched 'open' on the communication panel, and waited for the caller to identify their self.

"Franko," a grizzled voice promptly stated.

"I already paid," he said, assuming the voice belonged to a collection agent. The voice had a familiar sound and he tried to put it to a face. He waited for an introduction, and when nothing was said, he continued. "Who is this?"

"Franko," the voice droned in the exact same timbre and time.

"Synthetic," Janus muttered angrily, and immediately thought of a typical marketing slogan for diamond-carbide laized synthetic brains: "Synthetics now have feelings, too."

"Franko," it repeated.

"Yes, I'm Franko," he said feverishly.

"I have been," the voice started, but was interrupted by a chime-in from the media company that provided his free service.

"Please stand by for a commercial interruption." The voice was sweet, bright, and possessed every loathsome quality of a corporate propaganda spokesperson.

"Din ji!" Janus swore, using the most vile profanity ever invented by space-faring cargo pilots. There had been a time when he would have shied away from using those words, words that were wicked and acidic, but he had managed to use them more often in the last eight months. He pounded the wall with his fist, forced to listen to an advertisement for a deodorant 'engineered for the athlete living in high G.'

"What do you want?" Janus asked, perturbed.

"I have been asked to extend a personal invitation to the Welch family's Summer Festival."

He looked around for the brochure, found that he was still holding it, and waded it up. Janus crammed the paper wad against the phone's built-in receiver. "Hear that? That's the part that reads I need a synthetic date. Good bye." He punched 'close' and turned away from the phone.

"Signed communications cannot be closed by the receiving party," the phone instructed him.

Janus glared at the phone and saw that the 'open' button still glowed, indicating the caller was still connected.

"Janus Franko?" Another voice, one he couldn't place.

"Another party has entered the conversation. Please stand by for a commercial interruption." Another commercial started playing, but halted less than five seconds into the minute-long program.

"Communication is now secured," the phone instructed him, and the line clicked.

"Free phone service," the new speaker said with disgust. "Janus, this is Victor Welch."

Janus bit his lip and felt his heart race. The voice belonged to one of the wealthiest citizens of the Cascadia Chateau, and the head of the only family that did not sever contact after his pitch caused the Chateau's team to lose to the British team. "Mr. Welch," he said, mustering a polite tone to mask his previous outburst.

"Janus, I called under the ruse of inviting you to my family's party. However, I have another matter that I wish to discuss with you. If you could join me for a brief conversation, I believe it would work out to benefit both of us." Victor Welch's voice had a commanding and refined tone, but came across as benevolent.

"Mr. Welch, I appreciate your hospitable offer, but I'm not sure I'm in much of a position to help myself, much less anyone else."

"Janus," he replied almost immediately. "The matter that I wish to discuss is delicate and one in which you are particularly knowledgeable. In return for your assistance, I will see that you are provided the material appointments you would require to attend my party, or some other reimbursement if you decide that your attendance is not in your best interest."

Janus cupped his palm over his forehead and shook his head again. "Mr. Welch," he started, then decided to investigate the offer rather than express outright denial. "Very well. When should we meet?"

A CONVERSATION ABOUT BASEBALL

"Franko," the synthetic with the grizzled voice from the phone conversation said and motioned him towards the office suite door. Victor Welch's security team had gone to great lengths to create a socially acceptable bodyguard, but there was no mistaking that the synthetic was built around a war chassis. The behemoth's integrated arsenal left few sinuous, human-like lines. Janus now recalled having seen the security guard at various games.

Janus nodded and entered the palatial suite. He was instantly brought back to the world he rued losing when he smelled the alcohol from an open decanter and saw the fine ornamentation embellishing the walls. "Mr. Welch?" he asked, when he didn't see anyone present. It was then he realized that he could not remember what Victor Welch looked like, or if the voice even belonged to the same family. The word 'fool' came to mind.

"In the game of baseball," the voice of the alleged Victor Welch said from the door. He shut it and walked over to a desk on the other side of the suite.

Janus found himself hanging on every word and could only watch the pasty-skinned, very obese Victor Welch make his way across the room.

Victor dabbed at his perspiring forehead with a well-used handkerchief. "The issue that weighs so heavily on my mind, Janus, is in the game of baseball .." he paused again. "I simply don't understand the physics." He turned and stared with an enigmatic expression. "Pardon me for drudging up a history that, I'm sure, you have revisited quite often. Since I have an economic interest in the outcome of many politi-cally-minded sporting events, I must admit I have spent a considerable amount of time studying the nature of the games."

"What happened? Is that what you want to know? Why my pitch sank too early?" Janus felt flustered and turned around, trying to quell an onrush of vertigo. Why indeed. He knew why. There were a thousand reasons why. Ten thousand, maybe. And he knew them all because he had to know. So much had been lost that a decent explanation was all that held his mind together.

"Yes," Victor said. He walked behind the desk and, with some dif-ficulty, sat in an oversized chair. "And no." Again, he wore an enigmatic expression. "Putting aside all external factors, what physical condition caused the ball to sink too late?"

Ten thousand reasons, Janus thought to himself. And the best ones that came to mind were, "Any number of reasons. Dust on my finger tips, a draft, something adhering to the ball."

Victor shook his head and his expression cleared, becoming calcu-lating, cold, and precise. "You are a doctor in kinetic energy and motion. Very specialized. Your thesis was on random disturbances along a known trajectory. Your body was so finely tuned the moment you threw that pitch that no machine on the planet could have matched its accuracy."

"Yes," Janus whispered, taken aback by the sudden change in Victor's attitude. "But not this time."

"What do you mean, 'not this time'?" Victor said excitedly. "What I want to know," he raised his thick hand and pointed a knobby finger at Janus, "and what I want you to tell me, is in the game of baseball, is there such a thing as chance?"

"No," he replied immediately. "Maybe a thousand or so years ago when it was first invented. Maybe five hundred years ago when baseball players were first genetically engineered. But not now."

"I'm glad we agree on that one point. Baseball is game of strategy. It is the only reason humans have not turned to war since it was first used to settle political and economic disputes." Victor mopped his forehead again. He peered at Janus intently, his expression lost within the sickly-white layers of soft flesh.

Janus suddenly felt revolted at Victor's appearance. Every party he had attended catering to the uber-pretentious was hosted by the Welch family. And now, with the host standing in front him, those parties suddenly became a joke. People would spend months preparing themselves to be as beautiful as possible, and for what? This disgusting individual.

"My dilemma, Janus, is if baseball is a game of strategy, and not a game of chance, then how should your throw be classified?" Victor sat back in the chair and folded his thick arms over his chest. "If baseball isn't a game of chance, that is."

Janus found himself suddenly speechless. He wasn't sure if Victor was implying some other misfortune, foul play on behalf of a third party, or that Janus meant to throw that pitch.

Before Janus could offer a reply, Victor continued. "But I don't want to spend more time than necessary discussing your misfortune. I asked you here to use your scholastic abilities in determining the outcome of a theoretical pitch." He made a gesture with his hand to trigger an optic-tracking device that would engage the 3D environment.

The entire room was immersed in a pixilated representation of a baseball diamond. A pitcher, catcher, and batter, all featureless, stood and squatted in their respective positions.

"Assume these are national teams," Victor said. He beckoned Janus towards the 3D mound. "And assume the catcher is experienced. Unknown batter at the plate," and Victor gestured to the model. "What conditions would this pitcher need to strike out that batter?"

"Drop the Wisomin," Janus said at once, pointing to the pitcher's mitt. "Hans and Kluudner."

Victor frowned, perplexed. "Yes, yes. Very expensive, but not the most popular."

"A good pitcher needs a low profile mitt with a shielded jammer." Janus stood next to the 3D model. "But only the Hans and Kluudner mitts include a vector tracking unit. They aren't meant to be stylish, which is why most pitchers don't use them. You can count on any national league pitcher to use one because they're beyond caring what looks good."

Victor nodded an acceptance of the explanation.

"Shoes are ok, and the optic visor is a good choice. Just make sure the dominant eye isn't covered." Janus pointed to one of the model's eyes. When Victor looked skeptical, he added, "as you said, we're finely tuned. Better than a machine."

He gave the model another quick survey, then pointed to the pitching hand. "Lose the pitching glove. There shouldn't be anything between the pitcher's hand and the ball."

Victor nodded. He withdrew a remote keypad from a pocket and sent updated instructions to the 3D display. Janus' suggestions were incorporated into the pitcher model.

"A hypothetical scenario, then. It's the fifth inning. Doesn't matter what half, doesn't matter who is ahead. One team adds a legal side stake on the next pitch. The other team accepts. Given these three models, and using your knowledge in this field, what are the expected results of the next pitch?"

Janus nodded slightly to affirm he understood the question and then walked around the pitcher model. Next, he walked towards the grainy representation of home plate and studied the batter and catcher. Finally, he looked to Victor. "What is the pitch?"

"Would it matter?" Victor asked.

Janus paused, then shook his head. "No, I guess it wouldn't."

"Then you've made your estimation?"

Janus nodded. "The batter will miss. That much is obvious. If this model is an accurate representation, its weight is slightly off. It's obvious the batter wants the pitcher to think he is ready to swing high, but the axis of his body leads me to believe the hardest contact would be made only on a low pitch. Either way, he'll miss."

"How can you be so sure of that?" Victor asked.

"Batters, much like pitchers, are very well learned. Unlike pitchers, batters don't have the luxury of time. They study the posture of the pitcher and attempt to deduce where the ball will fly. It is also a matter of matching a batter to a pitcher. This batter favors a line-drive hit." Janus pointed to the representation of tensed triceps on the batter's arms. "You can tell by the muscle use. Once again, even that doesn't matter because the pitcher is going to throw high and this batter won't have the reflexes to hit a fair ball."

"I agree," Victor said. "A very thorough analysis, though I'm not sure I agree with the part about favoring a line-drive. That could simply be a ruse."

"It could at that," Janus said. "Is this what you needed my help with? Baseball 101?" He felt slightly annoyed now at the simplicity of the question.

"Not exactly. Let's have this pitch go through." He pressed a key on the remote and the pitcher erupted into action. The pitch was perfect, as expected, and the batter swung low, as Janus had surmised. But where he expected to hear the simulated sound of a baseball snapping in the catcher's mitt, he only caught the sharp crack of a bat.

Janus blinked. "Apparently I missed something. Again."

"Yes," Victor said sullenly. "But no one could have gotten this one." He walked towards the plate and stopped halfway between the pitcher and the batter. "You thought the batter would swing and miss. Either the pitch was off, or you were wrong. But, as we discussed, baseball is not a game of chance. At least not anymore. That clears you and the pitcher, leaving only the ball."

"It would show up in the playback," Janus argued. "I know. Do I ever know. I've watched my last game hundreds of times, walking with the ball through each frame. If something disturbed the ball, it would have been caught."

"Janus," Victor said plainly. "Something did disturb the ball, at least in this scenario." The tone of his voice seemed to hint that it may have applied elsewhere as well.

Janus shrugged. "The ball is perfect, the pitch was perfect. Heck, even the batter did a crackerjack job, assuming this was a real game."

"And assuming we can ignore the minute detail of a foot or two in the height of the ball at the time it crosses the plate, which we won't ignore. That pitch should have been higher. You thought so, I thought so." Victor had begun to act flustered and exasperated. "Even this kinetic field thinks so!" He said. Victor pressed another key and a wafer-thin red field was drawn just off the mound.

"No human and most machines can't see or sense it. Very few people know it is even possible, theoretically. And yet here it is."

"In all its 3D splendor," Janus said with heavy sarcasm.

"In 3D splendor, yes." Victor agreed. He changed 3D view from a simulation to an actual ball game.

"That wasn't some play you cooked up, was it?" The game looked fairly recent, possibly one that took place in the last few months judging by the advertisements on the outfield wall. Though, he wasn't sure as he had not been affording much attention to anyone, or anything, other than his misery.

"Are you beginning to understand, Mr. Franko?" Victor said, suddenly becoming very serious and calm. "It wasn't chance."

"Then what?" Janus demanded, enraged at the thought that his pitch was not as errant as he had believed.

"Diamond-carbide bonding. Faster computers." Victor flashed a wicked, albeit temporary, grin. "Lots of money." His anger returned. "My money!" He turned off the 3D display. "I've lost more than fifty diamond mines to political struggles between the Chateau and other nations in the last year. All to the game of baseball. All coming down to one errant pitch." He gestured wildly towards the room. "All to a kinetic energy field that no one can prove exists."

"Then how.." Janus started.

"Trust me," Victor said matter-of-factly. "When it comes to my money, I'll go to great lengths to find out who is stealing from me."

"You know who did it?"

"As these are political struggles, the only publicly acknowledged entity that would gain from my losses is Britain. But that means very little because international law stipulates that a country cannot retain private ownership of property seized from the resolution of a dispute. It would have to be sold. Even the inevitable buyer can claim no knowledge of any wrong doing. In order to identify any conspiracy, the saboteur and the buyer have to be identified before the first transaction is completed."

He sighed and walked behind his desk, then sat down in an overstuffed chair. "I do not know specifics, but I do know these key facts. One, a kinetic energy field was used to thwart an otherwise successful pitch. Two, someone directly involved will be attending my party. Three, I am of the opinion that you may know this individual." Victor returned to his chair. "I lost the first set of mines to your pitch, Mr. Franko, and began my investigations immediately afterwards. In three days, when my party is over, the transaction will be complete, Britain will be permitted to put the mines up for auction, and I will have no legal recourse to regain ownership of the first set of mines. In addition, any facts I may discover afterwards would be considered tainted since the buyer would then be known. My proposal, therefore, is fairly straightforward. Attend my party, find out who is responsible, and I will see to it you regain employment, recoup your status and lost salary, and include a handsome fortune."

"And if I say no?" Janus ventured.

Victor shrugged. "I'll pay you for your services." His lips turned into a gruesome smile. "But wouldn't you rather find out who is responsible?"

"This party," Janus said, almost choking. "It's a synthetic party."

Victor nodded.

"I hate these," he admitted. "The whole point is to be seen with the best looking companion. I mean, you can't turn around without running into someone swapping out parts just so their synthetic has a bigger bulge in its pants or a larger chest."

"Quite sick." Victor added.

"Then why do it?" Janus asked, peering at the disgusting man of incredible wealth.

"Because the distance traversed by the wealthy to maintain their pretense amuses me," he admitted.

MEETING THE EX AT THE SYNTHETIC PARTY

As the chauffeur guided the hovering limousine through the front gate leading to the Welch estate, Janus realized how unprepared he was for the evening. His 'date', what seemed to be a Transynth Series Two, was woefully outdated by several years, and Janus could not keep his mind off the hundreds of petty details that made one's evening successful at a synthetic party. Even its clothes hadn't been in style for over a year. He wondered whether Victor intentionally requested his services only to meet with failure, or if Vincent himself was out of touch with contemporary vices.

The chauffeur looked back at Janus with a wry smile. "The Welch estate, sir." He tossed in a smirk at no additional charge.

"Yeah," Janus muttered. He tugged at his chin with his thumb and index finger, then sat back in the seat and made no motion towards the door.

"Having seconds thoughts?"

He shook his head. "I'm probably the only one here who has to be." His 'date', having already been given explicit instructions to remain quiet, continued to do so.

"It's won't be that bad," the chauffeur offered.

Janus raised an eyebrow and looked at the chauffeur in disbelief.

"My presence with this," he gestured at the Series Two, "will be a laughing stock."

"Then chop it," the chauffeur said matter-of-factly.

"What?" he asked in a tone that reflected his horror at the suggestion.

The chauffeur fell silent, then motioned towards a patch of shadow on the side of the mansion. "See that woman?"

Janus squinted, then nodded. He watched as the woman wrestled with the lower anatomy of her synthetic date, dropped something in the bushes, and then turned towards the house as though nothing had happened.

"Five-to-one odds she just dropped a Patterson-made Pro-performa."

Janus shook his head. "What?" he asked again.

"A dong," The driver said. "I bet she just pitched a brand new Patterson-made Pro-performa ball and socket set. You know," and he made a lewd gesture.

"And you know this because," Janus prompted.

"Because I've worked here before. Look, you must know what goes on here. And, you must know that people can't walk around with spare parts all night. They get as far as the lobby, see what everyone else has, then run to a secluded spot to change parts. And by my count so far," the driver rustled with several items on the front seat, then held them up for Janus to see clearly, "the ladies definitely are not favoring the Patterson's tonight. Even though parts and clothes are changed and thrown away, they are still very much in fashion. Even these Patterson's are in their prime, so to speak."

Janus looked dumbfounded at the handful of synthetic male genitals in the driver's hands. As he felt a swell of disgust in his throat, clarity found its way into his moment of desperation. "And all of the parts that are thrown away are kept where?"

The chauffeur laughed and then guided the limousine away from the curb. They drove around to the back of the house, and the chauffeur hustled Janus towards the service entrance.

"You definitely do not want to be seen back here, so move it."

They walked quickly through the kitchen and into a storage room. Janus was immersed in a small warehouse of the latest synthetic parts. He bit his lower lip, then looked at the chauffeur. "What would it take to let me run through here?"

The chauffeur smiled then clapped his shoulder. "Courtesy of the host."

Janus felt fooled again. "I don't understand. Why?"

The chauffeur stopped him. "The Series Two, I'm assuming by her frame, has the best chassis of any synthetic for hot-swapping parts. Its packaged peripherals suck, but if I had to outfit someone with the best possible synthetic for a party like this, I'd send them along with a Series Two and have them raid the trash bin, so to speak." He gestured towards the storage room, "So, with Mr. Welch's best wishes."

"Why didn't you take me here directly?" Janus asked.

The chauffeur shrugged. "I was instructed to let you make your own decision on this matter. Maybe because if you were a genuine fool, you would have deserved to walk through the front door as-is. Maybe you aren't that stupid. I'll be waiting for you in the limousine. Keep it short." And, he left.

Janus spent several minutes sifting through assorted appendages before he remembered that he was out of touch with recent fashion. He hurried back to the kitchen, where he had noticed a few panoramic displays of the party, and watched the women for several moments. It took him a while to discern the real women from the synthetics, and then some minutes longer to identify the common fashions. When he returned to the storeroom, his sense of fashion felt refreshed.

The chauffeur met him at the limousine door as Janus hurried out the back of the mansion with an armful of replacement parts and a long evening gown draped over his shoulder.

"Amazing what people just throw away," the chauffeur commented, helping Janus into the back.

Janus quickly pushed his armload of materials onto the seat, and spread them out so the synthetic could see them. "Change your chest, posterior, thigh buffers, shoulder slats, lower jaw, ears, then put on the clothes."

As his date silently upgraded herself, Janus started to wonder how he could identify a person on a shoestring collection of facts. "Any recommendations on finding a particular person in a party like this?" He asked while working on the synthetic.

"Does this person have a name?" The chauffeur asked.

Janus shook his head. "More to the point, I need to ferret out a particular person."

The chauffeur paused then shrugged. "I guess it would help if you could identify what you are looking for."

Janus nodded in agreement. "Good point. I imagine it is someone who will be surprised to see me here. And who probably doesn't think too highly of your employer." Janus set the evening gown in the synthetic's lap. "Put this on," he said brusquely.

"You ready?" When his passenger nodded, the chauffeur started the vehicle. "It sounds like you're looking for someone who probably doesn't belong at such a party."

Janus quirked an eyebrow. "How do you mean?"

"These parties cater to those who are beyond wealthy. They are for people who use their wealth to define their lives." The chauffeur let out a deep laugh. "I've spent many hours discussing this with the rest of the staff during these events, you understand. So, maybe you should just look for the couple that doesn't belong."

"But I'm only looking for one person," he said.

"Right, but since this is a synthetic party, everyone here has a date. And part of the climate is that every person is suitably matched."

Janus glanced at the synthetic at his side, then looked at the road ahead. "That's certainly one thing to look for." The suggestion didn't seem at all plausible, but he did think the general goal was the right one. It wasn't as simple as finding the out-of-place couple, but it might still be possible. "Baseball," he whispered as a muse. He smiled and directed the chauffeur to let him off near the front gate without yielding an explanation.

When the limousine stopped, Janus escorted the synthetic to the walk and strolled slowly towards the front door, giving everyone outdoors the opportunity to see the new arrivals. It also gave him the chance to remember his social graces. He drew the synthetic's arm close to his and gripped the ceramic-textured fabric tightly. It was the first time he had actually touched her, and her skin felt a lot more human than he had anticipated. She responded, as expected, with a curt smile.

"Track conversation," he prompted, using a high-level instruction language for natural robot programming.

Without breaking her slow walk, the synthetic replied in a whisper, "topic?"

"Baseball. Kinetic energy. Diamonds." He said the words very softly, then escorted her up a large marble staircase that lead into the Welch estate.

Janus paraded the synthetic through the foyer, feeling nervous with so many eyes that were apparently on him. He wasn't sure what to think, so offered a subtle nod when his eyes met with another's. Whatever he was expecting a synthetic party to be, it was so much more. And so much less. Perfectly matched pairs strolled, danced, and dined. They looked like proverbial matches made in heaven. It was a sham on a magnificent scale, and Janus idly wondered how much these people bought into it.

He readily identified several national league players who had either forgotten him or were simply not interested in engaging in any conversation. He started to guide the synthetic towards the ballroom when she balked and directed him with her eyes towards an expansive hall containing a library and sitting area.

Giving the ballroom a quick surveillance, Janus guessed he would have wasted his time. Couples seemed more inclined to parade than converse, and he didn't think the person he was looking for would be there. Apparently, the synthetic had come to the same conclusion first. As he turned to escort the synthetic in the suggested direction, he noticed Victor Welch in the ballroom. It wasn't the mere presence of the large man that caught his attention, but his escort: an equally obese woman. Individually, both were very unpleasant to look at. However, as a couple, the match was impeccable. Janus walked from the ballroom with a vague feeling of amusement tugging the corners of his mouth into a slight smile. Briefly, he wondered if Victor Welch's date was a synthetic. He had always assumed the luxury synthetic models would be slim and attractive.

The overall mood of the party changed as he entered the library and sitting hall. The occupants appeared much more relaxed, going as far as to have their synthetic dates stand at the back of the room. Though, those that did so seemed to be given cautionary stares from the other couples.

"Partial match," the synthetic whispered into his ear from the corner of her mouth. "Baseball and diamond mines. The two couples by the hearth."

Janus started towards the hearth when a familiar voice caught him off-guard.

"Well, if this isn't Janus Franko, it certainly is a passable copy."

Janus swallowed and produced a curt smile to the debutante who had spoken. "Priscilla," he said amicably. His eyes scanned either side of his former girlfriend for her escort, then took in the site of the finely tailored mannequin that accompanied her.

"I didn't expect to see you here," she whispered so no one else would overhear them and flashed a cutting smile. "I didn't think this would be your scene."

"Well," Janus said slightly louder, looking away from her, "I've been enjoying myself so far." He felt pressured by time and was quite disturbed by Priscilla's presence, more so by the thought of a protracted conversation. The memory of her company overcame him and he struggled to remain composed.

"I didn't know you were playing again." Priscilla slipped her arm around her escort's waist. "At least, I haven't heard anything."

"I've had other pursuits occupying my time," he lied. "And you? I thought you hated these things?"

"When it was fashionable to hate them," she demurred, and sized him over without bothering to pretend she was doing otherwise. Then she asked with a subtle barb, "How is your game?" Her eyes wandered across his chest and waist as she spoke.

Janus' lips were pursed, ready with a curse, when his synthetic slipped her arm around his elbow, nuzzled his jaw with the tip of her nose, and coyly asked, "You weren't privy to know he was back?"

Janus felt smug with his synthetic's beautifully timed and articulated response.

Priscilla's face flushed slightly, not expecting a response from what she assumed was his synthetic date, but then she laughed gaily. "Oh, yes. I'm quite sure he is back. Minor League is it?"

"Playing for local disputes, are we?" Priscilla's beau added lamely.

Again, before Janus could respond, his synthetic raised her arm and she touched her fingertip to Priscilla's synthetic's chest in a benign gesture. "Oh, stop! You are such a comedian." She withdrew her hand and patted Janus on the chest, though looking directly at Priscilla. "But seriously, the voter-approved initiative that was passed a few months ago would make that, well, illegal."

Now, Priscilla gaped, glaring at the synthetic.

It took Janus a moment to realize what had happened. His synthetic had, in a few terse sentences, socially trounced Priscilla and her date by demonstrating that neither human nor synthetic were aware of local politics that had been in effect for over two months. He was also quite surprised that his synthetic was so astute.

Then, he remembered a social grace and smiled apologetically. It wasn't good form to leave another couple on a sour note. He took his synthetic's hand and started to walk away. As he passed Priscilla, he remarked, "You have chosen a very suitable match."

When they were out of earshot, his synthetic whispered, "Ouch. Nice parting shot, while socially acceptable." She seemed to have become much more conversational than she had been earlier.

"Thanks," Janus replied, and started feeling better.

The couple Janus intended to investigate had moved during his interlude with Priscilla, so he kept walking towards the far end of the hall that contained the library. As they approached a more secluded section of the library, Janus made a subtle gesture directing the synthetic to sit. He sat beside her, took her hand in his, and kissed the backs of her fingers. It was important to act as though the synthetic was an actual person. As he did so, acting and kissing, he whispered, "At first, I thought you were a Transynth Series Two. But I think you just proved me wrong. I should know your model anyway."

His synthetic offered a softened smile and touched his cheek when he kissed her fingers. "I think it is a good idea if you go with your original assumption," she spoke while standing up, contrary to his recent instruction to sit. "But you should refer to me by name." Her eyes twinkled; another sign that she was certainly not a Transynth model, but something more advanced. "And you never asked. It's Anastasia."

Janus also stood, though just looked at her. "Anastasia. Alright." He thought for a moment, "I'm starting to feel like I'm the synthetic here. That, or ..." but he stopped when she put her finger up and touched his lips in a gesture for silence.

"I am a synthetic, if that was to be your question. You watched me strip myself down, after all." She turned and looked towards the foyer. "Was that an ex?"

Janus nodded. "Yeah," he muttered.

Anastasia snaked her arm around his waist and gave him a gentle hug. "Don't fret."

"She's a deceitful bitch," though the same moment he spoke, Anastasia's tongue flicked over her lips and he didn't hear himself cuss.

"White noise," she explained. "Don't swear." She continued giving him a supportive hug with her arm. "She behaved more like a socialite. And her age is starting to show. She's on her way out of her game."

"She's not that old," Janus said defensively.

She raised an eyebrow. "Don't bet on it. She may have the surgery and cosmetics to look twenty, but she is closer to fifty."

Janus shivered, but no longer felt concern for her, which surprised him. He started to reconsider his options, and mused aloud. "It would take a lot of money and muscle to fix a baseball game. And chances are the person responsible is smart enough not to bring it up, at least by name."

A warm, supportive smile brightened Anastasia's mouth and she nudged him. "Would you like to try a different tactic then, other than baseball and diamonds?"

He nodded. "Yes, but I'm not sure what. Although, I noticed a lot of surveillance monitors in the kitchen. I suppose Mr. Welch has been recording those, and probable from other cameras as well. Do you have access to those records?"

Anastasia's smile managed to brighten further, and she nuzzled his cheek with her nose again. Her playfulness was starting to irritate Janus since, after all, she was a synthetic. Nevertheless, she played the game that well! Most synthetics he had encountered were not able to make such timely gestures. "We'll just see what happens if I ask nicely."

"Ah, yes," she said almost immediately thereafter. "I do have access."

"Then shall we dance while you read?" He smiled and even gave her a quick peck on the cheek. After his synthetic had trounced Priscilla, and now knowing that he wouldn't have to hunt and peck through every conversation himself, he was feeling a lot better now. He led Anastasia towards the ballroom, whispering through the side of his mouth as they sauntered.

"Can you try filtering all of the conversations for anyone using a lot of metaphors, and also using a highly skilled vocabulary? Elements that might indicate education?" He patted her hand as they walked, nodding to several other couples as they passed.

Anastasia nodded to him, and also to the other couples walking by.

It was then that Janus noticed that her neckline had plunged dramatically, and the opacity of her gown had diminished enough to be quite revealing. Anyone could see that she wore nothing beneath the dress, and Janus felt somewhat embarrassed.

"What are you doing?" he asked harshly.

She replied pleasantly, "The dress you gave me is meant to shift in spectrum and opacity. I've also noticed that the other ladies are preferring a less conservative wardrobe." She tipped her head to indicate one woman who now appeared all but naked.

They stopped at the ballroom entrance, and Anastasia turned to face him. She placed her hand on his shoulder, and was ready to be lead onto the dance floor. "Janus," she spoke softly, "I'm well aware of your dispassion for synthetics."

"Wha…" he started to argue, but she shook her head to silence him.

"Sauntering about the sitting room and library is one thing, but on the dance floor you will have to put aside your disdain and treat me like a real woman. If you expect others to think you are genuinely interested in trying to make us appear as the perfect couple."

He remained silent, though looked puzzled.

"You are going to have to touch me," she said. "You have to behave like you are attracted to me, and not be so standoffish."

They started to dance, but Janus began to argue her recommendation almost immediately. "I'm not sure putting up any pretense is necessary now that you have access to the recordings. I don't see how playing out this sick game will help me now. I'm here, and you can help me find the people who ruined me. Why should I have to play along anymore?"

Anastasia frowned and danced with him, but her movements were less fluid than they had been; more mechanical. "Is that all I am to you? Some robot?"

"No, you're on-loan too," he said bitterly.

"Real classy," she snapped, then turned and walked away.

Janus' jaw dropped, and he quickly walked after her. He saw several wide stares, some disapproving, and his confidence quickly dissipated.

Anastasia stalked through the hall towards the dining room, then out onto the terrace.

CONFESSIONS ON THE TERRACE

Janus approached Anastasia and stood by her, resting both palms on a thick cement railing. "Look, I'm sorry I said that."

"But, you meant it," she muttered, and dabbed her eyes. They were glistening, and a few tear streaks marred her cheeks.

"Don't you think you're taking this a bit too far? I mean, with the crying and storming out of the house? You're a synthetic. Aren't you supposed to act properly and not behave like a little kid?"

She turned to face him and shook her head bitterly. "Synthetics are more than just human simulacrums, Janus. They have become much more than mere replicas of emotion and physical traits. Most people only think of synthetics as they were a couple hundred years ago, they have advanced to the point that the latest models are not that far removed from human."

Her eyes cinched together and more tears were wept. "I have instructions I must follow. I won't ever get sick, grow old, or succumb to a lifespan. I have an owner. And, by literal interpretation of the law, I am a slave. So, yes, I could turn around and act 'properly'. But my owner has not placed me under such orders, nor do you have the authority to give such orders. And I choose not to."

She angrily pushed Janus away from her and pointed at him accusingly. "You think that because I changed parts for you means you control me? That you can treat me poorly?"

"Look," he said sheepishly, though unmoved, "I'm not used to dealing with this whole 'Synthetics now have emotions, too' thing."

She turned her back to him, shaking her head. "Try thinking of it in terms of the 'Humans are such assholes' thing. It's a fact of life you'll just have to get used to."

"I've only known synthetics as the rest of the world has known them," he admitted, "and they've never been anything like you. They've been a soulless voice peddling advertisements, or a bulky drone doing menial labor. Even these parties, where the synthetics are supposed to be the best models, I've only heard that they are nothing more than expensive expressions of pretense. Like Priscilla's synthetic." He tried to touch her shoulder, but she brushed his hand away.

"Not knowing is no excuse." She peeked over her shoulder. "I wanted to help you tonight, I asked to help you tonight. The truth," she paused and turned to face him, "the truth is that I've known about you for quite some time."

He remained silent, not sure what to think of her admission.

"I knew who Priscilla was," Anastasia continued, "and, tonight, I know what is at stake. I wanted to help you because I didn't think anyone gave you a second thought."

"Pity?" he frowned and leaned against the rail. "My position is so bad that the synthetics are pitying me?"

"For someone who is supposed to be as smart as you, you really are a fool," she retorted. "I did it because as I learned more about you, I became more attracted to you."

"Pardon me?" he asked, now surprised. "You were, pardon me?" Silently, he couldn't help but feel reviled at the thought. Anastasia was unlike any synthetic he had ever met, but that did not mean she was anything more than a robot. He still wasn't able to come to grips with that.

She looked saddened, but still quite irritated. "I like you."

Janus was awe-struck. "I guess I'm not sure how I'm supposed to respond to that."

Anastasia held up her hands and then looked out over the garden. Most of the couples were inside, and the moonlight cast lonely shadows besides a few individuals walking across the wide expanse of the lawn. She folded her arms and leaned against the railing, her shoulders hunched together.

Janus was so taken by the natural pose, his immediate reaction was to take off his jacket and lay it across her back. Only after he had done so did he feel foolish, and he stammered, "you looked cold." He muttered apologetically, "I forgot."

She touched the lapel of the jacket and then drew the garment over her arms. "Synthetics don't feel cold," she answered rhetorically. She didn't tell him that she did feel cold, or that her arms were covered in goose bumps. "Besides, it's the gesture."

A long silence fell between them.

"What I don't understand," he started to ask, but then added in hastily, "if you don't mind my asking, is why a synthetic would be attracted to a human?"

"I can't answer such a blanket question. I can only answer for my-self," she sighed. "But I won't massage your ego with a plethora of compliments to your character. I've already told you that I became attracted to you as I learned more about you. I didn't say I loved you. It would be quite ridiculous for me to state such a thing."

"So," he said while making a leading gesture, "you're just saying you like me. Nothing more?"

She rolled her eyes, "Yes." She turned her back to the garden and faced him again. "Though I'm still mad at you."

Janus looked back towards the house, then at her. "In the car, you acted exactly how I had expected a synthetic to act. Now, you're not acting like a synthetic at all. Why the change in behavior?"

"Because Mr. Welch had me outfitted with outdated components in order to observe your reaction. Granted, you were prompted to re-configure my attire and physique. If I didn't act like a synthetic, you wouldn't have thought of me as one. It was crucial for everyone in attendance to believe you were with a synthetic."

He laughed with disdain. "You're mad at me because I treated you like one, yet .."

"No," she interrupted him. "I didn't say treat me badly. Just that you had to know I was a synthetic."

"Why?" he asked, still perplexed.

"Because I like you," she replied with a tone of desperation, "and because I didn't want you to think I was organic and then feel deceived when you found out otherwise."

Janus nodded, and looked at her. Although he found himself feeling slightly less repulsed by the thought of a synthetic being attracted to him, he still found it difficult to identify Anastasia as a person. Hadn't he selected several primary traits himself? Then, he smiled softly.

"You find this humorous, then?" she asked with a snide tone.

He shook his head and said "No." Her gown was still semi-translucent, and he touched the collar seam. "I was just thinking that the woman you pointed out earlier in the near-nude dress seemed neither popular or attractive."

Anastasia sniffed and smirked. "Really," she stated.

"I was also thinking that you might have a much better fashion sense than I do. Perhaps you would feel more comfortable in a gown of your own choosing?" He asked.

"Perhaps," she agreed.

"What I was really thinking," he sincerely added, "was I don't know what you look like."

At that she raised an eyebrow, and seemed to have understood the question, but waited for him to elaborate.

"What is your ideal or chosen physique? Did you ... " he paused and groped for words.

"Ship with a default set?" She asked, though her tone was somewhat warmer and she did manage a slight smile. "No," she answered. "But I do have my preferred stock."

"Would you like to, um, be yourself then?"

"Why do you care?" she asked, her tone suddenly short.

A cool wind brushed through his hair and he found himself capable of putting his feelings into words. "I didn't mean to act like an asshole." His eyes felt red and raw, and now a slight tremble palsied his lips. "You and Mr. Welch have been the only people who have said more than two words to me in the last year. I've been a pariah, no one has wanted to have anything to do with me. Then, out of the blue, Mr. Welch thinks there may be a way to get out of this hell, and a synthetic," he paused, the corrected himself, "and you not only try to help me, but manage to like me. I won't pretend to know why because I've got nothing and if you didn't notice the stares inside, I have no friends left, either."

"If you like me, synthetic or not, I should be grateful that someone in the Universe doesn't think I'm a complete and utter failure. I was thinking I should at least be thankful for your generosity and I shouldn't have stuck to my misconceptions."

Anastasia dabbed her eyes, and then took his arm in hers. "I think I'd like to get changed now. We still need to solve your problem." She started to lead him towards the house, but he balked.

"I am sorry," he said ruefully.

"I know," she replied. "Are you still up to your challenge?"

"Would you think less of me if I just wanted to go home?" he asked.

Momentarily, she looked hurt, but she conceded. "I would be disappointed. But, it's your life, Janus."

He nodded, then smiled. "Then lets go."

Now, Anastasia stopped and looked at him. "Where?"

"You wanted to change, didn't you?"

Both human and synthetic smiled and walked towards the house.

...

AN ENCOUNTER IN HER BEDROOM

Janus assumed Anastasia would be headed for the storeroom in the kitchen, so was surprised when she shook her head and guided him upstairs.

They walked hand in hand up the narrow staircase near the kitchen, climbing to the third floor. At the top of the staircase, they came eye-to-eye with one of Mr. Welch's bodyguards.

Janus started to say something, but the bodyguard simply nodded to Anastasia, saying, "I'll unlock your room."

She lead Janus to a grand door halfway down the hall, opened it, and then motioned him inside. After she entered, she closed the door and activated the electronic lock.

Janus stood agape, both at the extravagance of the room, and at not realizing it belonged to Anastasia. "I didn't know you lived here." He said, then asked, "You live here?"

She walked across the room to a large closet and opened two doors. She softly laughed, and nodded.

"You live here," he said again, and then motioned around the entire room, then out the window. "With Mr. Welch?"

Again, she nodded. She selected a long, conservative black gown, simple black shoes, and some less conservative under garments, then walked across the room to the bed and set them down. "Yes," she finally answered, though now seemed somewhat distracted. "I live here. I've been on Mars for the last nine years working for my father."

Janus sat down on the edge of the bed and watched her, completely perplexed. "I'm baffled," he admitted.

"Give it a moment, you'll eventually draw the correct conclusion." She now walked to another closet and open it. This one was filled with tightly packed, sealed containers.

"Mr. Welch is..." he prompted.

"Correct," she said distractedly as she began pulling several containers from the closet.

"But you're a ..." he started.

She returned to the bed. "I don't think the present is the right time for family history," she said.

"Ah," he submitted.

"Janus," she asked, "As you've already changed my parts once I won't let any pre-conceived sense of modesty affect me. But, I don't want you to see anything you don't want to see."

He raised an eyebrow. "What else is there to see."

"This isn't my," she started, and motioned to her body with her hand. "I am unlike most models and can completely refit my build, but changing it is the really icky part."

"I don't mind," he said, completely unprepared for what she would do.

"Some people find it quite gruesome," she said.

He shrugged, and actually found himself fascinated. "No, it's ok."

"Alright," she conceded, and she immediately slipped out of her gown.

The room was light with small candle-like fixtures around the walls, and her body, the body Janus had selected, was finely sculpted. But she neither demurred nor posed, and quickly began stripping away everything. Her hair, her entire face, all of the slats, and her breasts were disconnected and tossed into a basked at the foot of her bed. She slipped out of her pelvis as she would a pair of panties, and unrolled her leg shells like a pair of nylons.

Anastasia stood in front of him, a skinned human, a robot chassis completely covered in cellulose gel. And that, too, she began to peel off.

Janus grew nauseous as Anastasia tossed pieces of cellulose into the basket, though he bit his lip. He had never known that synthetics used such a complex mechanism to shape their bodies. "Are synthetics androgynous," he asked with a guarded tone.

"No. There are distinct male, female, and asexual frames. I have a female chassis. And my subconscious processes include behavioral programming for a feminine gender role. If I tried to use a male physique, I surmise I would look like a homely transvestite. Now, I need my shape," she said, and then walked into the bathroom. She was gone only a few moments, and returned with a new cellulose gel encasing her body, giving her a completely different dimension.

As quickly as she had disassembled herself, she began to add features back to her physical self.

"Priscilla used to spend more time in the bathroom than it took you to become a completely different person," Janus said in awe.

Anastasia smiled and gave him no time to admire her completed form in the buff, though she remarked, "My body has changed, but I am still the same person." She donned her under garments, and then slipped into the black dress.

Still, an entirely different person stood in front of Janus, and he was amazed at her sinuous, exotic beauty, and surprised to see how well her physical appearance fit her personality. He found that her new physique was more appealing to him than the one he mistook as a Transynth Series Two. He was so used to judging synthetics by looks and voice alone that he had a difficult time reminding himself that he didn't like synthetics. Anastasia was certainly unlike any synthetic he had met or imagined.

"The sight of me naked didn't detest you?" She asked, now fully dressed. She touched his shoulder and then walked back towards the bathroom. "Still need to fix my hair," she called over her shoulder.

"No," he answered, a bit louder. "It was, um, interesting." Just a little gross, he thought. "I didn't know that synthetics could change shape like that."

"No commercial model can," she called from the bathroom. "I'm what you could deem a unique design. Or custom design," her voice trailed off, "not sure which is the best description."

She returned, her hair brushed and drawn back into a French braid. She turned around for him. "How do I look?"

"Beautiful," he said.

"Thanks," she said, and she blushed.

"So, what did you do on Mars?" he asked.

"In a matter of speaking, I worked on myself. My studies overlapped with my own design, so I'm pretty much wearing my work." Now, she demurred. She sat down next to him on the bed and slipped her shoes on.

"What kind of work do you do? I'm assuming something to do with synthetics."

"Part of the time I work on the technology used to create my cellulose gel frame, and also with behavioral programming using proto-type chip sets," she responded with pride.

"Why on Mars, though?"

"Because the diamonds found on Mars have the best structure for use with diamond-carbide bonding," she prattled merrily. "My gel frame and chip set require the Martian diamonds."

"Yes, I was wondering if synthetics had frames like yours. I guess they don't. Are there any advantages besides being able to change your frame dimensions?"

She nodded and picked up a the pelvis from the basket. "Most synthetics have a standard male or female chassis. Slats and buffers can be added to fill out some parts, and identifying characteristics can be changed." She pointed to portions of the pelvis, then dropped it back in the basket. "But the base chassis remains the same. That's why it is so easy to identify a synthetic because once you've see a model, you can easily identify the uniform build. Plus, the lack of an organic layer makes it very easy to identify a synthetic using a thermal scanner or x-ray."

"So that gooey stuff under your skin is organic tissue?"

She made a face and shook her head. "No. It looks like it is to a medical scanner, but it is not living tissue. Besides, trying to make a cyborg out of a synthetic is very impractical. Synthetics with modifica-tions like mine gain many of the benefits a cyborg would have, but with-out actual tissue."

"There are others like you then?"

She nodded distantly. "I am a unique entity, but there are other synthetics that use similar techniques."

"How do you know when you meet another synthetic like your-self?" He asked.

"I don't know. Other synthetics are easy to spot using tissue and thermal scanners, or just analyzing their speech and behavior. But my model is very different in those respects." She checked her clothes and then looked at Janus expectantly. "Still, I'm a synthetic. Are you ready?"

"In a moment," he said. He stood and looked at her, drinking in her finely crafted features. She was perfect in that she wasn't too perfect. Then, he started to think about the implications of what she had told him. "If Mr. Welch, er, your father, loses these mines.." he paused and looked at her, and then felt a very mellowing sensation. "Legally, are you the property of the Mining division that manages those mines, or of Mr. Welch?"

She looked crestfallen. "The mines," she said. "Yes, I will be the property of the new owner."

"And Mr. Welch?" he asked, now beginning to draw a partial conclusion. "Where are his mines?"

"I'm not sure ..." she started.

"Is Mr. Welch like you?" He asked. "Is Mr. Welch a synthetic?"

She didn't answer, or give any indication to the contrary.

Janus studied her carefully, the continued. "Supposing Mr. Welch is, and I'm not sure how he managed it, but just supposing, then he has probably circumvented the issue of ownership by having one of his own mining divisions own his own synthetic title. I don't know how he would have been able to avoid the publicity of his nature, but I'll assume he was able to do that as well."

Still, she was silent.

"Also a Martian mine, then? He would lose himself and you?" Janus asked.

A slight nod, but no sound or sign of emotion.

"He said that he knew the culprit would be here tonight, and that I knew him or her. Perhaps he intended to imply that someone would need access to me to make the deception possible." Janus said. Now, his mind raced and he thought back to the kinetic energy field that Mr. Welch had mentioned to be the cause of his pitch. "He also said most synthetics can't see a kinetic energy field, but I think he could. I'll bet you can, too. That is how he knew it existed and why he started investigating right away. Also, the field probably needs a point of reference. Something I was wearing?" he asked, not specifically to Anastasia.

"Priscilla could have planted something," he continued, musing aloud. "And if so, that could be the reason why he thought I knew one of the culprits."

"We can't admit to seeing the field," Anastasia said earnestly. "If we do, everyone will know what he is. He will be discredited."

"Don't you think some people already know?" Janus asked.

"How could they?"

He took her hands in his and gripped them loosely. How human her hands felt, how human she was making his heart feel. Though he still felt antipathy towards synthetics in general, he could not dismiss the growing ambivalence he felt towards Anastasia. She was a synthetic. But, he had to admit to himself he liked her.

"Anastasia, they know. I believe they've known for a long time."

"How can you make such an assumption?" she argued, though flexed her palms in his.

Even after the way I've been acting tonight, she still likes me, Janus thought. Or, at least wants me to think so.

"Because owning you and Mr. Welch, er, your father, is far more valuable than mines. They may ultimately be out to own the blueprints for your construction. Your father said that there was a lot of money in diamond mines, but there is even more money in synthetics."

He looked down at their hands folded together. "In my doctoral thesis, I studied random disturbances along a know trajectory. Consider the fact that someone knows as the random disturbance. The trajectory begins with your father and you being the property of your own company, and ends with someone owning your company, and therefore owning you. The potential buyer, who we won't know until it is too late, is the ultimate conspirator, and the co-conspirator is the person we need to find tonight. If we find that person, we may be able to prove that the kinetic field exists and was used during my last game."

"But how?" she asked. "We don't know how. That's why my father asked you. You were the first victim of this ruse. And your studies also make you likely to make more sense of the situation than we have."

He then realized a potential truth. "Perhaps Priscilla was involved. If so, maybe her employers positioned her near me, got us married, and she was able to plant some device to act as a reference beacon for the kinetic field generator. And her employer, then, is most likely the person who will own those mines as of tomorrow morning."

"But without proof, what good can be done? Where can we find the proof?" she asked earnesty.

"Simple," he said. "We'll prove Priscilla is a synthetic."

A FACADE OF LOVE ON THE BALLROOM FLOOR

They walked hand in hand, and were met with more than a few intrigued glances. The Anastasia the crowd had previously seen with Janus had disappeared and was now replaced with a completely different person. Janus felt more confident after observing that most of the people didn't mind, and Anastasia's earlier outburst on the ballroom floor seemed to have been forgotten. Most of all, he just felt more comfortable with Anastasia as herself, in a body of her own choice.

Anastasia held his hand as they walked into the ballroom. The ballroom was quiet and only Mr. Welch and his date still danced away. Anastasia faced Janus and took his hands in hers. "I still need to sort through the security recordings," she whispered. "But, even if your conjecture is correct, we will need to take added precaution in playing out our roles for the party. We must not allow anyone to assume we're here for an ulterior reason, or they may simply leave and we'll miss the opportunity."

Janus nodded an agreement, and then placed a light kiss or her jawbone.

Her eyes darted over his face and her lips fluttered in a slight, cynical smile. "You don't have to be too smoochy-faced when dancing," she commented in a dry voice. "This is more about touching and holding your partner as you execute each step."

"Maybe I wanted to do that for the sake of doing it," he said.

"Why would you want to?" she asked, not sure what to make of the gesture.

"I'm okay now," he assured her, nodding slightly as he spoke.

She observed him for several moments, and then asked, "Earlier, you seemed quite adamant in your position on synthetics. Now you've seemed to have changed your mind."

"I've learned more about you, and I feel more comfortable with you in your own physique. I guess the act of changing synthetic parts makes them seem more inhuman rather than more perfectly human."

With their hands gently pressed together, they started dancing to a brass symphony that echoed from the walls, bass that pulsed in the cherry wood planks under their feet, and strings and woodwinds wafting down from the ceiling. Though Janus was not an experienced dancer, his life as a professional athlete helped, and Anastasia contributed by teaching him the appropriate steps. She made sure to keep slow the speed of her dancing, and to guide him so he didn't make too many noticeable mistakes. When she turned her head, her sandy hair drifted across the pale skin covering her high cheekbones, and a faintly rose-colored lipstick glistened on her pursed and pouting lips.

Janus' chest tightened and he found himself feeling the uneasiness he always felt when he liked a woman, and slowly began to find it harder to express his interests and affection. Telling a synthetic it looked good was one thing, but telling the same thing to a human was completely different. The dance Anastasia helped him through required their hands to be clasped, then his hand on her hip and hers on his chest. His hand would slide from her hip to her shoulder and then down the length of her arm so their hands were together once again.

Yet dancing with a synthetic was not as hard as he had thought it would be, and he was able to touch her as a woman and not an object of carnal lust. Anastasia also seemed more relaxed as her own self, and for a time the two enjoyed each other's company on the dance floor. Anastasia was a synthetic, though, and so was able to analyze the security logs in a separate process while she danced, but still committed a substantial number of cycles to Janus.

"If you two keep this up, you'll make us look bad," Mr. Welch jested as he and his partner danced close by.

Janus blinked and caught himself gazing starry-eyed at Anastasia. He nodded to Mr. Welch, "I have to try harder to make up for my previous performance on the dance floor," he said and grimaced, referring to the earlier spat he had with Anastasia.

Mr. Welch smiled warmly and seemed much more cordial than he had been when Janus had last met him. "How have the two of you been this evening?"

Janus nodded, not quite sure how to respond. "Very well."

"A bit puzzled," Anastasia said after looking around the ballroom to see if anyone else was close by. Her dancing with Janus degraded to a stationary sway and round-robin steps.

"Yes?" Mr. Welch prompted.

"Priscilla," she paused and glanced at Janus, then continued, "has spent a lot of time milling about the library and study, and going outside to change the configuration of her partner. But, they appear to have on ongoing conversation when they are alone, and have confined themselves to those two areas of the house, even while others have left to eat or walk about the garden."

"So she is a bore," Mr. Welch said, adding a shrug and a nod of sympathy towards Janus.

"What are they talking about?" Janus asked.

"An upcoming game between France and Japan, and the stakes being an underwater research platform." She danced more actively with Janus, though still near Mr. Welch.

"And outside, in the front garden where most of the synthetics are reconfigured, she appears to take special precaution so that she is facing away from the house. Her motions indicate that she is putting something on her face. This pattern of behavior recurs throughout the evening, and her synthetic companion alternates between changing his genitals or adjusting pectoral slats. He too is obscured from a direct line-of-sight with the camera."

Janus smirked at her last remark. "So long as he doesn't use a Patterson Pro-Performa, right?" He couldn't help but snicker.

"I don't even want to know why you knew he wasn't wearing one," Anastasia jested, though gave Janus a strange look.

"It does seem strange that someone with her perfect complexion would need makeup so soon" Mr. Welch's date offered.

Janus raised and eyebrow and looked between Anastasia and Mr. Welch's date. "Didn't you say she was looking ..." he struggled for the right word.

"Ancient!" Anastasia said and made a disgusted expression.

"She looked quit fetching when I saw her, which was recently," Mr. Welch's date said.

"Interesting," Mr. Welch mused.

"Wait," Janus said. "Anastasia, you said her date wasn't wearing a Patterson. Did he add or remove it?"

"He added it," Anastasia replied, then she raised her eyebrows. "I think I know what you're thinking." She turned to Mr. Welch and explained. "When we arrived and the chauffeur prompted Janus to, eh," she made a gesture down the length of her body and Mr. Welch nodded knowingly. "The chauffeur noted the general trend for the evening was the Pattersons were not the preferred assembly for male companions."

Janus shrugged and asked, "Maybe the ladies decided they were back in style? Can you check to see if any other synthetic male put a Patterson back on?"

"Doubtful," Mr. Welch said. "Any spare parts are quickly policed and are considered non-retrievable."

"A moment," she said, and then shook her head. "No, you're right. That is the only instance where that particular item was added."

"I think that is puzzling," Janus said. "Her date is very much out of fashion, and she doesn't seem to notice." He looked at Mr. Welch, "Isn't that against the grain of the party?"

"But," Anastasia interjected, "also remember that both of them did not seem all that prepared for the party when we met them earlier. She was openly hostile, and seemed quick to duck out of any confrontation." Then she tipped her head to Mr. Welch.

He nodded pensively. "Yes, her actions on both accounts were not conducive to the atmosphere of the party. If she was engaging in an act of subterfuge, she may not have prepared herself for the party, and she may have instructed her date to change something without paying attention to what her date actually changed."

"Then why is she here?" Janus asked, then he looked between Mr. Welch and Anastasia, but fell silent.

"Anastasia, what puzzled you about the recordings?" Mr. Welch asked.

"The underwater platform is a research facility for silicon polymer, potentially a competing product to our work with cellulose gel. I never thought anything of it because it is too unstable for extended use unless constantly replaced."

"That would certainly explain why she was in the bathroom for so long," Janus joked, though with a dark tone.

"It would explain it," Mr. Welch's date said matter-of-factly. "And it would explain what she was doing outside. She may have been changing her face."

"An interesting supposition that she is a synthetic," Anastasia stated and looked directly at Janus. "You may very well be right."

Mr. Welch's eyes glimmered, and Janus took note of the reaction. "If she is a synthetic, and she was created by a company that is a competitor of your synthetic research facility on Mars," Janus suggested to Mr. Welch, "and she was married to the pitcher who threw the one errant pitch that cost you your mines, then wouldn't that be cause for further investigation? And if she plans on acting as a representative for a potential buyer, perhaps she is here to take immediate possession tomorrow."

"Yes," Mr. Welch agreed, though his temper now simmered. "But the security footage and speculation is not enough. If she is a synthetic, she has to be ferreted out, in public for all to see. And it does sound reasonable that her only intention for being present is to serve as an advance agent for 'collecting' her employer's new property, come the morrow. A moment while I check with my legal team."

With a subtle gesture, Mr. Welch cued a new song, and an airy melody began playing in the dusky light. Some couples stopped at the entrance, watching with genuine interest; a perfect opportunity for them to play 'spot the synthetic'. Janus and Anastasia, and Mr. Welch and his date, danced slowly to the music, their conversation paused while Mr. Welch consulted with his lawyers and the onlookers paid notice to their countenance.

Janus interlaced the fingers of his leading hand with Anastasia's, and they swayed close to each other. He enjoyed the feeling of being united with someone without care or concern for what transpired around him. It was not his current predicament, or the possible troubles Anastasia and Mr. Welch may experience if they could not prove their case. The feeling was a lack of pretense; at that moment, he simply did not care what others might think of him dancing with a synthetic. He had only known synthetics as a cheap parody of life used for commercial gain. But this synthetic, the woman he now danced with, was nothing like his original definition of synthetics. Though the thought of Priscilla being a synthetic revolted him, it did not make him feel ill because she was a synthetic, which surprised him.

His wife deceived him. She used him. Though he did not let her leave with a sheepish grin as his goodbye, but a torrent of insults and angry accusations, that had been the sum of his anger and outrage. He had wasted the last eight months trying to forget her because he could not let himself forgive himself for the penultimate mistake of not leaving her earlier. That, and he admitted he never should have married her, regardless of whether he knew she was a synthetic.

He was not a synthetic scientist, and did not know how synthetic behavior was programmed. But Anastasia had demonstrated the ability to be devoted to him out of simple blind affection, the type a child would have when they first experience infatuation with another, and she was able to forgive him for his transgressions and shortsightedness. While she may have acted as though she liked him, and possibly played coy games to the contrary, she was able to interpret his unspoken feelings; something no synthetic was supposed to be able to do.

Anastasia was a synthetic, and while they danced, he felt his chest clench as he found his thoughts arrive in a rare moment of clarity: he liked her.

Janus kissed the back of her hand as they danced, and he commented quietly so the onlookers would not hear, "You are an amazing dancer."

"Thank you," she whispered.

"I'm surprised there aren't more people dancing."

"Most synthetics make terrible dancers," she explained. "Even two synthetics designed to dance together tend to be very artificial, even if they are precise."

"And yet there are three synthetics dancing, and I'll wager everyone thinks you're human."

"Three?" she asked and gave him a coy smile. "My father may or may not be a synthetic, I don't believe I gave you an explicit answer when you asked. And his date is most assuredly human. Ms. Adley is a behavioral scientist. She is an amazing woman." Anastasia glanced over at Mr. Welch and Ms. Adley. "I think my father is sweet on her, and she wrote my soft logic."

"She programmed you?" Janus asked, also looking over at Ms. Adley. "I thought synthetics were produced from a mold."

Anastasia shook her head. "The synthetics you're used to," she snorted, but gave him a comforting nudge. "Component-based synthetics are ideal for mass production, but not for truly unique sapient designs. Ms. Adley designed a brain based on imprinted behaviors and growth patterns. It mimics how a human child is raised, and so far is the only brain that can host a unique individual personality. In the simplest terms, writing soft logic is equivalent to creating a detailed lesson plan for how a child will be raised."

"You weren't just turned on with a full program then?"

Again, she shook her head. "No. I was self-aware when activated, and I could download any type of information I wanted, but I had to learn to interpret that information. Everything I learn and experience affects my soft logic in some manner."

They danced close to each other, their arms twisting and intertwining about their bodies in time with the music and to the rhythmic motion of their steps. On a whim, Janus spun Anastasia round and then leaned her back into a stationary pose, his face hovering near hers. It was the classic position in contemporary ballroom dancing where the leading gentleman kissed his partner. Yet Janus paused.

From her reclined pose, Anastasia looked up at him and whispered. "I don't mind if you kiss me. I think that's what everyone expects of this move."

But Janus just smiled and held the pose, and held her in his arms, before drawing her to her feet. He stepped behind her and whispered into her ear, "I do want to kiss you, but not for a tradition or because it is expected."

"You're old fashioned," she quipped, then lightly kissed his cheek.

Mr. Welch and Ms. Adley danced closer, and Mr. Welch whispered, "Even if the other hypotheses are incorrect, the fact that she is a synthetic would cast significant doubt on the legality of the transaction. First, it would make Janus' marriage invalid as she falsified her status as a non-human. That might be grounds for an additional argument that he was ineligible to play. Second, if we can demonstrate that she does have some knowledge about what may have caused Janus' errant pitch, then the transaction will be postponed indefinitely. Even if you can only demonstrate the former," now he looked directly at Janus, "that will be enough to buy more time. But, if you can prove the latter, then you will shift the burden of responsibility onto her. I am concerned that if she is exposed, she will take flight, or be deactivated, before any incriminating evidence can be extracted from her memory."

Ms. Adley looked at Janus with an even gaze that reminded him of Mr. Welch. The similarity was uncanny. "If you risk exposing her, it has to be public with as many witnesses as possible."

Janus nodded his understanding, and the couples returned to their dancing. For a time he danced in silence, keeping Anastasia close in his arms. Then came a pause in the music, and he stopped and led her to the edge of the floor. He took her hand and looked at her solemnly. "What will happen after tonight?"

She looked at him with a somber expression, studying his face and the way he continued to hold her. Her expression brightened. "It's not like I'm dating anyone right now," she said, and then laughed.

THE AUTUMN ENGAGEMENT

Though Anastasia had stripped to nothing more than her chassis while in his presence, which was much more exposed than a naked woman could be, he had not really taken stock of what clothes she was wearing. As she walked a few paces ahead of him, her simple black gown plumed at the hem and billowed around her calves with each step, and her shoulder-length hair swished against her shoulder blades. His growing attraction to her led him to take stock of himself.

He had selected a very conservative pair of flat black slacks and a charcoal jacket. But his attire did not trouble him as much as his physical appearance. Over the last year, he had not stayed in shape and his square jaw had become smooth around his chin, and his eyes appeared gaunt and jaundiced. Seeing the perfection in Anastasia and hoping that their association would not end after the party, he felt bad knowing that his physical appearance was not as sharp as it had been. He wondered if any part of her attraction to him was physical.

Janus reached forward and took hold of Anastasia's hand. "Do you have any ideas?"

"I've been thinking about the lighting," she replied.

"Yes, it looks alright, I guess."

She prodded him with her free hand and stopped, motioning to the ceiling. "The lights simulate natural sunlight and emit a range of bands that emulate the affects of solar radiation."

"Ah," he murmured, then was more intrigued. "Maybe that was why Priscilla was having so much trouble with her face. That dress she is wearing covers just about everything else."

"That was my idea. I've analyzed the frequency that she has had to take corrective action, and she has been consistent at about two hours. She is outside fixing her face now." Anastasia smirked. "Now that I know what to look for, they aren't being all that subtle about it."

"Can you increase the amount of radiation from the lights?" he asked.

"Yes, I was thinking as much."

"But would she notice the change?"

Anastasia shook her head. "No, not unless she is looking for it."

She put both hands on Janus' shoulders and said, "Dear, we may have advanced computers in our bodies, but we are not walking probes."

He nodded. "But we still have to side track her long enough for the lights to work, and it would be helpful if we could somehow box her in so she couldn't run."

Her face was pensive. "That would be a problem. Her beau is sure to signal her that something is amiss, and there really is no way to restrain her."

"I don't mean physically restrain her," he said. "If we approach her from the front of the room, and slowly work her into a corner, she will have to get around us. Also, once in a corner, we can use a little subterfuge to trick her into staying in the corner."

"What kind of subterfuge were you thinking about," she asked.

"A kinetic field," he replied with a grin.

"We don't have one," she admitted. "Nice idea, though."

"It doesn't have to be a real one," he explained hastily, "just something that looks like one. You can see one, and I'm certain Priscilla must be able to see one."

She fell silent, and glanced towards the ballroom. "I'm asking my father if such a thing is possible." After a brief pause, her face softened and she shrugged. "He thinks it could be done. I'm wondering if it will have the desired affect. He wanted me to remind you that it is not a force field."

"Ah," Janus said, "but did you know that until he told you?"

She shook her head. "I never considered the matter."

"Then Priscilla may not know either."

"We're not the same, Priscilla and I," Anastasia said sharply.

He took her hand in both of his and held it to his chest. "I know you're not the same. You're not like any other."

"We'll try the simulated field," she conceded, and then her eyes begun to twinkle. "But I will introduce the topic of conversation."

Janus noticed the look of mischief on her face, but just nodded. "Um, ok."

They waited until Priscilla and her date returned, and once they were well inside the house, Janus and Anastasia started walking towards them.

When Priscilla noticed them drawing closer, she struck an arrogant pose with her date and started to walk away.

"Priscilla," Anastasia called too loudly, the tone of her voice quite saccharine. She made sure that everyone heard her, thus making it harder for Priscilla to snub them right away.

"Yes?" she asked, her tone icy and empty.

"I apologize for his oversight earlier," Anastasia said and tipped her head towards Janus. "He didn't introduce me. I'm Anastasia."

"Lovely to meet you, Anastasia," Priscilla's beau said. "My name is Rube."

Priscilla fumed silently, though her expression made her feelings obvious. "Yes, salutations. We were just on our way too the garden."

"It is a wonderful garden. Before you go, though, there is something that Janus and I would like to tell you." She had become very excited now.

Janus felt his eyes narrowing as he awaited what was to come next. She hadn't told him how she planned on stalling Priscilla.

"I'm completely dispassionate ..." Priscilla droned, but was again cut off.

"We're wanted you to be the first to hear our good news; we're getting married." She draped her arm around Janus and gave him an over-exuberant hug.

Janus coughed and looked at Anastasia.

Priscilla's face turned red and appeared maniacal. She said in a harsh whisper to Janus, "Not that I really care what floozy you decide to marry, but you know it's completely inappropriate to bring a human date to Mr. Welch's parties." Now her movements became exaggerated, and she looked all about her. "An embarrassment to everyone here, that's what this is. You just had to try some stupid stunt like this to get headlines. Well," she jabbed a finger at him, "you've made a mistake. You'll be blacklisted." She smiled cruelly, and spoke in merriment, "I'm actually glad I get to see you fall flat on your face a second time."

Janus was certain he would explode with a torrent of vile curses at his ex-wife, but he reminded himself of what he was trying to do. And he had to admit Anastasia did a remarkable job of starting a conversation that would get Priscilla's dander up. However, his blood was on fire with rage and his jaw was agape.

Anastasia touched her finger to his mouth and gently pushed it shut. "He's so ecstatic, he's speechless."

Now, Janus realized that the time to act was now. All he had to do was to keep Priscilla distracted. But how? If he debated with her, she would have won her argument and just saunter off. If he didn't say anything, she would still win. Then an idea entered his head and it seemed absolutely ludicrous given the circumstances. So utterly cliché and mundane that he thought it would show a complete lack of respect to everyone who most certainly were now eavesdropping on the conversation. But, it also made the most sense to him. The problem was a matter of logistics. Now that Anastasia had dropped a proverbial bomb on Priscilla, and on him, he had to contribute to the effort and not only distract Priscilla, but keep her from leaving.

"I'm a bit parched," he said. "Dear," he added what he thought was an appropriate level of saccharine to his voice, "Would you ladies care for something to drink?"

Priscilla shot him an odd look; she was at a loss as to why he would make such an offer.

Anastasia immediately responded, though also seemed unsure of what Janus was planning.

Before Priscilla made a negative reply, her date said brightly, "A beverage is surely in order. We should give them a toast," he said to Priscilla.

"Rube?" Janus started walking towards the bar, "would you help me carry the drinks back?"

"Of course," he said. "I won't be a moment," he said and winked to Priscilla.

Later, Janus would give a full account of what made him ask if the women wanted a drink. First, he expected Priscilla to say no, but was hoping her date would answer first. Second, he could then invite Rube with him to help carry the drinks. Lastly, he could waste a lot of time at the bar and Priscilla would be stuck with Anastasia.

At the time, though, Janus felt that his nerves would give out and he would succumb to violent shaking. The bar was on the far side of the hall, and though it took no more than thirty seconds to reach it, he felt ready to collapse at any moment.

"Some party," Rube said once they reached the bar. He knocked on the hardwood top and signaled the bartender. "I've never been to one of these before. How about you?"

Janus looked at him dumbly. "Neither have I."

The bartender nodded to both of them. "How may I help you gentlemen?"

Janus started to speak, but Rube asked hurriedly. "What kind of ambers are on tap?"

"I have a nice Martian lager," the bartender suggested.

"Two of those," he said and beamed. "Priscilla seems like the kind of woman that can appreciate a good beer," Rube said to Janus.

Janus just about fell away from the bar in a fit of laughter. Priscilla hated beer. He decided not to say anything.

"Scotch, single malt," Janus said. "And, what're the ladies having tonight?"

"Lazy Janc's," the bartender said, describing just one of a million mixed drinks.

Janus considered then shook his head. "A Sun-Dried Galaxy."

The bartender nodded. He served the two beers and the scotch, and started the tedious process of making the mixed drink.

While Rube nursed one of his beers, Janus looked towards Anastasia and Priscilla. He was happy to see that both were where he had left them, and they appeared to be glaring intently at each other.

"That's a good beer," Rube said and set down the empty stein. "Better fix me up another."

The bartender nodded, still working on Janus' order.

Janus glanced at Rube. "So, what do you do, Rube?"

"I work on an off-shore plant." He looked around the room, then said, "You know the kind." His allusion to a synthetic plant was quite blatant.

Janus nodded. "Good work, then?"

"Oh, yeah. You don't have to be a rocket scientist to do my job, but the pay's good."

"As long as you're happy, that's what counts." Janus continued to watch Rube and started to rethink his conclusion that Rube was a synthetic. His posture and mannerisms better fit the description of hired muscle that would follow orders and not understand what was going on around them. If he was a synthetic, his manufacturer went to extraordinary lengths to make him seem blue-collar. Janus imagined that a common cognitive ability would be harder to program because basic concepts may be black and white, but more advanced issues could not simply be calculated. That would be the mark of a genius. Rube's working-class demeanor suddenly felt much more believable than Priscilla's personality as an educated socialite.

The bartender set the mixed drink on the bar, and then drew another lager for Rube.

As they started walking back, Janus paused and said, "Rube, I don't want to go on putting airs or anything, but I'm starting to wonder if Priscilla might like something else to drink?" He wasn't so much concerned with what Priscilla wanted as he was not having her become too angry too quickly.

Rube shrugged and kept walking. "She just needs to loosen up."

"Hah!" Janus laughed and clapped him on the shoulder. "That's good."

When they returned, both Priscilla and Anastasia were still staring at each other with a deadpan expression. Whatever they were doing, Priscilla had been significantly distracted from the condition of her skin; the affect of the lights was taking its toll.

"Dear," Janus said, offering the mixed drink to Anastasia.

"Thank you," she said, her face relaxed and she smiled.

"Priscilla ..." Rube said, now having noticed her face.

"Yes?" she seethed in a whisper.

"Your drink," Janus interjected and took one of Rube's beers and started to hand it to her.

Janus cast a glance at Anastasia.

Priscilla's face darkened when she saw the beer, but she reached for it. "It seems you haven't forgotten my tastes," she said acidly.

When the stein was near her finger tips, Janus dropped his arm, pretending as though a force had pushed down on it, and let the stein fall to the floor.

Anastasia and Rube both reacted in startled fashion.

Janus clapped his hands to his chest and quickly apologized, adding, "I'm such a klutz. It felt like something knocked it out of my hand."

Whatever Anastasia and Priscilla had been doing while Rube and he had been at the bar had already had Priscilla worked up into a frenzy. Now, she was openly hostile and snide. "Are you that stupid? You're genetically engineered, you moron. Your motor skills are more precise than most machines." She fumed. "For heaven's sake, it's the same thing that altered your pitch ..." but she stopped and put her hand to her mouth. She looked around the room and was overcome with dread when she realized that many people were looking, and listening, due to the ruckus created by the spilt beverage.

Both Anastasia and Janus were silent, and they both shared a common thought: not enough. From their vantage, her skin had deteriorated to the point of looking bad, but she still looked human.

Priscilla shook with rage, but she didn't move. She behaved as though she was unable to move beyond a certain point. "I don't know what little scheme the two of you have concocted..."

"Oh, God," Rube said loudly, and made a disgusted expression. He pointed to her face and looked defeated. "Dear, your face is falling off."

Priscilla became shocked and put her hands to her cheeks and started to feel the skin. But, in doing so, it became detached in some areas.

Now, Rube looked outright nauseated. "Oh, now I can see the yucky parts."

Several people in the hall started whispering, and the word 'synthetic' could be heard. Anastasia and Janus looked at each other, at the people in the hall, then at Priscilla.

"Is that it?" Janus asked.

Anastasia nodded.

"Let's get out of here," he said, and felt like he was going to collapse

She took his hand and they walked out of the hall, out of the house, and into the calm, clear evening.

EPILOGUE

On the night of their first real kiss, one of affection and passion, Janus put his arm around Anastasia's waist and looked at her with a clear conscience. He said, "I once read a cheesy science fiction story about a guy who hated synthetics but wound up marrying one." Then he placed his lips to hers and their mouths melted into an earnest kiss.

Soul of an Artist, Brain of a Geek
William A. McKee

There's a place I want to be. It's in a state of mind that produces art. But I am far from there: I create software. The best I can hope for is to create the perfect program. It would be invisible, transparent because the user wouldn't even know that they are using something I created. They would simply do what they wanted on the computer unencumbered by the buttons and menus that just get in the way. By hearing the sounds and seeing the gestures of a user, the perfect program would correctly interpret the input and act.

The art I create is in the patterns of logic that make up the algorithm that shape the behaviour of a piece of software. No one can "see" this art but only experience it second hand by actually using the software. But art is a tangible component of what I do. My work is creative and has style and structure.

Creatively, I go through five stages: conception, expression, execution, reflection and depression. When I execute my art, I go through four additional stages: design, implementation, testing and documentation.

The conception of an idea is the greatest joy. It makes you want to run down the street naked shouting "Eureka!" Often, the inspiration comes from others; a conversion leads ones thoughts down a new road to discovery. I find that left alone my own thoughts are tired and repetitive. Others bring a fresh set of eyes to old patterns and a new way of looking at a problem leads to revelations.

Raw ideas must be moulded into a recognizable form. I express myself using logic as my medium forming algorithms and bits of code in my mind. I add syntax and grammar so that the ideas are in a language that I can share with others. This process also acts as a sieve where by so called "good" ideas get sifted out as unworkable and we are left with a pearl formed from a grain of an idea polished with layers of logic.

Design is the act of putting pen to paper (or fingers to keyboard). The specification for a piece of software forms the basis from which the expression becomes reality. The art is there but in an encoded form. The meter of a good program is that can you write it down in clear English statements so that even a non-technical person can follow the logic.

I then implement the idea in the form of source code.

Testing is a critical part of the process. Literally, you must criticize every aspect of the software. Also, in a more philosophical sense, if your software doesn't do what you set out for it to do, you have failed as a programmer.

Documentation takes two forms. An explanation so that others, like your boss or peers, can understand what it is that you have done. And, a set of instructions to "condition" the user to make full use of your software. Of course, the perfect program would not require user documentation.

Often, after a project is complete, I reflect on what I have done. Could I have done it better? What will I add in the future to improve it? Does this lead to other new ideas or should it simply be written off as "finished"?

Inevitably, there is a period of post project depression. I'm not sure why I'm sad after a project is completed. Maybe it's the sense that yet other great idea is now just another tired and repetitive thought going through my mind. I crave new ideas and when I think of all the time I spend on just one of them, I sigh and think there is never enough time to accomplish the prefect program. Or, could it be that my art will never be properly appreciated?

My soul cries out but my brain keeps telling it to shut up.

The Last Step
Michael E. Thompson

John Mallory shivered slightly as he stepped out into the cold autumn morning. The air had that crisp quality that lets you know that winter can't be far off. "I should have worn my coat," John said to himself, "Oh well, it won't matter for long."

"What a view," John thought as he looked around. He could see the bay from his vantage point and the Golden Gate Bridge. He could hear the sounds of traffic and off in the distance a church bell was ringing. John shivered again as he stepped forward.

"Bang! I got you, Johnny!" Pete yelled, stepping from behind the tree with his cowboy pistol in his hand.

"You missed me! Bang! Bang! I got you!" Johnny yelled from behind the car.

"No way! You cheated! I got you first."

"You did not!"

"I did too. Shot you right in the head."

"Did not!"

"Did too!"

"Johnny! Time for dinner!" Johnny's mother called from the front porch. "Come in and get washed up."

"Aw, mom! Do I have to?"

"Yes, you do. Now get in here."

"Can Pete stay for dinner?"

"Well, I suppose so if it's okay with his mother."

"Come on, Pete let's call your mom. Race you!"

"Did you get them, John?" Pete asked as John ran up.

"Yeah, they're in my pocket," John replied, looking over his shoulder.

"Let's go down by the pond," John said, leading the way down the path. Twenty minutes later they were sitting on a large rock beside a small pond. The woods around them were alive with the sounds of crickets.

Pete, slapping at a mosquito, asked, "Can I see them now?"

"Sure," John replied, reaching into his pocket he withdrew a small plastic bag with a pack of cigarettes and a book of matches.

"You sure your mom won't miss these?" Pete asked.

"No, she always has a couple of cartons opened up around the house. She'll never miss one pack." John peeled the plastic from the pack and tore open the paper underneath, and shook out two cigarettes, handing one to Pete. He opened the matches and struck it against the gritty strip. He held it up for Pete to light his cigarette, and then lit his own. He inhaled the acrid smoke, only to start coughing violently. Across from him Pete was also coughing. John tried to inhale from the cigarette again as his coughing subsided. By the time the cigarette was burned halfway through, John was beginning to feel nauseous. Looking up, he noticed that Pete looked a little green.

"Maybe this wasn't such a good idea." Pete said.

"Oh, John! It's beautiful." Kate cried out as she looked at the purple orchid wrist corsage. "It goes perfectly with my dress." She held out her left hand as John slipped it around her wrist.

"It sure does." John sighed as he looked at Kate's dress. It was lavender with spaghetti straps and he thought she was the most beautiful thing he had ever seen.

"All right now. You two stand over here and let me take a few pictures." Kate's mother pointed to a spot against the living room wall.

"Mother, we don't have time for that now."

"You can spare a few minutes for a picture. After all, this isn't just any dance, it's your Senior Prom and I want pictures. Now, if you please."

Kate smiled as she moved to the spot her mother indicated. "Come on, John. If we don't humor her she'll never let us out of here." She took John's hand as he stood beside her.

"Smile now!" Kate's mother said as she raised the camera up to shoot.

...

"You know if you faint or throw up out there I'm sending the tape to *America's Funniest Videos*." Pete chuckled. "Who knows, I could win the big money!"

"Just shut up and help me with this damned thing," John said, taking his hands away from the limp bow tie around his neck. "If I do throw up it'll be your fault."

"Hey, nobody forced you to do that many shooters last night. I wish I could have gotten a picture of the look on your face when the stripper showed up." Pete laughed as he stood in front of John and started working on the bow tie.

"Let's just not ever mention last night again, especially when Kate is around. If she ever finds out she'll kill us both."

"Look, all you did was let a mostly naked woman sit in your lap." Pete said with a smirk. "A stripper is traditional for a bachelor party, and what kind of best man would I be if I broke with tradition? There, that's got it." Pete stepped back and pointed to the mirror on the wall. "You look fine."

John looked at his reflection in the mirror. "Still, let's just keep the stripper a secret, all right?"

"That could be a little difficult since I uploaded the pictures to my web page this morning" Pete grinned.

"You what!"

"Just kidding. But I may have to blackmail you for them later."

They both turned at the sound of the door behind them opening. They could hear the organ music clearly as John's father stepped into the room. "It's time, son."

John felt a slight wave of nerves as they stepped into the church and walked over to take their places in front of Father Flannigan. The organ music changed to the Wedding March as everyone stood and turned to look down the aisle toward the back as the flower girl turned the corner at the front of the procession.

"Damn you! I'll never let you touch me again, you bastard!" Kate groaned as she crushed John's left hand with hers. Sweat was dripping from her hair as she grimaced in pain. Looking down between her spread legs, she pleaded with the man standing there. "Please! I'll give you anything you want. Can't I just have something, an epidural, or morphine, anything?"

"It's too late for that now, you're crowning." The doctor replied. "Now, push!"

"I can't push anymore! It hurts too much."

"Come on, Kate! You can do this! Just a few more pushes!" John encouraged.

"I can't! It hurts too much!"

"Kate, you have to push! Now push!"

Kate grit her teeth, took a deep breath, and pushed hard. "Aaaaargh!!!"

"That's it! Here comes the head!"

"Daddy!" The little girl squealed as she ran into John's arms. He scooped her up and held her high in the air.

"How's my Jennifer doing today?" he asked, giving her a noisy wet kiss on the cheek.

"Stop it, Daddy, that tickles." Jennifer pushed John's face away with her hands. "I thought Mommy was picking me up from daycare today."

"She has to work late so I'm afraid you're stuck with me for dinner."

"Can we go to McDonald's?"

"You know Mommy doesn't like it when eat fast food."

"We don't have to tell her do we?" Jennifer smiled.

"It'll be our secret."

"Mr. Mallory these officers are here to see you," said John's secretary from the doorway of his office. "They said it was important." John looked up as two police officers entered his office and walked over towards his desk.

"Are you John Mallory?"

"Yes, I am officer." John said standing. "What's this all about?"

"I am sorry to have to tell you this but your wife and daughter have been involved in a serious accident."

"Oh my God. Are they all right? What happened?"

"It appears that the brakes failed on a delivery truck, causing it to hit your wife's car broadside. I am sorry, sir, but your wife was killed instantly."

John's body went numb as he sagged back into his chair.

"What - What about Jennifer, my daughter?"

"I don't know her condition, sir, she was taken to San Francisco Memorial by helicopter."

"I - I have to get there."

"I am very sorry, Mr. Mallory, but she has severe damage to her brain. It's a miracle that she's even alive."

"But she will recover, won't she?" John asked, looking through the intensive care window to where his daughter lay with so many tubes and lines, her small body so battered that she was unrecognizable.

"No. Mr. Mallory, I'm afraid you don't understand. There is nothing else we can do for her now. She's brain dead."

Through a fog John heard a sound. Then the sound went away. In moments the sound returned. John lifting his pounding head from the pillow, knocking over an empty whiskey bottle as he fumbled to pick up the phone. He finally got the phone to his ear.

"Hello, hello?"

"John, where are you? The meeting with the client starts in ten minutes. We need your report. John? John, are you there? John!"

Letting the receiver fall to the floor, John laid his head back down on the pillow as his eyes closed.

"You wanted to see me, Mr. Peterson?"

"Yes, John, come in and have a seat. I don't know how to say this other than to just come out a say it. John, I know things have been difficult for you since the accident. Everyone here at the firm has tried to be understanding, but it's been almost a year and you're not getting any better. You're constantly late, if you show up at all. You're obviously drinking too much. John, you need professional help."

"Mr. Peterson, I know I've had problems but I assure you that I will…"

"Stop, John. I can't listen to any more of your excuses. We're letting you go. If you get the help you need there may be a place for you here again someday, but for now I must ask you to clean out your desk by the end of the day. I am sorry, John."

"Officer, keep those people back." Steve Montgomery said, pulling rubber gloves onto his hands. He turned to the grisly scene in front of him. "You know, Terry, even after fourteen years you never get used to this."

"I know what you mean." Detective Terry Summers replied, looking high up over his head. "What is that about, 18 stories?"

"Something like that, maybe 20. It sure is a hell of a long way down." He carefully inserted his gloved hand into the body's suit coat pocket and removed the wallet. "Driver's license says this is John Mallory, age 28- his address is only about twenty minutes from here."

"Maybe he worked in this building."

"You ever wonder what goes through their heads on the way down?"

"They say your whole life flashes before your eyes right before you die. But who knows? The coroner should be here shortly to take the body."

Joy Juice
S. Seiferling

It was Saturday, a day just like any other – except for the fact it was the last Saturday in the month. That meant party-time in the Boy's Club. The party began in the evening at 8pm. However, most of the boys did not arrive until about nine or nine-thirty. Each boy who wanted to join the party had to pay a guy, named Jeffrey Miller, six whole dollars before they were allowed in. Some of the boys who knew Jeffrey better could also give him the money afterwards. Jeffrey was a tall, well-built boy of about sixteen or seventeen years. He was the one who organized the party. But it was also Jeffrey who was sitting in the corner shortly before midnight, stoned and lulling to himself.

For my friends and me, it was not too much of a problem to scrape six dollars together for each of us. We all got two dollars for milk money each week, but we didn't save one cent of it. After all, we did not want to starve at school. Tommy and Mickey did the newspaper rounds every day in our area and both earned fifteen dollars each month. Johnny mowed lawns and washed cars for a few snobs outside the area. He earned the most. John earned roughly thirty dollars a month. And what did I do? I tried working as a waiter in Rusty's Restaurant, on the corner of 47th Street and 9th Avenue. Nobody could wait tables better then I could. I was an absolute crack at it. All in all, I earned up to twenty-five dollars a week – but only when the people who came were in a very generous mood.

The boys brought part of the money to me, as they were afraid of their older brothers and sisters taking it away from them. I think I was the youngest keeper of secured funding in all of Hell's Kitchen. We took the rest to the bank where each of us had a savings account, because of the interest we could gain. Mostly we drew out the money for very special occasions like parties, movies and so on. Sometimes, we spent it on comics and baseball cards though – after all, we were children and not bankers!

~

Some of the boys did not have any money and they did not even know who Jeffrey Miller was. It was, therefore, logical that these boys did not come to the Boy's Club and the party. We turned up at around nine thirty. Jeffrey stood at the entrance door of the Boys' Club. He took one glance at us and wanted to send us away. Tommy had the money on him. He took it out of his trouser pocket, held it under Jeffrey's nose and said, "Is that enough?" Jeffrey took the money, counted it and let us in. The room where the party was held was decorated with lanterns, string lights and balloons. The air was already stale and smoky but that did not matter to us. At first we thought six dollars seemed a rather large chunk of money for us to be spending, but when we found out that the drinks were free, except for alcohol, we found six dollars quite reasonable.

At eleven o'clock the room was packed full, and at midnight things were really under way. It was absolutely great and well worth going there. We played rodeo on floor-waxing machines that looked like vacuum cleaners while the music boomed from the boxes. During the entire evening, we drank Coke until it almost came out of our ears. At around three in the morning, when we were almost high on caffeine, Johnny pinched five dollars from some drunkard lying next to the restroom, after he had emptied his stomach. And, of course, we could not think of anything better than to buy four bottles of beer with it. We knew that this was illegal as we were only twelve years old, but at that moment we didn't care at all. Neither did the bartender who gave us the beer. We snatched our four bottles of beer and disappeared to a basketball court nearby. We did not know the effect alcohol would have on us, as we had never had this stuff in our hands before.

We had only heard about it. But we thought that what everyone else can do, we can do, too. After all, we were almost *grown-up*. We all drank together from each individual bottle. That meant that each of us had one bottle of beer, more or less. This stuff tasted awful. It was bitter and smelled revolting, and as we had never drank alcohol before. We were, of course, full to the brim. Johnny already gave up after a good half bottle. And although it was not that much, he had drunk so much he was sizzled more than the four of us put together. When Johnny stood up to tell us that he wouldn't drink one drop more, he tripped over his own feet and fell over. Actually, we wanted to help him get up, but our stomachs hurt from laughing. Johnny made the most stupid face of the year when it dawned on him that he had fallen over.

After we had quieted down, Johnny pulled himself together and sat down with us. While we were drinking our beer, we couldn't care less what it tasted like now, we told our greatest adventures. Many of them were just made up, but who cared? The main thing was, they were funny.

Tommy was the first one who had to go to the bathroom. He stumbled his way somewhere and pissed against a fence post like a dog. When he came back again, he had a basketball in his hand that he had found on the court somewhere between a few trashcans. Actually we weren't in any state to play basketball, but since we were already there and had a ball we thought that we should at least give it a try. You could not exactly call it "playing". It was more a question of, *"How can I get this ball in that crummy basket without falling over"*. It was really a scream.

The alcohol gave us the feeling that we were floating, which meant that we were not only drunk; we were somehow high, which I couldn't quite really understand. We laughed at everything, regardless, even when we fell over. And we got more bruises than we probably ever would have done if we'd been in a fight. At five in the morning we decided to make our way home, giggling and singing.

When I got in I tried my best not to make a sound. After all, I didn't want to wake Dad. When I tried to go up the steps I stumbled at least three or four times. And then it became clear to me that I would never be able to grasp any of the four banisters. Each time I fell over I began to giggle although the knee I'd fallen on hurt like the devil. And when at last I had reached my room, I slammed the door behind me by accident. My dad wouldn't possibly have been able to hear that. I heard my dad's bedroom door open and footsteps towards my room. He popped his head into my room to make sure that I was okay. He did not make any attempt to help me. And when he saw me kneeling in front of my bed he came into my room and helped me up. I don't think he did this out of pity. He just didn't want me to sleep on the floor. Stoned as I was, I just don't know how I could have managed to heave my tired bones into bed, as they were like lead.

I slept like a log that morning until about eleven-thirty. When I woke up, I could have kicked myself for drinking alcohol. I was sick and every sound seemed so loud that I thought my head would explode at any moment. Actually, I did not want to get up as I felt I was on a carousel with every move I made. But then I was dying to go to the bathroom, and not just to empty my bladder.

I held my pounding head and swayed into the bathroom. And then when I came out again a short while later, my dad was standing there, leaning with his back against the door of my room. He had a glass of water in his hand with an Aspirin dissolved in it. "I was just coming to ask you if you were going to get up soon!" he said, in rather a loud voice. He probably thought that I was deaf. At first tried not to let anything show, but not managing it, I gave in. "Please Dad, could you speak a bit quieter? I've got a whale of a headache!" My dad didn't say another word. He just looked at me in a way that said, *"I know what you've been doing"*. Then he pressed the glass into my hand and said, "Drink that, and you and your head will soon be feeling better."

He did not ask me if I had been drinking any alcohol, as that was unnecessary. I must have stunk of it so badly that you could have smelled me from a distance of a hundred yards, just from one bottle of beer. I had overslept and missed church. As a rule, my parents always forced me to go. However, I still got the "The Word on Sunday" preached to me. And not just me! My friends and I weren't allowed to go to one more party again for a whole month. As if that wasn't enough, we had to clean the school toilets after school for a whole month, when everybody had gone home. A grand job, that was! And there was no possibility of saying, " I haven't got any time today" because if just one of us had tried to get out of it, the whole thing would have gone for another month. We were quite certain that our parents had planned this together. It was a conspiracy, so to speak. But we stuck together, just as one would expect real pals to do!

After this episode we didn't drink alcohol again for a long time. For as they say, one learns from experience.

Ashley
Elizabeth Lamb

She was alone. These days she was always alone. She stared out her bedroom window, watching as the sun set. Wind rattled the pane, and a blue jay called for its mate.

"Stupid bird," she thought bitterly. "Your mate isn't coming back! He left you pregnant, high and dry."

She heard the door slam, and then footsteps on the stairs. The door opened slowly, and there was Anna, looking at her with a sad smile.

"Hi, Ashley," Anna said. When Ashley said nothing and continued to stare out the window, Anna came up behind her and rested her arm on Ashley's shoulder. "How are you feeling?"

Finally, Ashley turned to face her. "I have bad cramps."

"Have you heard from Mike?"

Ashley stiffened at the question. "He doesn't know yet."

"What? You haven't told him?"

Ashley nodded and looked out the window again. She hated lying to her best friend, but felt as if she had no choice. She called Mike three weeks ago; after she found out she was pregnant. She remembered it like it was yesterday. She'd been nervous and almost hadn't been able to get the words out.

"Mike...I'm...I'm pregnant."

"It's not mine."

Ashley was shocked. Of course it was his, what did he think she was? "I've never been with anyone else!"

There was a long pause, and then, "Get rid of it."

Mike hung up, saying that his wife was coming. Ashley stared at the phone in shock. She didn't know what she was going to do, but she knew she couldn't get rid of it, just like that. It didn't feel right. She also knew it was wrong to love a married man, but she couldn't help herself. Mike was special. He told her that he loved her, but that he had a responsibility to his family.

"Someone has to hold the family together, because my wife certainly doesn't." She thought he was a very caring man, considering the circumstances. "I know that my wife is cheating on me," he said. "No one spends that much time at the office!" So she understood his insistence that she keep this quiet.

She remembered back to a year ago when she'd seen the ad in the paper. "Baby-sitter wanted," it read, "Afternoons and Weekends for three sturdy children." She laughed when she saw that, but she needed the money so she called for the job.

The phone rang several times before Mike's wife, Lauren, answered the phone.

"Hello?" She was breathless, and kids were screaming in the background.

Ashley faltered a moment before responding, second-guessing her decision to call. "Hi. I'm calling about the ad in the paper."

Ashley's determination to buy some boots that she had seen in the mall won out.

"Oh, yes." Pause. "What's your name dear?"

"Ashley Campbell."

"Hello Ashley, my name is Lauren." There was another pause as the screaming in the background intensified.

"Boots. Boots. Boots." Ashley reminded herself.

"Are you there dear? Maybe we should set up an interview. Things are a bit...chaotic here today."

"Just today?" Ashley thought as she choked down a snicker and agreed to meet Lauren the next day.

Ashley hadn't expected a Greek God to answer the door, but that's what she got. Mike towered over her petite frame by at least five inches and his teeth were blindingly white; he had a beautiful smile.

"Ashley, I presume?"

She could only nod.

"Mike. Mike Cannon." He held out his hand and Ashley stared at it dumbly before her hand got the message to shake. The rest of the interview was a blur; she could barely remember her own name. All she saw were Mike's blue, blue eyes and white teeth.

...

She remembered the exact moment she fell in love with him. He had been standing in the doorway on his way out that first night. He looked handsome in his tux and was waiting for his wife to come downstairs. He winked at her as he called for his wife, like they shared a special joke. That's when she knew she was falling in love with him. She knew it didn't make sense. She barely knew him, but she was falling in love. On the other hand she was becoming fast friends with his wife. They talked and giggled together on those rare times that Lauren ended up waiting for her husband. She would tell Ashley about her job and Ashley always wondered if she really was cheating on Mike. One night Ashley asked her how she could stand to be at the office 24/7. Mike's wife turned to her, and replied with a coy smile, "Who says I was at the office?" Then she laughed as if it had all been a joke, but Ashley was never sure. After that, Ashley wasn't very interested in being friends with her. She felt sorry for Mike, struggling to hold the family together. Maybe he really did need her, something that he never hesitated to tell her. It was nice to be needed. That's why she started sleeping with him; he was her first.

It was about six months after they met. He was driving her home late one night when he started to rub her thigh. She knew it was wrong, but she didn't stop him; she liked it. She trusted him because he was her friend. Mike listened to her and treated her like an equal. He gave her advice and asked her for some. He shared his problems, mostly about his unhappy marriage. Mike made her feel like she was special. It was nice to have a male point of view; she'd hardly seen her father since her parents divorce two years before. Her mom tried to give her a stable home life, but wasn't home much. Not by choice, of course, she just had to work hard to support them both. Ashley became accustomed to being alone. Mike changed all that. He spent as much time with her as he could and she felt, for once, that her opinions really mattered. He never lied to her or gave her reason to distrust him. That's why she believed him when he said the risk of her getting pregnant was low, so they didn't use protection. They had sex several times after that. He was adamant that she couldn't get pregnant; he always pulled out. But here she was three months later...alone and pregnant.

"Ashley? What are you thinking?"

Ashley was startled; she had forgotten that Anna was there.

"Have you told your mom yet?" Anna asked gently. Ashley shook her head no. Anna opened her mouth to say something but closed it again.

A few days later Ashley's mom was putting laundry away when she heard Ashley throwing up in the bathroom. She dropped the clothes and ran to her daughter.

"Baby, are you O.K.?"

Ashley shook her head and started to cry. Her mom hugged Ashley tight and brushed hair off her forehead.

"Baby, please tell me what's wrong. Let me help you."

Through her tears, she managed to tell her mom that she was pregnant.

"What? You're only 15!" and almost in the same breath said, "Who's the father?"

Ashley stiffened and kept quiet.

"Ashley? I said who's the father?"

"You. You don't know him. He moved here in the middle of eighth grade, and just moved again a month ago. His name was...Nicky."

"Nicky who?" Her mom demanded.

Ashley opened her mouth to answer and immediately vomited again. Her mom decided not to press the issue for now.

The next day her mom insisted that they see a doctor; Ashley found herself in the doctors examining room.

"Well everything looks good," said the elderly doctor.

"Is it a boy or a girl?" Ashley asked eagerly.

The doctor laughed and patted her knee. "I'm afraid it's a little too soon to tell. You are only 12 weeks." He then prescribed some medication for Ashley's cramping and told them to come back in a month.

Ashley's life had changed considerably over the next few months. She was almost six months along. She could no longer play tennis or sleep on her stomach, two things that she loved to do. She was too tired to do anything after school - not that she had anything to do. She had never been the most popular kid in school; in fact most of the kids laughed at her because her family didn't have much money. Now that she was pregnant, they had even more reason to ridicule her. They laughed at her in the hallway and were quick to point out her noticeable weight gain. Her only friend was Anna.

Anna would come over and rub Ashley's back and talk and laugh with her like nothing had ever happened. Ashley was grateful for Anna's company and tried to show it by not complaining about her aches and pains all the time. Aches that she was a bit worried about, not to mention the occasional spotting. But she didn't want to complain, so she just reasoned that she was having a harder time with her pregnancy because she was so young. Even though Anna and Ashley had been friends since before they could walk and had grown up next door to each other, sharing everything, she still hadn't told Anna about Mike wanting her to get an abortion.

However, Anna knew about everything else, how Ashley felt about Mike, the feelings that she hid from everyone else.

One night Ashley and Anna were having a serious discussion on who was hotter, Ben Affleck or Josh Harnett, when Anna suddenly asked, "So are you going to tell Mike?"

Ashley became quiet and frowned.

"I suppose I will when the time is right. I know he'll take care of the baby and me. He'll know what's best." She looked at her hands as she spoke, unable to look Anna in the eye. Oh God, she thought, maybe he does know what's best. Should I get the abortion?

"Ashley!! You can't let him run your life. He's a married man! He won't just drop his family to marry you and claim the baby."

Just then Ashley doubled over and gave a sharp cry of pain.

"What's wrong?" Anna cried. She didn't wait for Ashley to answer but immediately ran for help.

The hospital waiting room was brightly lit and empty. The footsteps in the hallway echoed in Anna's ears. It seemed like years before Ashley's mom came out, red eyed and lad Anna to Ashley's room. Ashley looked small sitting in the big hospital bed, with the pillows fluffed up behind her. She knew, even before Ashley said it, that the baby was gone.

Ashley's life seemed empty without her baby. She never told anyone, but she had already picked out a name. Jackson if it was a boy and Victoria if it was a girl.

She was now able to do all the things she did before she got pregnant, but they somehow had lost their appeal. She hadn't heard from Mike in a long time, even after she told him that she lost the baby. She thought that would make him happy, but he had been as rude and abrupt as when she had told him she was pregnant.

He told her that it was for the best. And that was that. So she never expected to talk to him again, but God how she missed him. She felt emptier than before. She was upset with how Mike had treated her, yet still yearned for his touch. Nothing was the same anymore, nothing. Then one night she got a phone call.

"Hey baby long time no see." It was him. Mike. Ashley froze and almost dropped the phone.

"H...Hi Mike" she managed to get out.

"I need a baby-sitter for Saturday night. Are you available?" Ashley almost dropped the phone again, but caught it just in time.

"Sure Mike. I'll be there." She hung up the phone and walked to her window. The sun was setting and Ashley saw a nest of blue birds on a nearby tree. She stood there looking out, not seeing anything, just staring, until her mom called her for dinner.

Hurtful Stories
Mark Carpenter

Little Sally watches from her seat on the swing as the other children play a game of tag in the grass nearby. She thinks about how much fun in would be to join them in their school-yard games, but she's afraid. She doesn't want to get hurt again.

She knows her real name is just Sally, not Little Sally, but everyone still calls her that. She lets out a small sigh as she looks down at her tiny frame, little legs like matchsticks dangling over the edge of the swing seat.

"Make sure the little one doesn't get hurt," she mumbles to herself. It's a phrase she's overheard often enough, whispered in hushed tones. She really doesn't like getting hurt, and not just because of the pain.

Last summer a dog bit her on the hand. It was the neighbor's dog from down the street. She had gone up to pet it one day and it had lunged for her, snapping its teeth and snarling. She wasn't quite sure what happened next, but she felt a sharp pain in her hand and then felt herself being pushed to the ground. When she dared open her eyes again after what seemed like forever, she no longer heard the growling and howling that had so terrified her. In fact, she couldn't even see the dog anymore. The chain it had been leashed to now ended in a twisted link and lay limp on the ground. In a frantic worry she glanced behind her in case the beast was ready to pounce on her again, but she relaxed after a moment when she saw that it must have run off somewhere. It was then that she finally looked at her hand. There was blood coming from a pair of holes between her thumb and her first finger, but she didn't cry. She took out her hankie and wrapped it around her hand before running home to show her mother.

Later that evening, her father had gone to talk to the neighbor about that dog. He said he was going to make sure that it never bit anyone ever again. When he got home, Sally listened at the kitchen doorway as he told Mother that they didn't need to worry about the dog bothering Little

Sally any more. The neighbor had found it a few houses away. It must have gotten into a fight with a bigger, meaner dog — a much meaner dog. He wouldn't talk about it any more when Mother asked him what he meant by that, but Sally saw the scared look on his face as he glanced to the doorway where Sally stood.

Little Sally hops off of the swing and slowly walks over to the sandbox where a young boy is making a small mountain with his toy bulldozer. She sits on the bench and watches him for a bit while making S shapes in the sand with her foot

"What do you think, Max? Is it high enough?"

She glances up to see the boy pause a moment, then nod and go back to dozing more sand up the side of the mountain. Sally can't see the person he is talking to, but that doesn't mean that there is no one there. She knows all about friends that no one else can see. She has one herself. She knows from listening to the other children that he... she's pretty sure it is a "he"... that he isn't much like the other children's friends. For one thing, he never, ever talks to her. Sally only rarely sees him, and even then only in the shadows. She doesn't know what he really looks like, but he is always there, watching; waiting in some dark nook or corner.

Sally had tried to tell her mother about him once, but her mother said that she mustn't tell stories. They have had to move yet again because of the stories. They live in the city now. Her mother had grown tired of the small towns. Sally had liked the towns because she could go off to play in the woods or in the streams and whatnot, but her mother had said that they were "gossip mills". When Sally had asked what that meant, her mother had told her that they were places where people told mean and hurtful stories about each other, and her mother was tired of being hurt. So they had moved to the city in the hope that it would be better here, that the neighbors wouldn't stop their conversations to stare at them with dark expressions as they walked past on their Sunday strolls.

Sally kicks at the sand, thinking about the last town they were in.

There was a mean little boy that she had gone to school with there. His name was Pete, and Pete was a bully. He was always calling her names and running up to her yelling "Boo!" really loud in her face. One day he did more than just yell; he ran right up and hit her. He hit her so hard that she fell to the ground crying. The teachers yelled at him and sent him home, which was the last time Little Sally ever saw Pete the Bully.

Her parents had told her that Pete wasn't going to be going to school there anymore, that he had gone far away. The story that she had heard later from the kids at school was that Pete was dead, and that Sally was the one that had killed him. Sally was certainly shocked. She was fairly certain the she would have remembered something like that. They said that Little Sally was cursed, a witch, or a maybe a demon even. They said that Sally had killed him, just like all the others. Anyone who hurt Little Sally ended up dead.

But it wasn't all just gossip. Sally knows that now. It was only a few weeks ago when she realized that all the stories about her were true.

Sally was sitting on a bench waiting for her mother to pick her up from school, amusing herself with a small wooden puzzle her uncle had made for her. As she heard the sound of a car pulling up and stopping in front of her, she looked up in the hopes of seeing her mother's car, but instead it was one she didn't recognize. It's passenger door swung open.

Inside a man smiled at her with a sad and worried face and told her that Sally's mother couldn't come. She had been hurt in a car accident and he was going to take Sally to see her. Sally looked at the man closely. Her mother had told her to be careful of strangers, and that Sally was never to go with anyone who did not tell her the secret password. But if her mother was really hurt, she might not have been able to tell anyone what the password was. What if she didn't go with this man and her mother was really hurt? What if she was dying and Sally did go!

As she began to get off the bench, a steak of shadow rushed out from underneath, racing past her feet and into the car. Sally saw a look of surprise and then terror cover the man's face before the passenger door slammed shut and the car started to rock and bounce on its springs. She heard a muffled shriek and then the windows were covered from the inside with a bright red and bits of things Sally didn't want to remember. With a sudden lurch, the car slammed onto its side with the sound of bending metal and breaking glass. Rolling, it came to a stop on its roof... and then silence.

Sally sat and stared for a long while, unable to look away. Finally, she picked up her puzzle and raced back into the school. She didn't scream. She didn't even cry until she got home later that evening, after talking to the people at the school and to the police officers that came. She only told them that she had seen the red. She knew that they weren't interested in listening to "stories". She didn't want to make them mad. Later that night, as she lay in bed, she cried quietly and fitfully into her pillow.

As Sally's attention drifts back to the sandbox, it now appears to her that Max and the boy have decided that the mountain is, in fact, too tall. The boy is removing great gouts of sand with wide sweeps from the bulldozer, accompanying the effort with loud bulldozer-like noises. Hearing a little snuffling noise, Sally turns to see that a sad-looking puppy-dog has walked up beside her. It sits down on its haunches and lets it's tongue hang out, panting in the way that dogs do, obviously looking for attention.

Sally looks down at the poor thing and shakes her head. "Go home puppy-dog. Go on home. I want to give you a pet. I really do," she offers with a sad smile. "But I'm scared you might bite me, and I don't want to get hurt. I don't want to get hurt ever again."

Aspirations
J. Grady

To be near here was to be near the very essence of perfection. The way she floated past, her long blonde locks bouncing behind her. I yearned for the day we would share a moonlight tryst, and she would remove her garments so I could visually admire her captivating beauty.

I waited, watching her secretly from my room. Timing her journeys to the market, so that I may escort the fair maiden. Having summoned up the courage, I opened up a communication between us. Madeline, such a name was indeed befitting a princess.

Yes, Sardonnicus, it was a dream, but one worthy living. At night staring at a picture that had found its way into my possession, thinking only of her, and me together. Not much sleep was had during those dark nights, I longed for daylight so that I might see her again. Twisting turning, sleep was not something I could easily execute. Lying in bed, I read, making the most of my time. The words were a medley of confusion and nonsense. My mind wander from the stories in the bounded text to the fantasy I wanted more than anything.

Sardonnicus, you would never know the pain of needing someone so much; lucky you are. For two years I have waited, ever so patiently, ever more eagerly. Madeline wanted no more than to be companions, I figured this was the easiest way to achieve my goal. Going to the market, we perused the merchandise. Jesting like a couple of fools, we walked the streets of our neighborhood and went to the theatre together. Those were happy times, Sardonnicus, but who can be truly happy when their desires go unsatisfied.

By the end of the first year I had known about every major event that affect her deeply. Her best friend moving away and her cat Snuffles, leaving its earthly body to begin life anew with Saint Peter or Francis, I forget which. She was ecstatic when she had ventured into this relationship.

I, on the other hand, was anxious as well as expectant. How long would it take? I wondered to myself when we sat together at dinner. Why can't I indulge? I thought as we sat at the theater.

As the days wore on Madeline kept becoming more and more visually arousing. Oh God, I needed her!!! Late at night, I thought I would go mad with desire, take her in my arms and luxuriate in the pleasures of the flesh!! Sardonnicus!! I cried, why couldn't I have her!!!

Barely surviving the night I awoke at the approach of sunlight. A message was placed on a nightstand next to my bed. I rubbed my eyes and gasped at the yellow leaflet. Upon it were the words Madeline wants to speak with you. I rushed to her house; she was waiting at the top of the wooden steps that led to the foyer. I went to her side.

She cried with a sorrow I had never bore witness to. Her tears were warm as they dripped onto my arm. Sardonnicus, I have never lost a loved one, but I can tell you that even though I did not know her mother, I still felt a void had opened up in my heart. Madeline placed her head on my shoulder; I ran my fingers through her soft golden hair. Reaching for a tissue, I placed one gently into her hand. Not a word was spoken, but we knew exactly what each other were thinking. After awhile her tears ceased and her head rose quietly from its resting place. Gazing into her hypnotic eyes she mentioned the four words that I had longed for all this time, "Make love to me." She was serious, I knew from her tone. A smile widened on my face! Finally, after all my hardships!! MY mournful attitude diminished as the thoughts of what would transpire punctured my brain. Sardonnicus, I cried! Sardonnicus, can it be true? I turned to face my newly appointed lover. My jubilant gaze met her dark hypnotic eye. My chance had come! I opened my mouth to say the greatest three-letter word in existence.

"No."

What! Was that spouted from the very lips that so wanted to touch my princess, taste her wine and feast upon the beauty of her soul? No?!?! Had I been overtaken by some primitive demon unaware of human biological urges and equipped with an extremely limited vocabulary?

I looked at the maiden once more; the answer was plain.

"I'm glad you said that, " She gently wrapped her arms around me, resting her head in my lap. I smiled. Twas no demon, twas no mistake, she was my friend and I wasn't going to let anything ruin this.

She inquired if I wanted to stay the night, playing games and reading, I declined. Sardonnicus, some men it would kill to be that close to a dream and not achieve it. Not I, I had come so far with her that indulging in those sophomoric fantasies would have ruined everything I had worked so hard for.

Closing my eyes for the first time, I drifted to sleep lulled by the sounds of Sardonnicus warm, soothing purring

Discipline
K.A. Thompson

The woman could have been a linebacker. At first sight the question crossed my mind: how many men have been snapped in two by those thighs?

How many actually gave her a shot at them?

Case in point: the woman terrified me on sight. Easily 5'11", she was huge, not fat so much as all there, muscle rippling in currents under too-tanned skin. The diet soda in her hand could have easily been a 20 pound barbell; I had no doubt she could sling either one across the room with the same casual attitude as an eight year old flicking boogers onto the blackboard.

Still, she had a quirky, curious appeal. She left little to the imagination as she sauntered onto the apartment pool deck in bleached white band-aids substituting for a bathing suit. No modesty, just a sense of complete authority. Control.

Amazon.

Her name, I came to find out, was Megan Russell, Rusty to anyone she gave half a thought to. The body, the nearly chiseled features, came from the daily practice and dedication to her profession.

"Taekwondo. Black belt," she said, without any hint of bravado. "Sixth degree. I instruct."

"Sensei?"

"Sabonim," she said with a hint of laughter. "I could teach you."

Teach me what? I wondered, trying not to be too obvious, lamely fighting the impulse to stare at the tits and not at the face.

The look said it all: Not what you're thinking, dickhead.

I swallowed hard and found myself nodding. "I'll just bet you could."

The studio – not a dojo, she groaned – was lodged inexplicably between 7-11 and Auto Zone at the strip mall. The private world of martial arts that I had imagined, secretive men zipping through the air in their pajamas behind cloistered walls, turned out to be eight and ten year old boys sweating it out in front of the glass walls for every mall rat to ogle and laugh over. Every mistake, every fall, every jiggle was there for the whole world to see.

There was one lone adult braving the audience, some poor overweight woman with a beet red face trying hopelessly to keep pace with the innately agile. One harried housewife didn't stand a chance against fifteen sugar-loaded little hornballs.

"Balance," Rusty was telling them, her voice bringing them to rapt attention. She stood on the blood-red mat, balancing nearly six feet of herself on one foot, her other leg bent waist high. She stood there for what seemed an eternity, delicately, almost with a modicum of femininity.

Then she struck forward, snapping the foot out in a blinding kick.

Fifteen little feet imitated their instructor with amazing precision; one quite large foot raised up tentatively, teetered, and fell unceremoniously. Did she realize she was being watched? I wondered. Did she care?

Rusty's left foot never touched the ground.

"Balance."

"You need curtains. Something. Anything."

Rusty handed me a Budweiser, popping open a Diet Coke for herself. She had practically yanked me off the parking lot, greeting me like the long lost friend she hadn't seen since junior high. I was surprised that she remembered my name, much less that she'd met me before.

"Zach. By the pool. You live two doors down. Quiet little guy."

Mind like a steel trap.

"One way mirrors. The kids watch themselves work out, tone their form, and their parents get to sit outside and see what they're paying for."

"And the whole world gets a cheap laugh at some poor old broad's expense."

"That poor old broad probably stumbled into the studio the same way everyone else does. She was out spending too much money, wolfing down bad food, when she waltzed by and saw all those healthy little monsters pinging off the walls. It intrigued her. That's how I get most of my students. Out of curiosity."

"And they don't mind being cheap entertainment."

She shrugged off the notion. "Kids love it. And the grown-ups know what they're getting into."

"Why do they do it, then?"

"The kids all want to be ninjas," she laughed, "and the adults all want to get laid." She stood in the middle of the living room, dropping instantly into full splits. "It's an incentive."

The thought of her snapping someone in two popped into my mind again. "What's your incentive? Besides the money."

She chuckled, sliding up out of the splits as easily as she had dropped into them. "Why not just money? Lessons don't come cheap, you know."

I rolled my eyes. "You furnished this place"—I gestured to the entire room—"in Early American Garage Sale. My gut feeling is that money isn't at the top of any of your lists."

She followed the gesture. Small black and white TV, old army trunk as a coffee table, knock-down couch and loveseat; fifty bucks probably furnished the entire room. "Don't like the decor?"

"I didn't say that. I just don't think you're money hungry."

"You're right." She bounced onto the couch next to me. "What are you hungry for, Zach?"

Loaded question.

I groped for a safe answer.

"Balance."

I shared evening beers and belches with Rusty for six weeks without learning much about her. She'd been practicing her martial arts for twenty of her twenty six years. She wasn't married, never had been, never mentioned any ongoing relationships. She wasn't gay, I learned that emphatically by being tossed on my ass for even thinking it. She didn't seem lonely, yet she was eager enough for adult companionship in the evenings after work. She ignored passes from other men, groaned at the ineptly bad ones, avoided making any of her own.

She evaded questions that bordered on intimate with the same skills she could avoid a kick or blow. Block and parry. Get too close, buster, and your balls will find a neat trajectory through your body cavity and out your nose.

She also knew little about me, other than she wanted to teach me. "Give it a month. One lousy little month to see if you like it. I bet you will."

"Bet what?"

She thought for a moment. "The lessons are free until the end of the month. If you like it, they stay free, you study for as long as you like. If not, you pay double the monthly rate."

"What's my incentive, then? All I have to do to avoid paying up is swear I love it, hang around for a while and then quit. Regardless."

She shook her head. "You're not a liar."

"How would you know?"

"I just know. We on?"

Never pass up a sure thing. "You're on."

Two days later I found myself standing on a thick red carpet, surrounded by floor-to-ceiling mirrors, dressed in someone else's overgrown pajamas. "There's no place to hide," the woman to my left said. "Believe me, I've looked."

We stood in the back, separated from Rusty by a mob of young boys shoving and punching at each other, restless to begin. The shrill volume of prepubescent voices was beginning to drive me straight up the wall, yet when Rusty turned around they all stood stock-still, hands clasped behind their backs, dead silent.

She exchanged bows with the students, recited the class creed, and began.

Evenings spent on Rusty's couch swilling Budweisers could not have prepared me for the agony she inflicted. I discovered that beads of sweat come in ten different sizes and they all leap from your face into your nose. Rusty's version of Taekwondo involved twenty minutes of heavy calisthenics designed to separate the men from the boys.

And the goddamn boys won.

"It's the cartilage," the woman beside me, Diane, huffed. "Those little rats are like Jello on the inside. You and I have already turned into petrified wood."

"Then why are we doing this?"

She grinned. "We're gluttons for punishment. It's the adult mentality. If it hurts, it must be good for you."

I wiped the sweat off my face and looked at Rusty. She didn't seem to be in any pain.

Saving it for the rest of us. Nothing but the best for her students.

Wonderful.

...

Rusty knew few of the day to day details of my life. She didn't know that I had married young. She didn't know that I had been widowed young. I never told her what I did for a living, what other interests I had besides how cold the Budweiser was, I never told her much of anything.

We talked mostly about ideals and values. Rusty could change her mind without so much as a blink; she sided with whichever point of view could make for the best argument.

Most importantly, I never told Rusty about Rebecca, my permanent yet very much adored headache. Becky was sixteen and the mirror image of her mother, a woman she barely remembered. She was five when her mother died; I was barely twenty-two.

It was a shotgun wedding without the firepower. Rachel was eighteen, I was sixteen, and my father was pissed as hell, though after the initial shock he never showed it. Always, he sighed repeatedly, accept accomplished fact. Finish high school, college, hold a job, and you can have my support; blow it and you're on your own.

We never had the chance to blow it.

We never had the chance for much of anything.

I graduated; my wife and daughter sat in the front row with my father, loudly cheering me on as I stumbled across the stage to accept my diploma. It was a simple piece of paper that fulfilled a promise and garnered a scholarship, yet it was the world wrapped with a small red ribbon and celebrated with a mortarboard thrown into the air.

Two days later that little world meant nothing, was little more than hard wrought toilet paper. My exhilaration over accomplishing what 500 other seniors in my school had crashed and buried itself ten feet under ground.

The condition itself I never learned to pronounce; I only knew that it meant I had as little as a year, at most two or three years, left to find out what marriage and commitment meant to me.

Rachel was dying, bit by bit, her brain invaded by microscopic predatory cells that held no mercy.

Two months after my twenty second birthday I was standing in front of a marble headstone, groping to find the right words to tell a five year old that her mother wasn't ever coming home.

Eleven years later I still don't remember what I said.

Becky seemed to be a healthy, reasonably well-adjusted teenager, as well adjusted as someone in the throes of rampaging hormones could be.

She was a beautiful, sensitive kid. A pain in the butt sometimes, but nothing out of the ordinary.

I kept my pain in the butt to myself.

I kept her away from Rusty.

"Psychology 12," I heard myself saying for what felt like the hundredth time. "Ethics. If you're not at least a sophomore, let me know now. If you're a sophomore and haven't completed psych 1 and psych 11, speak up, because you won't get credit for this class."

No hands went up. I stared into a sea of disinterested, glassy-eyed and dazed nineteen and twenty year old students. Most of them, I had learned over the years, signed up for the course assuming it was an easy A. Others took it because it was a requirement for their major. A few odd ones were wheedled into it by their career counselors; accounting majors, education majors, automotive mechanic majors.

"All right." I took my familiar spot, sitting on the desk, heels clicking against the metal where the legs were screwed in precariously. "The difference between an ethic and a moral. Explain." I pointed at random, settling on a bewildered looking young man, his fingers clenched over the pile of notebooks and textbooks on his desk. "Mr...?"

"Woodward," he squeaked. "Jeff."

"Jeff. Give me a definition."

"I don't know."

I nodded; I hadn't expected an answer, I knew better than to expect anything out of them for weeks to come. Twenty poor souls whose confusion would only mount over the coming semester.

That included their instructor.

"By the end of this semester," I announced, "you will most definitely be able to explain the difference between a moral and an ethic. And you will do it in two sentences or less."

I remembered the first class I had been left in charge of, offering them my challenge. Explain ethics and morals. Be brief.

I still wanted to throttle the lousy little shit who came up with my own definition and blew the entire semester.

There was nothing to teach. He summed up an entire textbook and a summer's worth of notes and research in two lousy little sentences. I vowed from then on to pose the question to the least likely candidate and hope for the worst.

I was rarely disappointed.

At least, not in the classroom.

"It's not like I'm asking you to go off and get married, for Pete's sake. Why won't you even think about it?"

"I don't," I told my daughter, and not for the first time, "need help finding companionable women."

"Could've fooled me."

"Becky, I meet women all the time. I'm just not interested in settling down."

"Who said anything about settling down? God, just have date. Get naked or something."

"Becky!"

She sighed and went back to her book, a massive tome that would have frightened me away by sheer size. The angry furrow across her forehead softened suddenly, and she looked back with wide eyes. "You like women, don't you?"

"My God, Becky."

"Well, you don't date. Your big thrill in life is watching Monday Night Football with Uncle Scott and Grandpa. I mean, if you don't like women, I'll shut up."

"I like women," I groaned, staring out the living room window, watching little drops of water ping off the glass. I wondered what she would have done if I had told her she was right on the money, that women were not the objects of my desire.

Without so much as the blink of an eye my liberal, headstrong daughter would have set out to find a more likely masculine candidate.

I looked back over at Becky, her nose buried in the book. She looked like her mother, emerald green eyes and dark brown hair, a smile that was as suggestive as it was shy. I didn't need to stare at the photograph by my bed to remember the woman I had lost; my daily reminder was blossoming into womanhood herself. She was precisely the same age I had been at her birth.

I wondered about the men in her life.

We were getting too far out of touch.

"You're staring at me," she accused, barely glancing up from the book.

"Just wondering if you're feeling all right. I mean, it's been at least five minutes since you said a word. I thought you might not be feeling well."

"Funny, Dad."

"You don't usually give up so easily."

"What's the point? You won't listen to me. You'd rather spend your evenings planted in your chair in front of the television set. You're only thirty-two years old and your life is already over. Why should I care?"

"My life is far from being over."

"Really? Could have fooled me."

"Becky…"

Those green eyes flashed at me in a rare display of anger. "You might as well be a priest. Hell, Dad, I won't be here in a couple years, sign up for the seminary now! You've got the celibacy part down pat!"

I leaned forward in my chair, curious instead of angry, and surprised at all the passion leaping from my daughter's mouth. "Is that so wrong?"

"Not for an old man," she challenged. "You're not really happy. You're lonely as hell and you don't even know it."

The fire in my gut spread, and I couldn't even swallow.

"Not as lonely as you think," I told her after a while. "I'm just careful, Becky. No, I don't date. I haven't had a girlfriend since your mother died. The women I meet aren't much older than you. Dating them hardly seems appropriate."

"What about the lady down the hall…?"

"Rusty?"

"I don't know her name. I've just seen her talk to you. She likes you."

"Megan Russell is just a friend. And my karate instructor. I don't think she's looking for a relationship, either."

She shook her head. "Dad, you wouldn't know a real pass if it reared up and bit you on the ass."

~

"Becky doesn't remember Rachel," I told my brother, Scott, over a cold beer. For once the TV was off and strains of Mozart filtered through the stereo. "She doesn't understand how I feel."

"Neither does anyone else. Rachel was terrific, but she's been gone for twice as long as you were married. Come on, Zach. The rules don't say one to a customer. You're allowed to at least look around."

"But I don't really want to."

He shook his head. "You're turning into exactly what Rachel was afraid of."

I asked in spite of my better intentions. "And what's that?"

"A bitter old man."

"I'm not bitter."

Scott took a long, slow sip of his beer, his sigh deliberate and calculated for effect. "Why were you in love with her?"

"What?"

"You heard me. Why did you love Rachel?"

"Because she was my wife, dammit! Because she loved me back. Because she gave me the most wonderful daughter in the world!"

Sixteen years ago I could have answered him calmly and given him a lengthy list of reasons that would have made him gag from the sticky sweetness of far too much saccharine. Most of those reasons were faded, blurred memories crowded out by the simple fact that what I expected to be my world was no longer where it was supposed to be. What was left, the reason that stood out among them all, was a sixteen year old bundle of angelic hellfire.

"Know why I love my wife?" Scott asked. Without waiting for an answer he plunged on. "She knows what she wants out of life. She's fiery and she's sexy and she doesn't take any crap from me. She keeps me on my toes and lifts me up by the bootstraps whenever life seems impossible." He crumpled his can and tossed it smoothly into the trash can across the room. "Who does that for you, Zachary?"

"I'm thirty four years old, at least thirty pounds overweight, and I have two rambunctious little boys to chase after. Why else would I be here three times a week? I have to get in shape just to keep up with them."

Diane was splayed out on the floor of the karate studio, staring up at the ceiling. Jason, a tiny eight year old, ran over and offered to help her up.

"Not yet, dear," she sighed. "Just let me die right here."

"Miss Russell don't like people dying in class," he informed her.

"He has a point," I said. "If she thinks she's gotten to you..."

Diane nodded and crawled up onto her knees, and then stood. "God knows I don't want to give her a reason to work us that much harder."

"Thank you."

"So what possessed you, Zach? Newly divorced? On the prowl?"

"Hardly. She lives down the hall from me. She didn't think I'd survive a month here, so..." I shrugged. "I'm here to prove her wrong."

"Is she ever wrong?"

"I wouldn't want to be the one to tell her if she was."

"Speaking of whom," she muttered, standing behind Jason, the class falling into place for warm-ups. Rusty went through her usual routine, bowing to the flag, reciting the class creed, and then went straight into conditioning exercises.

Diane moaned a few times during the twenty minute torture session, but she kept up with the little hornballs.

When it was all over, Rusty gave her a thumbs-up sign.

She shook her head sadly at me.

"You aren't trying hard enough," she told me later over coffee. "But you," she told Diane, "are coming along great."

"I've gained weight," Diane moaned. "I thought this was supposed to help me go in the opposite direction."

"It'll happen," Rusty assured her. "The weight gain is pure muscle."

Diane sighed and sipped at her coffee, black, no sugar—"though I'd kill for about a quarter cup of the stuff..."

"You should stop weighing yourself. The actual pounds don't matter. All that matters is that you get into decent shape and stay there."

"I think your shape is just fine," I said to Diane, hoping to buff Rusty off her fitness attack. "I can see you wanting to keep up with your boys, but if you think you're not attractive, think again."

"You're too kind," Diane said softly, blushing.

"No, I'm not. I mean it."

"Zach doesn't lie," Rusty added for me. "It's against his better principles."

"Well, I appreciate it." She gathered her purse and jacket. "You're sweet, Zach. And I've got to get going or the little monsters will tear down the house."

Rusty watched her walk out of the cafe. "Diane is precisely the kind of student I would like to have more of," she said.

"Really?"

"She doesn't have any pretensions of becoming the next Chuck Norris or Bruce Lee. Diane does it for all the right reasons."

"And me?"

"You have no reason. You're just out to prove some macho point."

"Machismo has nothing to do with it, Rusty. You wanted to teach me, so here I am."

"And what have you learned?"

I rubbed at sore muscles and admitted, "I've learned that my body doesn't like me very much."

"It'll come," she promised.

"My body, maybe. But what about the rest of my life?"

"I can picture you here," Rusty said, looking around my office, "but I can't picture you in front of a room full of teenagers preaching psychology."

I settled in the chair behind my desk. Rusty dropped onto the leather sofa pushed up against the right wall, her eyes darting as she surveyed the room. "Most of them aren't teenagers anymore. And I don't preach. I teach. There's a difference."

"To a point. You try to make them see your point of view, what you believe to be the truth of psychology. That has an element of preaching, don't you think?"

"Maybe," I allowed. "What about you? Don't you think you preach your point of view?"

She nodded. "Definitely. But my point of view supports finding the balance between what's inside a person and outside. You can learn what I believe, and you can take pieces of it as your own, but you can't take me. Not all of me. At some point each of my students—those who stick with it—find where the martial arts belong in their lives and use bits and pieces of it to create themselves."

"Not much different than what I do," I said. "You teach the balance between mind and body, I teach the balance between right and wrong."

"Perceptions."

"That's all there is."

"You could have been a minister, Zach, you know that?"

"My daughter seems to think so."

Rusty sat up straight. "Daughter? You have kids? Are you an old married man?"

I shook my head. "I have one, a sixteen year old. And no, I'm not married, not anymore."

"Divorced," she guessed.

"Widowed."

She got off the sofa and went over to the bookshelves across the room. She ran a finger along one shelf, flicking dust out of her way. "How long ago?"

"Does it matter?"

"Maybe. I don't know you very well, but I do know you're a hell of a lot different than most men I've known. I've been trying to figure it out."

"Ten years. And don't bother with the mental math. We married when I was sixteen. She died when I was twenty two."

"I'm sorry."

I leaned back in my chair and watched Rusty look at the pictures on the shelves and walls. That wasn't the typical 'I'm sorry.' It was genuine, almost anguished. She picked up a frame, traced her finger over the edges. "Is this your daughter?"

"Becky."

"I've seen her. I didn't know she was yours."

"Well, she is. And she has accused me of the horrible crime of being celibate and lonely."

She put the picture back in its place. "Are you?"

"Which one?"

"Both. Either."

"I suppose."

"Suppose? You don't know?"

"You really want to know?" Of course she did. I wasn't sure if she was nosy or concerned. "All right. Sure, I guess. It's hard to feel lonely when you've got so many people surrounding you, but yeah, I guess I am a little bit lonely most of the time. But I think most people are."

"Maybe." She glanced over at me, a tiny grin tugging at the corner of her mouth. "And that's all."

"What else do you want?"

"Just for you to satisfy my curiosity," she said honestly.

"Why should you care about my sex life?"

She shrugged. "I probably shouldn't. But I would think at the very least, you should."

"I'm glad the lawn isn't mine," I said, standing at the window. "I'd be pissed as hell if it was."

Becky peeked around me. "It's not a lawn, Dad. It's a lake."

"We're not supposed to get this much rain this time of year."

"I dunno. I think it's appropriate. I mean, the beginning of school, lousy weather..."

"Makes you feel better?"

"What the hell, it can't make me feel any worse."

"What the hell, fersure," I teased.

She thumped my arm and dropped onto the couch, loudly shuffling textbooks, pretending to agonize over her choice of subjects.

"You have an English paper..."

"Don't remind me." The shuffling of papers stopped, replacing by the sound of impatient page-turning. I stood in front of the window, feeling the chill seep through the glass, and listened to her indignant huffs and sighs as she read through several pages of Chaucer. "I met your friend today," she grunted with a pencil in her mouth.

I glanced over my shoulder. "Which one?"

Her eyebrows knotted together. I could tell she was thinking 'he has more than one?' "Rusty," she said. "Strange woman."

"How so?"

"I dunno. She seems... I dunno. I couldn't place my finger on it."

"Distant?"

"No." She took the pencil out of her mouth. "No, just the opposite. She was a little too friendly. She acted like she'd known me all my life. I dunno, I guess it bugged me because at the same time it was like she didn't know jack shit about me."

"She doesn't know jack shit about you, other than the fact that you exist."

"You hate it when I do that, don't you?"

"Do what?" I dropped into the blue recliner across from the sofa.

"Swear."

I shrugged. Becky's sudden spurt of foul language sort of sailed right over my head. I assumed she would either outgrow it or weave into her own vocabulary. I never presumed that I was to be consulted on the matter.

She started to go back to her book. "You're staring at me again," she accused, trying to find her place. "It bugs me."

"That's my job in life."

"You're awfully damned good at it."

"What'd you and Rusty talk about?" I asked.

It was Becky's turn to shrug. "I dunno. She asked a lot of questions about you. Wanted to know if you were dating anyone. Like I would really know."

"I'm not."

"You're not dating her?"

I shook my head.

"Shit, the way she acts you'd think she was three pizzas and a movie away from a ring on her finger. What the hell is it you two do?"

"Talk. Bullshit mostly."

"Do you plan on dating her?"

"No. Why?"

She tossed her book down, staring at me. I felt like a bug three inches long with wiggling antennae. A curiosity to be examined closely before being squashed. "You don't get it, do you? Dad, you can't string a woman along, make her feel like there's something there, if you don't have any intention of following up on it. It's cruel."

"Since when is trying to be someone's friend cruel?"

"She obviously thinks you want to be more."

"I talked to her, Becky, that's all. I accepted her offer for karate lessons. We had a few beers, coffee once. How the hell is that stringing her along?"

"Maybe that's all she's got."

"Could be she's just desperately lonely. Or maybe there's something about you she can't resist."

"Oh, come on," I groaned. "There's nothing about me women find irresistible. That's never been my problem."

Diane sighed, a simple, what-the-hell kind of sigh as she reached for the sugar and poured it liberally into her coffee. "Rusty strikes me as the sort of woman who goes after what she wants. And if she wants you, you may have no say in it."

"Bullshit. Megan Russell is not my type of woman."

"Oh, really?" She grinned. "Just what is your type of woman? You don't like the long-legged, self-assured, sex-starved type?"

"I don't like women who manipulate. And if she's snooping around about me through my daughter, that's exactly what she's doing. I tried to be her friend, nothing more. She had Becky thinking I was on the verge of proposing."

"But proposing what?" Diane said, waving her spoon at me. "That's the question that remains to be seen."

"What, sex? If that's what I was after I'm sure I could find a more suitable partner."

"Who's more suitable? Rusty could probably grind you into the mattress."

"I don't want to be ground into anything." I took the sugar container and followed Diane's lead, dumping a heap into the middle of the cup, stirring it slowly. "Diane, I haven't slept with anyone since my wife died. I never got into bed hopping or anything like it. I had a little girl to protect, for Christ's sake…"

She was shaking her head. "You're the psychologist. Were you protecting her or yourself?"

I didn't answer.

"And now? She doesn't need that kind of protection. It would probably be a relief to her to know you had someone in your life. Maybe now Becky's just a good shield."

"I don't," I said emphatically, "want to sleep with Rusty."

"You have no desire for sex."

"That's not what I said."

"Then what do you want?"

I had no idea, but I didn't think I would find it chugging beer and trading barbs with Rusty. I didn't think I would find it by leaping around her karate studio in overgrown white pants and bare feet.

The confusion was a strange feeling.

It occupied the spaces inside that for years had felt completely, utterly, dead.

...

I handed her a check. Double the usual rate, exactly one month to the day later. She stared at it for a long time.

"I don't get it."

"I'm sorry, Rusty, but I never got into it. Whatever it is that attracts you to the art holds nothing for me. I really am sorry."

"Not as sorry as I am," she muttered. "I really thought you had it in you, Zach. You have the right kind of body, the right kind of soul…"

For what?

I peered through her office window. Diane was sitting on the carpet, stretching out, her head bent down to her knee; Jason was standing behind her, gently putting pressure on her back, helping her stretch as far as she could.

"I don't think I wanted it bad enough," I said. Maybe not for the right reasons. Diane hopped up, lifting her arms above her head, leaning to each side, gracefully, pulling the muscles taut. "At least not as bad as some of your students."

She shoved the check aside.

"Still friends?"

"Our friendship never depended on you getting your black belt," she laughed, reaching for her own. "You're forgiven."

"Am I really?" I looked into her dark eyes, wondering what it was I saw there.

Hurt? I didn't think so.

She tied the belt around her waist carefully, tugging at the hem of her uniform to snap it into place.

"I suppose I'll have to figure out another way to find my balance."

Her hand was on the doorknob. "Balance? Zach, what you need is discipline."

The door clicked shut behind her.

I got it, finally.

I had taken Rusty's little test, and I had failed miserably.

Jeff Woodward stood by his desk, pen in hand, looking me straight in the eye. He could, he was sure, give me a reasonable definition. "A difference in morals," he said confidently, "is a question between right and wrong. A difference in ethics is a question between two rights."

Little shit.

"All right, Mr. Woodward, take your seat. You've summed up the entire semester after only one month."

He beamed.

"And quite possibly," I went on, "my entire adult life."

Becky leaned against the breakfast bar and waited. I had started the conversation and now that she was listening I wasn't sure I wanted to go through with it.

I took refuge in playing with the ice cubes in my soda.

"I miss her, Becky. Even now. I loved her so much... We never had the chance to find out how good we really would have been together. We were two kids playing house and she was gone before either of us had an honest chance to grow up. It hurts that the chance was taken away from me. I will never know how good or bad a marriage it could have been."

"If you loved her..."

"But that's not always enough." I leaned across the bar and touched the back of her hand. "I was sixteen and in love with the idea of being in love. It was a fantasy and it was fun, but I don't know how far beyond that we grew."

"Is that it, then? You're afraid to find something better, aren't you?"

"Sweetheart, I'm terrified."

"Don't you think she'd want you to find something better?"

Of that I had no doubt. But did I want something better? For my daughter, sure. For myself...?

Maybe there was no separating the two.

Balance.

When the phone rang and Becky pushed off the counter to answer it, I turned my head to look out the window. The rain had stopped, stars splashed across the sky like spilled glitter.

"Dad?"

I broke out of my reverie; Becky was holding the phone out to me. "Some woman."

I raised an eyebrow.

She put her hand over the receiver. "So just who the hell is Diane...?"

How A Computer Works
William A. McKee

The year was 1978. I remember the first time I saw a computer. It had a bank of switches on a sloping panel and row of lights across the top. Inside it was a mass of wire and integrated circuits. The owner, Mr. A, was a retired electronics expert who use to work for an observatory. He built it from a kit as an exercise to learn about computers. You see, I had a crush on his daughter and shamelessly used that as a pretext to look at his computer.

Anyway, I was 15 and I didn't have a clue how the computer worked. I barely knew what digital electronics was. The only logic I knew was what I'd gleamed from digital electronics. But, Mr. A was a kind old gentleman and he had learned all he was going to from the dark box so he generously lent it to me. The great thing was that it came with a bunch of instruction manuals with everything from how to build it to how to run it; all laid out for a young mind to absorb.

Well, the first thing I learned was what all those switches did. There was the memory switches arranged in two panels of eight switches across and eight rows down. Imagine, you could physically set each bit of memory; a whole sixteen bytes of it. That's what I call ROM with an attitude. Then, there was the Reset button, the Step button and the Run button on the right about half way up the front panel. There was also a speed switch for fast or slow beside the buttons. Below these were eight address/data switches and two buttons: one for setting the address of the instruction pointer and other for writing eight bits of data to one of the 16 bytes of RAM. There was also a Power switch down in the lower left-hand corner. The first thing I learned was when you turned the power on, you could give yourself a small, non-fatal shock by touching the frame of the computer. You see, when Mr. A built the computer, the power supply had not been grounded properly.

There was also a cryptic table stencilled onto the front panel just right of the memory switches and just above the other buttons and switches. I later learned that it was the op codes for the limited instruction set you could use to program the computer. Fascinating. A secret language that only a few special people knew. Every kid's dream.

Now to the lights. There was the accumulator (ACC): eight lights on the left. One light was the carry bit and another the zero bit. The instruction pointer (IP) was the next five lights. And last was the fetch/execute light. The lights were mesmerizing since when you pushed the Step button the pattern of lights in the ACC would shifted right, sometimes the IP would count upward (in binary) and the fetch/execute light would blink away. When you set the Speed switch to slow and press the Reset button then the Run button and it would come alive. I had no idea what it was doing or what it meant but it was a thing of beauty.

Putting it all together. I had achieved step one: I was a computer user. I could run the computer but that wasn't enough. I had to have control over what it did. Step two: becoming a programmer. I learned that by setting the memory switches with the correct op codes the computer could be programmed to do useful work. It took a lot of imagination but I could see patterns emerge from the mist of ignorance.

First, there's the computer's native language: binary. If you want to know how a computer works you have to learn binary. The only two digits in binary are zero (0) and one (1). By combining 0 and 1 in to a pattern of eight digits (called a byte) you get the decimal (regular, every day) number from 0 to 255. Now here's the neat part. The lights can be on or off. When a light is on it represents the digit 1 and when the light is off it represents the digit 0. So just by turning the ACC lights on and off you can have 256 different patterns; each pattern representing a number. Oh yeah, the same applies to the memory switches. When the switch is up (on) it mean 1 and when the switch is down (off) it means 0. Welcome to the world of digital electronics.

Let me digress for a moment. Now binary numbers are the same a decimal (normal) number because they are isomorphic. That is to say you can convert from one to another without getting all mixed up. Computers love numbers. Everything in the computer is numbers. Op codes are numbers; letters are numbers; the address of every byte of memory in the computer is a number. Even the pretty pictures you get off the web are really just numbers. The neat thing about numbers is that you can put them one after another to create a context in which the numbers give raise to meaning.

Ok. The foundation of computer's architecture is the hardware. This is the grossest possible context. It does everything that a computer is capable of doing. In the world of computer hardware, there are only switches (called bits) that can be turned on or off. Billions of them. Some work in unison like the video RAM to give you a screen full of information all at once. Some work by coaxing the various parts of your hard drive to spin and grind until it gets to a useful place where your pr0n is stored. Some you can set by typing on a keyboard or pushing your mouse around.

The next level in the computer's architecture is the software. This is a sequence of numbers know as op codes (collectively called a program) that tell the computer, given that some bits are on or off, how to turn on and off the various other bits. The op codes only make sense in the context of the central processing unit (CPU) which is at the heart of the computer hardware. Random access memory (RAM) is the very place where the op codes, among other things, are stored. This leads to levels with in levels since a small program (boot strap loader) can load a larger program (kernel) that loads a larger program (desktop GUI) that loads your favourite game.

The top level of the computer's architecture is the data. Data only makes sense in the context of a program and the "state" of the computer. When you type the "A" key on the keyboard, it eventually under most circumstances gets stored in memory as the number 65 (binary 01000001) and the only reason you can see it is because you are using a word process (or some such program) that tells the OS to draw a picture of the 65th image in the "Times New Roman" font onto the graphics screen. The actual data of the "A" you see is really just a bunch of bits set to look approximately like the shape of the letter "A". It has very little to do with the bits that were set when you typed the "A" except that the program interpreted the context and took appropriate action.

Let's get back to the story. Second, there are the op codes: instructions that Mr. A's computer can follow. All the op codes were one byte long and most had two parts: the instruction field (3 bits) and the address field (5 bits). The most useful instruction was LOAD. This would take the data at the specified memory address and move it into the ACC. There was also the reverse instruction: SAVE that moved the ACC to a memory location. (Of course, you could only do this with a RAM address.) One of the most useful instructions was ADD. It would take the data at the specified address and mathematically add it to the ACC. There was also the JZ (jump on zero) instruction that changed the IP to the specified address if the ACC value was zero but I'm getting ahead of myself. You see, the computer looks at the op codes one at a time. Only looking at the instruction pointed to by the IP. Since every memory location has a numeric address, it is easy for the computer to keep track of were it is currently working. The computer does its work in two steps: fetch and execute. In the fetch stage, the computer reads the memory location at the IP. Then, when executing, it is changes the ACC or RAM or IP: whatever the op codes says. After each fetch the IP is increased by one so that after executing the current instruction it will fetch and execute the next instruction. You can explicitly change the IP with a jump instruction, this is what we call flow control in a program and determines the order in which things get done.

So that's how a computer works. Things haven't changed much since 1978 except that there are more instructions, faster CPUs, more memory and a host of devices that extend the usefulness of your computer.

As for Mr. A's daughter, I never saw her much after I got my first computer. I hope she found a nice boy to marry and have lots of kids. I'll never forget her or Mr. A's computer. You never forget your first love.

Look Up At The Stars
Daniel W. Webb

When I look up at the stars, I think to myself that we are capable of so much. If the world just learned to pull its resources together, there's nothing that we couldn't accomplish. Instead we have to worry about politics, and war. We have to worry about our financial situations, and debt. We have to carry our butts to work every day, dreading the idea, because the only purpose our jobs serve is keeping the food on the table. We lack motivation. What can we do to change this?

When I look up at the stars, I think to myself that I really would like to go up there. If I lived two hundred years from now, would I be able to? Would I be the first human to walk on that Martian surface? How would I get there? How long will the trip last? Could I go other places? What would I discover? Who would I be going with? These questions can only be answered through exploration.

When I look up at the stars, I think to myself, "Is there any intelligent life out there?" There has to be. Space is way too big for there not to be; but how can we prove it? How will we make first contact? Will they contact us first? Will they be willing to let us learn from them, or would they be hostile? What would they think of us? What will we think of them? So many questions. I hope that one day we will know the answers.

When I look up at the stars, I think to myself, "I wish I had a star ship." Maybe I've watched too many science fiction movies, but it would be nice. It would be the ultimate get away. I would leave all my troubles behind, and explore everything that I could. I would take my discoveries back to earth, and maybe it would inspire more explorers to start their own adventure and live their dreams.

Look up at the stars tonight, and think to yourself.

Thank You
Jessica Hildbold

One of the greatest gift that I have ever received wasn't jewelry or a leather coat or a new car. It was two little words that I received from a friend of mine shortly before I graduated from college. It was a big year that year as our little group seemed to be going off in a million different directions. We had all lived in the same wing of a residence hall (not a dorm ~ dorms are where you stay; residence halls are where you live), but at the end of the year two of us were graduating, two of us were transferring, and all but two of us were moving to other living spaces, either other halls, apartments, or sorority houses. There were many good-byes to give and receive and many gifts to exchange. I remember receiving an alumni t-shirt, a candle, and flowers, as well as some of the most beautiful cards that I will keep forever. I also remember knowing that this was the last time that I would see many of these people. I found myself at a complete loss as to how to tell them just how much they meant to me and how much I was going to miss them all. I would miss the all night study sessions before finals; the championship video game tournaments; the Friday night parties. I would miss the security of walking out of my hall and knowing I could walk into any other room and find a friend. I would miss the lessons of humility, love, anger, and friendship that each one of them had given me. It tore me up inside that I didn't know how to say good-bye. I nearly graduated not knowing what to say.

But my friend did.

The day before graduation, my friend, Kimmie, was leaving for a weekend trip. She was spending the summer at the university and wouldn't be leaving for home so this was her only weekend to spend with her boyfriend. A fairly emotional girl, she was known for her good-byes and the way they always made you cry. There was something in her eyes, the loss of a twinkle, that made you break in two every time you had to tell her good-bye. That Friday, we stood in the hallway just looking at each other for a few moments. Neither one of us moved. I couldn't breath. This was my final opportunity to tell her, to tell her everything that she meant to me and I couldn't even move. The world seemed to be collapsing around me. I had known this girl for only three years, but in those three years we had been through so much together: the problems with her parents, several deaths in my family, the troubles with college tuition we both always had. She moved first, hugging me tight. Her entire body shook as tears flowed from every ounce of her. Never one to cry much myself, I openly sobbed. Shortly before she broke away to make a hurried exit, she whispered my greatest gift. "Thank you."

Thank you.

I stood there dumbstruck by what she had just said. I once again found myself unable to move as I watched her sprint down the hall. Thank you. Didn't she understand that I was the one who wanted to say thank you to her? Didn't she know how much she had helped me to grow? Thank you. Didn't she know that I was grateful to her for being in my life? Didn't she know? Thank you. That phrase stuck in my head, repeating itself over and over. What had she meant by that? Was it possible that I had helped her as much as she helped me? And, then, I realized that I had finally known the way to say good-bye. It was so simple. I just needed to say thank you.

Unfortunately, most of my friends had gone home by then. Our university did not allow for anyone other then seniors to stay on campus after finals. The lesson, possibly the last lesson that I learned from Kimmie, was to say thank you, as much and as often as I could. I still use "thank you" for the simple things in life such as someone holding the door open for me, but I also remember to use it for the big things. Every time someone complements the work that I have done, I say thank you instead of blushing with embarassment. If someone helps me, whether with the spelling of a word or moving into my new apartment or a personal crisis I just couldn't see my way out of, I say thank you. And the next time that one of my friends moves on in life, I will hug them tightly, tears flowing freely, and whisper thank you.

I may never know exactly what Kimmie meant when she whispered thank you to me. She may not even know herself, but I thank her for one of my greatest gifts. I had forgotten before that day just how powerful and positive some words can be. So, Kimmie, wherever you are tonight, thank you.

And thank you for reading.

SPARK
Miranda Hall

Did you feel it?

I want to ask him so badly...to know I'm not crazy, that I didn't feel the spark because I wanted to...I want to hear him say he felt it...

There...another glance, another touch, another spark — and I'm alive again. Does he know? I catch his eyes for a moment and have to look away before I fall into...his eyes...his stare...into him. Does he see it? Someone told me when I look at him, that my eyes and my heart open for all to see...and the light that shines from them is blinding...and it hurts, it's so bright. And I feel it. This time, it's all I think about...I can't see how he sees me, but I feel how I see him.

He asks me if I see the lightning in the sky...and I do.... I feel it — I feel it's intensity in his every word...and in the spark that passes between our skin in the slightest touch...he tells me that it would feel like your body explodes from the inside in a split second...and I know it would...it does...and the pain is exquisite.

And I know he felt it.

A Picture of Death
Donna Eyer

Kevin O'Brien maneuvered his Jeep Grand Cherokee down the Bennett Falls exit ramp from Interstate 82, relaxing slightly as he left the fast pace of the highway. At the bottom of the ramp, he turned right onto a very familiar stretch of state road. Seeing no oncoming traffic, he reached over and turned on the radio. As the sounds of the latest country hits began pouring from the speakers, Kevin leaned his head back against the headrest and grinned.

Kevin was now officially on vacation, having submitted his last photographs of the week to the newspaper office well under deadline. He'd been waiting for the vacation all summer, and finally, in late August, he got the good news. Now Kevin was headed for home to enjoy the weeks off and spend some time with his wife and kids.

Suddenly, his attention was called back to the road ahead of him, or more specifically, to the man walking along the shoulder. He was short and timid-looking, and his neat appearance was one of a man who should be sitting in front of a computer screen in a large office building in the city. Instead, he was out here on a road between civilization and the middle of nowhere, and he had just turned to face Kevin's Jeep as it approached. The man stuck out his thumb in the classic gesture of a hitchhiker, and Kevin immediately began to slow down. He flashed back to his younger years and the large part that hitching rides played in that time in his life. The man looked harmless enough, and Kevin was sympathetic, knowing that the weather was unseasonably cold that day. Without another thought, he pulled off the road as far as he could go.

The hitcher eased into the leather seat, resting a small backpack between his feet. With hands that were still shaking from the cold, he pulled the door shut and fastened his seatbelt, then turned to Kevin.

"Thanks, man," he said gratefully. "There's not much traffic out here. I thought I was going to freeze before I got a ride. What's up with this weather anyway?"

"Hey, no problem. Looks like fall's getting an early start." Kevin smiled and extended his right hand. "I'm Kevin O'Brien."

"Brady Dillon," the hitcher replied, taking Kevin's hand and giving it a hearty shake. Kevin noticed that Dillon wasn't wearing gloves. His hands were raw and red, as well as ice-cold.

"So, where are you headed?" Kevin signaled, then pulled back onto the road, being careful not to hit the patches of gravel at the edge. The Jeep was his pride and joy, and he wasn't about to be careless with it.

"I'm hoping to get as far as the Bennett Falls city limits tonight, then tomorrow morning, I'll be on my way to Seattle."

"I think you're in luck," Kevin stated amiably. "I just happen to live about a mile from the city limits. I'd be glad to take you there."

"You're kidding!" Dillon stared at him in disbelief. When Kevin shook his head, his passenger grinned broadly. "Whoever coined the phrase, 'this must be my lucky day,' should get a medal." They both chuckled, and Kevin found himself giving Brady Dillon the once-over.

Dillon couldn't have been more than five-and-a-half feet tall, and his weight matched his slight build. The clothes he was wearing weren't suited for walking outside in the low temperature and frigid wind; the navy blue sweater vest covered a thin, white dress shirt, and his tan Dockers were pressed and creased. His black leather dress shoes were "clarino"-finished, making it impossible to tell how old they were, but they certainly must have been uncomfortable when it came to walking long distances on the shoulder of the road. Dillon wore no jewelry that Kevin could see, and he glanced from the man himself to the pack resting on the floor between his feet. There were odd shapes poking at the sides of the bag, but Kevin couldn't place them.

Dismissing the pack, he focused on the road ahead. They were approaching the Bennett Falls cutoff. Slowing the Jeep, he made his usual turn and headed toward his hometown, which was affectionately known as The Falls. The sun was just beginning to set, bathing the entire area in a hazy, reddish glow.

"The city limits are about six miles from here," Kevin announced, breaking the preceding silence.

Dillon, who was resting quietly with his eyes closed, smiled. "I'm making better time than I thought I would. Maybe I'll stop somewhere to eat after you drop me off. Know of any good places?"

"Well, there's Norton's, which is basically on the city line. Since you'll already be there, that's your best bet. Other than that, there are some fast food joints about two miles into the city, but Norton's would be my choice. They've got the best burgers and fries this side of the Rockies, and that's no joke."

"Okay, okay, you've convinced me," Dillon laughed. "Norton's it is. Say, the food there isn't expensive, is it? I don't have all that much cash."

"Nah, don't worry about it. Norton is one of those great men who believe that if you keep the prices low and the food edible, you'll get twice as much business as your competitors."

"Oh, he's a genius, is he?" Dillon asked, a bemused smile playing at the corners of his mouth. They were now passing through the woodlands beyond the outskirts of town. The trees, which had always been a permanent part of the area, hadn't yet been disturbed by the technology that seemed to be taking over the small town. Dillon gazed out the window at the woods, taking in the scenery. Just ahead were the falls from which the town had taken its name. As Kevin approached the bridge, Dillon's eyes narrowed. He began to shake, not from the cold, but with nervous anticipation. He licked his dry lips and cleared his throat.

"Mr. O'Brien, do you think you could pull over here for a moment? I'd like to take a few pictures of the falls. I don't want to be any trouble, but I don't think I'll be getting back this way for quite a long time."

"First of all, call me Kevin. Second, you have a camera?"

"It's in my pack," Brady Dillon replied, gesturing toward the bag between his feet.

"In that case, I'll most definitely pull over. Call it a favor from one photographer to another."

"You're a photographer?" Dillon felt a twinge of guilt. Photography had been his hobby since late childhood, and he felt a comraderie toward others who had the same interest. Now he wasn't sure if he could bring himself to do what he had to do.

"I am," Kevin replied, smiling. "I work for the local newspaper, the *Bennett Falls Gazette*."

"I just take pictures as a hobby," Dillon told him, beginning to unzip the pack as they approached the side of the road. Kevin pulled off into a small parking area beside an observation point. Only locals visited the overlook this time of year, so it was no surprise that the parking lot was otherwise empty. He put the Jeep into park, pulled on the emergency brake, and unfastened his seatbelt.

"I think I'll join you. I need a little fresh air." He turned his back to Dillon as he unlocked the door and started to reach for the handle.

"Don't move," the man in the passenger seat commanded. Kevin was about to turn around when he felt the cold, metal barrel of a gun against his bare neck. "I mean it. Don't even flinch or you'll be a statistic."

"What – ?"

"Shut the fuck up!" Dillon screamed.

Kevin could feel the gun trembling against his neck and instantly knew that the hitchhiker was like a liquid explosive. One wrong move and he would be set off. "Shut the car off, then take the keys out of the ignition." The voice was softer now, but it still held the note of derangement that turned Kevin O'Brien's blood to ice. Trembling himself, Kevin reached for the keys. He turned off the ignition, then pulled on the keyring, feeling it slip loose.

"Drop them."

"Drop them where?" Kevin dared to ask, his voice almost a whisper.

"Anywhere, asshole!" Dillon slapped the keys from Kevin's hand, and they clattered against the dashboard before hitting the floor. "Now take out your wallet and give me all the money you have. Do it slowly. Don't try to be a hero. No one remembers dead heroes nowadays."

As Kevin reached for the wallet in his back pocket, a plan started to form in his mind. He opened the wallet and took out the money automatically, his thoughts focused on something totally different. He put the hand containing the cash behind his back, and the bills were immediately snatched from his grasp.

"Now I'm going to take the gun away, but if you so much as breathe loudly, I'll blow you away. I've done it before, and I'm not afraid to do it again. Am I being understood?"

"Yes, of course you are." Kevin was calmer now, but he tried not to let that show in his voice. He still wanted his captor to think he was just a helpless victim.

Brady Dillon put the gun on the seat between his legs and began to count the money. There was over a hundred dollars, which seemed to somewhat satisfy him. He quickly frisked Kevin O'Brien, searching his coat pockets, then his pants pockets. Finding nothing else of value, he pulled the wedding band from Kevin's finger and put it in his own pocket along with the money.

With Dillon momentarily distracted, Kevin saw his opportunity and wasn't about to let it escape. He turned around in the seat, swinging his left fist at the man across from him. A startled Brady Dillon looked up just at the right moment, and Kevin's fist connected squarely with his captor's jaw. Dillon felt it hit him like a freight train, and he was thrown back against the car door. Enraged, he lunged for the gun, which had fallen off of the seat in the commotion. Kevin swung his right arm this time, and he winced slightly when he connected with Dillon's nose, sending the assailant against the door again.

As Dillon tried to recover, shaking his head slowly from side to side, Kevin made a desperate grab for the gun. His hand closed around the barrel, but as he started to sit up, he felt an enormous impact on the back of his neck. Kevin fought the grayness that was closing in on his mind and tried to keep the gun in his hand. The adrenaline kicked in, and he launched himself backwards with what little strength he had left. His elbow caught Dillon in the stomach and knocked the wind out of him.

Brady Dillon struggled to breathe, not quite sure what had happened. This wasn't the way it was supposed to go. His victim was taking control of the situation. As Dillon coughed, trying to force air back into his lungs, Kevin regained his position on the driver's seat. In what seemed to be surreal slow-motion, Dillon could only watch as Kevin's fist slammed into his chin. His head snapped back against the window almost hard enough to shatter the glass. Brady Dillon's world faded into black nothingness.

For a moment, Kevin O'Brien couldn't bring himself to move. He sat sideways on the driver's seat and fought back the terrified sobs that threatened to burst their way from deep inside of him. He gasped for air, closing his eyes and clenching his fists against the panic. His mind was no longer comprehending the concept of time passage, so he had no idea how long he stayed there before finally shaking off the paralysis of fear.

When Kevin opened his eyes, Brady Dillon was still slumped back in the corner formed by the seat and the door. Thin lines of blood ran from his nose and the corner of his mouth, but his chest was still rising and falling.

He's not dead. At first, the thought angered Kevin in some way. Thankfully, a tendril of rational fear crept its way back in, and Kevin realized he needed to get away before Dillon regained consciousness. He didn't dare risk waking Dillon, so he left his money and wedding band behind. He grabbed the keys and the gun instead, then left the Jeep behind as well. Not knowing what else to do, he ran up the trail leading into the woods toward another of the town's namesake waterfalls.

The sun had gotten even lower in the sky by the time Kevin O'Brien heard footsteps coming up the trail toward him. He'd taken refuge behind a small windfall, hoping that it would be enough to hide him from Brady Dillon's view. Kevin knew these trails well, as he'd spent most of his childhood in this area, creating new and interesting adventures almost every day of summer vacation. He'd known that the windfall would still be in its usual spot, but he'd been much smaller so many years ago, and it didn't seem to provide nearly as much cover for his tall frame as it had back then.

While he waited, he'd managed to recover his senses just enough to mull the situation over in his mind. What would he do to Dillon? Would he shoot him? Could he really take another human life? What if he just shot him in the leg and wounded him? Why was he even sitting there waiting? Shouldn't he be running or getting help?

As the questions tumbled over each other in his mind, Kevin sighed and ran his fingers absently over the cold metal of the gun in his hands. He knew how to use it. His father, a former military police officer, had taught both of his sons how to properly handle and fire various weapons. He'd taken them to the local gun club and had practiced with them at the range.

Was that why he was waiting to confront Brady Dillon again? Kevin wasn't sure, but he realized that part of the reason likely involved revenge. Dillon had dared to compromise Kevin's safety, his well-being, and Kevin wasn't going to just let him get away with that. Even so, taking justice into his own hands seemed drastic. It was as these second thoughts started to nag at Kevin's conscience that he heard the footsteps.

Slowly, silently, he shifted just enough to peer around the brush.

Brady Dillon was moving carelessly, almost as if he wanted to be heard. There was a line of dried blood on his lips and chin, standing out against the paleness of his cold face. He was now carrying something else in his right hand. In the waning daylight, Kevin could just barely make out the form of a large hunting knife. Shuddering, he shrank back as far behind the windfall as he could manage. He held his breath and waited.

In the trees on the other side of the trail, a bird started chirping, followed by another. The steady rush of the closest waterfalls droned in the background. Something, probably a squirrel, rustled the leaves a fair distance away, and Brady Dillon's footsteps stopped. Feeling the terror inching its coldness back into his heart, Kevin stayed completely still, not daring to move.

The seconds ticked by in a way that was both nerve-wracking and reassuring at the same time. Just as Kevin was beginning to convince himself that Brady Dillon would never discover his hiding place, Mother Nature played a cruel trick on him. The wind suddenly picked up, whipping the collar of Kevin's coat against his cheek. Startled, he flinched and tried to stifle a gasp. His lower lip trembled, and he suddenly felt like a terrified child, hiding beneath the covers from whatever strange creatures lurked in the inky black expanse under his bed.

When he heard the footsteps approaching him, Kevin thought his heart would stop. He squeezed his eyes shut and tried desperately not to break down. *What have I gotten myself into?* Holding the gun tightly in his right hand, his finger hovering just in front of the trigger, Kevin willed himself to stop shaking and to get his emotions under control. He swallowed hard around the lump in his throat and opened his eyes.

Brady Dillon was standing right in front of him.

As the knife sliced through the air, Kevin lunged to the side, rolling out from under the blade. He scrambled to his feet and trained the gun on Dillon, grasping it tightly in both hands, his finger on the trigger.

"Don't..." It was all Kevin could manage, his voice breaking. His vision blurred, and he blinked furiously, suddenly sure that Dillon would attack him while he couldn't see. When his attacker stayed put, still brandishing the knife, Kevin sucked in a deep breath and forced himself to calm down. He had the gun. He was in control.

"Give me the gun." Dillon's voice sounded odd, almost friendly. His brown eyes stared deeply into Kevin's blue ones, and his look was one of reassurance.

Kevin shook his head. "Fuck you."

Dillon looked almost hurt. He took a cautious step toward Kevin. "Now that wasn't very nice. Look, I just want to talk for a moment. We have quite a bit to discuss, you and I." He ran his tongue over the small gash in his lip.

Again, Kevin shook his head, not just in defiance, but also in a futile effort to clear his thoughts. He couldn't let Brady Dillon get inside his head. Against his better judgment, he spoke again. "You tried to kill me."

The hurt look in Dillon's eyes deepened. "I wasn't going to kill you." He sounded astonished by the accusation. "I just wanted the money." He flipped through his mental file and came up with a common denominator. "We're both photographers. I'd never hurt one of my own. If I'd known it was going to turn out like this, I would've waited for the next car." He took another step toward Kevin.

"Stop it!" The sound of Dillon's voice was unnerving, and Kevin had only now realized that the man was closer than before. "Don't come any closer."

"Kevin…" His voice apologetic, Dillon took another step. He turned his free palm up in the classic gesture of someone who doesn't want to be perceived as a threat.

"No!" Kevin could feel the panic welling up inside of himself, and he struggled to force it back down without losing control of the situation. He kept the gun pointed at Dillon's chest. "I'll shoot, I swear I will. I know how." The words sounded weak and childish.

"I'll bet you do." Dillon tried to maintain the innocent expression, but the cold determination returned to his eyes, and his voice hardened. "Now give me the gun." He slowly slid his left foot forward. His grip tightened on the knife handle, his knuckles turning a ghastly white against the redness of his raw skin.

Kevin shook his head again. In his confusion, he almost missed Dillon's movement. Somewhere far back in his mind, the position of Brady Dillon's left foot was trying to connect with a word. It was the same feeling Kevin had when a word was on the tip of his tongue. What was it?

Kevin saw Dillon raising the knife upward, but it was almost as if he was watching a slow-motion replay. His fight-or-flight instinct kicked in, and he realized that his life was in danger, gun or no gun. He was almost surprised to find that some events of his life really were flashing before his eyes, just like he'd always heard.

He saw himself chasing his brother through the meadow behind their house, laughing as they dripped dry after a quick swim in the river. That faded into an image of his dad in an Army uniform, posing proudly with his sons in the front yard beside the Corvair. He watched himself bury his dog, Bear. He saw himself graduating from high school, then from college. He felt the joy of his first slow dance with his future wife. There was Jill with the rice in her hair, smiling at him through tears of love and happiness; Jill again, giving birth to their son, Jordan; little Mallie's birth four years later.

As the visions blurred back into reality, the word finally connected in his mind – leverage. Dillon had moved his foot to get leverage. The thought was confirmed when Dillon lunged toward him, the knife raised high above his head.

Kevin exhaled and squeezed the trigger once, twice. The panicked part of his mind wanted him to keep firing until the clip was empty, but his heart won the battle of morals. His shoulders slumped, and he let his hands fall weakly to his sides.

Brady Dillon felt the explosion in his chest. The impact knocked him backward, and he stumbled against the windfall, sitting down hard only inches from where Kevin had been hiding. The knife fell back into the brush behind him, lost in the tangle of debris. In astonishment, he looked down at the holes in his chest, then glanced back up at Kevin. The expression on the hitchhiker's face was one of utter shock and surprise. What went wrong? He'd done this before, and he'd gotten away with it each time. How was this time any different? He just could not figure it out.

Dillon became vaguely aware that he was having tremendous trouble breathing. He leaned back against the windfall and pressed his bare hands to his chest in a futile attempt to stop the bleeding. A black veil had fallen over his peripheral vision. As it closed in on the rest of his sight, the psychotic part of his mind took over and he managed a raspy chuckle. He wasn't sure why the whole situation suddenly seemed so funny, but it did, and he tried to laugh. The rattling response from his chest startled him, and he stopped and looked down at himself again. Then, as if someone had flipped a switch in his body, Brady Dillon stopped moving. He uttered one final breath and succumbed to the darkness that was waiting to take him.

...

Kevin watched the body of Brady Dillon float down the river toward the falls. His body and mind were numb. He had taken back his money and wedding band before dragging the corpse down the trail to the bank of the river. Giving Brady Dillon's body a hefty shove, Kevin had watched it roll down the short embankment to splash into the murky water below.

Now, as the body neared one of the waterfalls, Kevin fought the urge to jump in after it and pull it back to safety. Instead, he tossed the gun far out into a part of the river where the current was sure to take it over the falls. He walked a short distance upstream to a place where he could rid himself of what little blood he'd gotten on his hands. The blood washed away easily, the cold water pricking at his skin like needles.

The thing he could not get rid of was the tremendous feeling of guilt. He had killed this man in self-defense, so why should he feel guilty? Kevin couldn't find an answer, other than the fact that he had actually taken a human life, something he never thought he'd have to do.

Sighing, Kevin took one last look at the falls, but they held no answer. He turned on legs that were still shaky and made his way back down the trail to the parking area. That long-awaited vacation suddenly didn't seem so important.

Eight months later, Kevin O'Brien read the front page of the newspaper with a combination of fear and, once again, guilt. "Body of Mass Murderer Found in Yakima River," the headline proclaimed boldly. The article went on to say that dental records were used to identify the badly decomposed remains found in the Yakima earlier that week, which had apparently washed ashore due to heavy runoff from the melting snow. The body had been identified as that of mass murderer Charles Duncan, a.k.a. Brady Dillon. He had been wanted by Washington State Police in connection with at least seven different murders, but it wasn't immediately apparent how he himself had died. More details would be reported as they were uncovered, the article concluded, also informing the reader that further investigations were underway.

The accompanying photograph was rather standard, showing two men wearing coroner's jackets wheeling a stretcher away from the river's edge. In black-and-white newsprint, the remains covered by the sheet were barely discernable.

As he stared at the photo, the hair rose on the nape of Kevin's neck. All at once, he wanted to cry, scream, hold his wife and children, maybe even tell someone what he'd done.

"Kevin, honey, we'd better get going." Jill appeared in front of him in the kitchen doorway, their daughter in her arms. "You're parents are going to think we got lost. Besides, Mallie wants to see her grandpa, right, little one?" Mallie nodded, and her mouth curled into a precocious grin below her pudgy cheeks. She looked over at Kevin, opening and closing her little hand in a typical toddler wave.

Kevin melted at the sight, and he managed to return the grin. "Well, let's not keep the princess waiting."

Before throwing the paper in the trash and following his wife out the door, Kevin gave the article one last glance. The old feelings tried to resurface, but he refused to let them. His eyes flitted over the photograph and the photographer's credit, which ran in small type along the bottom of the picture. He didn't even bother reading the credit. He already knew what it said.

The line read simply, "*Gazette* photo by Kevin O'Brien."

Pima Road
Richard Ebert

I can't see the sun. It's either a dream or a memory, and I'm still not sure. Then I realize that the edges are fuzzy and I'm not sure where I am. In dreams, everything is sharp and razor-real, but memories are soft and out-of-focus, and in a dream though you can be lost, you're aware that you're *lost* with absolute certitude – it's as good as knowing where you are. But memory… there are times you don't even know you're lost – you just don't recognize where you are. This is a memory and I cannot see the sun.

The sky is gray with clouds and dust. The wind has picked all the loose dust from earth and wound it into a wall across the sky. The dust of the desert, of construction, of nations past fills the sky and fights the clouds for dominance. They merge into texture of gray eliminating color and shade from the sky. It is Phoenix in August and I cannot see the sun from the dust.

I hear the engine running now and remember where I am. My parents are driving and I am in the back seat. The car hums with the sound of the road and the whoosh of the air conditioner. Occasionally the car will swerve lightly as a great gust of wind hits it. I'm not afraid at all. My father drives, my mother talks, and the wind blows and blasts while I am warm and curled up in the back seat, mostly asleep, exhausted from a long day of being a child. I am content.

There is a change in the sound of the car. We are slowing, turning, taking a new way home. The disturbance in our routine penetrates my conscious and begins to rouse me. The rhythm of the drive has been broken and I want to know why. I try to wake to ask my parents. Mom does it for me.

"Is it still closed?" she asks Dad.

"According to the paper. Pima Road will be closed the rest of the week." Pima Road – named after the Pima tribe whose land it ran through.

This was Mesa, this was Scottsdale; this was Arizona where the game of "Cowboys and Indians" takes on a new tone, because the Cowboys, in the form of the City of Scottsdale were taking on the Indians, the Pima. It wasn't a new dispute – it was the oldest subject between the native tribes and the later settlers; it was over land. This time, though, there was no bloodshed, but there was a great deal of hot blood all around.

Pima road was anemic back then: two lanes, one north, and one south. It was heavily traveled at high speeds, and the asphalt was cracked, the paint was fading, and the road was a very dangerous place to drive.

Scottsdale maintained Pima road, and it was not happy about the condition. Scottsdale, Mesa, and Phoenix were all growing up – stretching out and maturing from the sleepy desert cities they had been and forming great communities and industry. They sprawled in every direction, building lavishly and quickly. To this day you need a car to get around the Phoenix Metropolitan area – nothing is close, nothing is convenient. Without a car you are trapped within the castle of your home.

Scottsdale, and its energetic and enterprising mayor, Herb Drinkwater, knew what was coming. They could see the formation of "bedroom communities" where the people would work far from the places they lived. Scottsdale saw the need for a new Pima Road. So they decided to rebuild the road and expand it to a true artery of the city. They merely forgot to whom the land belonged.

There is no malice in my memory – no hint of the betrayals of a hundred years ago, but there was arrogance and a lack of foresight. Scottsdale put their plan in motion to expand Pima, without asking. The Pima were outraged. Pima road ran along their cotton fields, ran through the edge of their land. Pima road was a border to the Maricopa and Pima reservation. They saw the encroachment, they saw the city, they saw the Cowboys trying to take their land. So they fought back. They closed half of Pima Road, creating massive inconvenience to anyone driving from Mesa to Scottsdale.

This was new – the history of the Pima and the America fueled by Manifest Destiny is a little different than the usual story. The quick and wrong way would be to say that the Pima never fought back – that they acquiesced and willingly placed their necks under the yoke the Indian Agents and the government. This is what I believed.

The true story is longer – the history of any people is greater than any simple paragraph, but this fallacy is quickly corrected. The Pima were not weak, nor simple, nor were they blindly giving up everything to the newcomers. They were not slaves; they were *allies*.

The Pima, the Akimel Au-Authm, the River People, the children of the Hohokam, joined the U.S. military, a tradition that still continues today. When you see the picture of the men planting the flag at Iwo Jima, you see Ira Hayes, a Pima man fighting along side other brave men. The Pima were invaluable to the United States cavalry and to the later settlers.

The Army, aside from using the Pima as scouts, saw them for use as a buffer against the implacable Apache. They were right, too, considering what happened to the Yuma. The Maricopa tribe had a grudge with the Yuma, a grudge that was going badly for them. So the Maricopa traveled to the Gila River where the Pima lived and sought asylum. The Pima readily agreed, and the Maricopa moved in.

The Yuma, however, were not impressed. They attacked the Pima, and lost. The attacking Yuma were slaughtered almost to a man. The Maricopa had sought shelter with the right tribe. But they would have to move again.

The Pima had used their land on the river wisely. They grew wheat and vegetables in such abundance that they could sell most of what they made to the settlers, enabling the newcomers to thrive as well.

The Gila River was too lush and rich for the settlers to ignore. They dammed the river upstream to use their water to power an ancient Hohokam technology: irrigation. This left the Pima and Maricopa without enough water for their farms, so they moved to the Salt River.

The Pima had the same success with the land on the Salt River. So much so that late coming settlers were envious and eyed the land greedily. They applied to the Indian Agents and the Indian Affairs department to move the Pima. The Army wouldn't hear of it.

General Irvin McDowell found the location of the Pima valuable for protecting settlers from the Apache. Indian Agent Stout noted that the number of people who wanted the Pima forced back to the dry Gila amounted to 16. They fought for the Pima, and won. The Pima are still on the Salt River, and they still own the land.

This time the Pima fought alone for their land: one tribe versus one city. Scottsdale was furious at being balked in such a manner. They complained to the state of Arizona who stayed out of the fight. I remember the fury – I remember the papers and the news and the radio all howling their opinions. I remember having to take a different way home from my grandparents every Sunday.

Then Scottsdale got mean. They called on the Bureau of Indian Affairs, a department that does as much harm as good. The people held their collective breath, waiting to hear from the BIA. Would they force the Pima off their land? Would they allow Scottsdale free reign with the road? Finally, an answer: deal with them yourself – this is a local problem, not a Federal one. The Pima won their standoff. Scottsdale would have to concede.

Today I drove from Tempe to Scottsdale along the freeway where Pima Road used to be. I see the shiny new casino sitting behind the dry cotton fields. I remember the road that used to be, feel the faint twinge of nostalgia at how the world has changed. Never again will I think the Pima simple. They are a complex people, wise: they pick their fights.

True Tales Of Horror: My Sushi Adventure
K.L. Pfaff-Harris

Sushi: for those who love it, there's nothing to compare. The delicate fish, the flower-like rolls, the harsh bite of the wasabi all combine in a breathtaking array of beauty and savor. One thing about sushi, however, which often goes unremarked, is the sheer amount of work that goes into it. Tell me the truth: do you have any idea how long it takes to make your own sushi? I mean, can you possibly conceive of the time investment?

Of course you can't. Usually, you go to a sushi bar, and everything's all ready: they just grab some rice, slice up some fish, stick it together, and poof! California roll. Zap! Unagi. Bam! Spicy Tuna!

It looks so easy.

Who knew, who could possibly know, the horror of making your own sushi?

Well, I, my friends, have returned from the abyss and can now tell the tale...a tale of First-Time Sushi Making!

Muwahahahaha!

Oh. Sorry.

Anyway.

"How long," you may well ask, "can it possibly take to make sushi? It couldn't be *that* long, now could it?"

How little you know. First of all, just making the rice takes at least two hours.

Two.

Hours.

Just to make the rice.

Before you even begin cooking the rice, you have to wash the rice for probably at least 15 minutes until the water runs clear. Why? I have no idea. I have read in at least four thousand, six hundred and seventy eight pages on the Internet that you must wash the rice.

That, in fact, it is *very important* to wash the rice.

A simple search, however, for "why wash the freaking sushi rice dammit" turns up nothing.

Nada.

Zilch.

So I don't know why. But I know that it is **very important**.

After you wash the rice, you must drain it.

For an *hour*.

Before cooking it.

Along about the time that I was washing and rinsing the rice for the 47th time, my husband ordered a pizza. I figured it would be a tossup which would be ready first: Domino's ordered at 7:00 on New Year's Eve, or Sushi Rice which must drain.

For an *HOUR*.

Before cooking it.

Did I mention that part?

Guess I did.

So, just about the time I'm ready to put the rice in the rice cooker, the pizza shows up.

I don't have any.

(Pizza, that is. I don't have any of the pizza.)

I am stalwart and strong, and will wait for sushi!

(Well, I'll wait for sushi after just a couple of bites of those cinnamon bread thingies. I'm stalwart and strong, but, I mean, come **on**!)

Another half an hour later, and the rice is cooked. Notice that I said "cooked" and not "done." No, it's not done. It's not *done* at all. It's not even *close* to *done*.

Now, I have to mix up the vinegar/sugar/salt solution to make it really and truly sushi rice. Little saucepan, low heat, 5 minutes, poof!

I have my friend Rob sprinkle the vinegar stuff over the rice as I stir and turn and fold and cut and try to get this stuff mixed. The rice, without this mixture, is already pretty sticky, but hey – got to follow the recipe.

The recipe is from StickyRice.com, and with a name like that, you know they've got to know what they're talking about sticky-rice-wise.

I'm sure we can all agree to that: Like my grandmother always used to say, "Never Argue With Recipes Found on a Website With the Word

'Sticky' in the Domain Name."

So, now we have a bowl of sticky rice, a pile of seaweed, the best, premium imitation crab, avocado, cucumber, tuna, shrimp, and unagi in the freezer.

Time to make some wasabi. This would most likely be the easiest thing we'd had to do all evening. We got wasabi powder: just add water, stir, place upside-down for a minute or so, and BAM! You have the fire-breathingest, mouth-poppingest, sinus-burningest little green pile of Japanese horseradish you've ever wanted to see in your life. We carefully measured, stirred, mixed, and placed it upside-down for a minute, after which, it was time to see if it was done.

Friends, important safety tip: when you've just made wasabi, do not, I repeat, DO NOT stick your nose an inch from the bowl of wasabi and take a deep sniff.

In Basic Combat Training, we had to stand in a room with tear gas.

Tear gas has nothing, *nothing*, on fresh wasabi.

You have been warned.

If you trust me about anything, anything I have ever said, trust me on this. I beg of you. The nose you save may be your own.

Now, where was I? Let's see: fish, crab, avocado, cucumber, wasabi and, most importantly, sticky rice.

Yup.

We've got everything.

Let's Roll.

(California Roll, that is.)

Earlier in the day, I'd taken a little trip to the local International Market. There, I picked up various and sundry items such as pickled ginger or "gari," the wasabi powder, and, of course, the bamboo sushi roll making thingy.

Now, the thing about the local International Market is this: it ain't Safeway. There are no bright, fluorescent lights that bathe everything in a somewhat sickly glow like a village of the damned. There are no nice, wide aisles with neatly stacked and logically arranged products all together with friendly tags warmly exclaiming "Condiments! Teas! Salad Dressings!"

No.

There's none of that.

Instead, the cramped and narrow aisles huddle broodingly to either side, miserly and sober, as if holding their secrets away from prying eyes. Curry from India, unrecognizable jellies from Thailand, and cans of bizarre beef-containing-product sit next to each other without visible connection. There are packages of beans, seeds, noodles, miso soup mix, and strange boxes with flowers on them.

I ... I think they're flowers.

In piles, and stacks, and half-emptied open boxes blocking the aisle, the packaging taunts me.

Dares me to find what I'm looking for.

In the International Market, you must be alert – observant. You must closely examine EVERY item on EVERY shelf or you will be lost.

And so I do.

I stalk carefully through the "El Productos Latno(sic)" section (the only section, by the way, which is labeled) examining items from El Salvador, Chile, Mexico, and other places south of the border. A lonely 5-pound jar of something labeled in Hindi sits in between various chiles and spices. I briefly consider taking it to its friends, but I have work to do.

At last, I find sushi nori – packets of dried seaweed sheets for making sushi rolls. At the same time, I realize that the evil organizer of the store has made her first, fatal mistake: she has stored the sushi rolling mats RIGHT NEXT TO THE SEAWEED!

This bizarre twist of logical product placement saves me another trip down the aisle.

Me: 1 International Market: 0

Things are looking up.

Halfway down the same aisle, I find wasabi powder. Incredible! A short way farther, and there are sesame seeds! Joy!

I'm on a roll now, feeling the buzz.

It feels good.

Now, all I need is some gari (pickled ginger) and I can take my swag and leave.

I chuckle to myself. And I thought this would be an ordeal – heck, all I need is some gari, and I'm outta here.

How hard can it be to find a single product?

How hard indeed ... Oh, would that I had not asked that simple question. But it was only gari, only gari that I needed. Just one thing, just one.

Gari.

That blessed, happy ambrosia of the Gods. Its bright, neon pink shading. Its delicate translucence. Its oh-so-peppy and zingy gingery goodness, cleansing the palate and aiding the digestion!

Do sushi without pickled ginger?

No.

The thought was inconceivable. Impossible! There are some things you just ... do not ... do. Sushi without gari garnish is one of those things.

And so, cursing the whimsy of the International Market's Dark Design, I searched through the aisles for that one thing.

Just one thing.

I searched through the kimche.

I searched through the curry.

I searched through things crackling, and bubbling, and furry!

All the Who's down in Whoville were laughing at me; they chortled and chuckled and cried out with glee!

Um ... oh.

Sorry, Christmas flashback.

Anyway...

To make a long story short, I wandered pitifully up and down the same six long and crowded aisles for about thirty minutes.

Back and forth, back and forth. Up and down, up and down.

My eyes were beginning to glaze over, when finally, hidden behind several large boxes of something with the word "Curry" on them, a jar caught my eye.

It was pink.

It looked like pickled ginger.

It said Ga Ri in Japanese syllabic characters.

Ga.

Ri.

Gari?

I stared at the jar, willing it to reveal its true shape if it were not, in fact, the Gari for which I searched, but the characters stayed constant, unwavering.

The Dark Mistress of the International Market did not reckon on my knowing how to read Hiragana! Hah! SCORE!

I stealthily snagged a jar, then one more. I knew the chances of finding it more than once would be astronomical.

I made my way to the checkout stand (which was, of course, covered with trinkets, ginseng gum, and bizarre herbal packets) and paid my tab. She met my eyes soberly and narrowed her gaze as she handed me my change, as if to say, "So, my old nemesis. We meet again. You have triumphed ... this time. But it is not over between us. It shall never be over!"

Or maybe she just had allergy eyes. Hard to be sure.

But this was all in the past. Now, it was rolling time.

For Christmas this year, my friends got me a little tiny book of Sushi, containing recipes for rice, instructions for slicing fish, and, of course, sushi roll making.

"Rolling sushi isn't difficult," the book informed me. "It's FUN and EASY!"

Yes.

After a ten-year apprenticeship under a master sushi chef in Tokyo, I imagine it would be FUN.

And EASY.

However, for a thirtyish Caucasian girl from Nevada, it was a bit different, as I would find out, all too soon.

"Place the mat on a flat surface, and cover with one sheet of NORI (SEAWEED)," the little Book of Sushi advised. (The little Book of Sushi had an inordinate fondness for capital letters, I noticed.)

Gotcha. I carefully placed the greenish-black paperish sheet on the little bamboo sushi roller mat thingy, taking great care to ensure that the edges lined up pristinely with the angles of the mat.

"Now, gently begin placing the rice upon the NORI, leaving a three-quarter inch edge uncovered," the book continued.

Not a problem. I reached into the bowl of prepared sushi rice, and picked out a small handful. It stuck together like mad. All according to plan! StickyRice.com had indeed given worthy and sage advice leading to rice that was ... well ... sticky.

Yeah.

I slowly and carefully pressed the rice into the NORI .. um, I mean, "nori," spread it a bit from side to side, then lifted my hand away from the rice-covered seaweed sheet.

That is, I *tried* to lift my hand *away* from the rice-covered seaweed sheet. Unfortunately, as the hand went, so did the rice, seaweed, and all leaving the poor bamboo rolling mat sitting lonely and forlorn on the counter, its tiny sticks and little strings mocking me with their emptiness.

The rice was sticky, all right.

A bit *too* sticky, if you ask me!

But no one did ask me, oh no.

No they didn't.

Certainly those people at StickyRice.com didn't ask me.

They didn't call me up and say, "Pardon me, Ma'am, but just how sticky would you like the rice to be?" When Grandma was raving about "Sticky in the domain name," she didn't ask me, "Honey, do you want the rice real sticky, or just kind of sticky?"

Suddenly, it was all so clear.

The webmaster of StickyRice.com, my Grandmother, and the Dark Mistress of the International Market were all *conspiring against me*!

This was serious.

It was a sushirama that could have only one victor.

My friend Rob looked at me.

Looked back at the piece of seaweed now glued to my hand by the sushi rice.

Looked back at me.

Silence fell over the kitchen like a dark cloud of impending destruction. Rob cleared his throat, but said nothing. A wise man.

He didn't laugh.

A very, very wise man.

I turned back to consider my dilemma, when a bowl of water suddenly appeared before me on the counter.

Rob said, "I think that may be the reason why those chefs at the sushi bar are always washing their hands every ten seconds."

Then he backed away slowly.

Yes. Very wise.

Carefully, and painstakingly, I freed my hand from the rice, grain by grain, until I could reach the water. I swooshed my now-ricey-gluey-hand through the liquid until it was clean, then pulled another handful of rice and attacked the nori once more.

This time, it was personal, but the water had done the trick! This rice had nothing I couldn't handle, **nothing**. It went on the rice smoothly and gummily, as rice so often does, until I had it. At last: a big piece of rice-covered seaweed!

It was FUN.

Dammit.

AND EASY, DO YOU HEAR ME??

EASY!!!

But, as we all know, a big piece of rice-covered seaweed is not sushi, anymore than a Maaco paint job is a car. The main task was ahead: actually making this thing into a roll.

That meant rolling it.

And somehow, keeping all the stuff inside while rolling it.

I could already taste the roll with its toppings of tobiko and toasted sesame seeds. I must act now, decisively, and without hesitation. Sure and swift and true like the wind.

I took a deep, cleansing breath.

"EASY!" I said to myself, like a mantra.

"FUN!" I repeated.

I reached for the premium genuine non-crab imitation crab flavored seafood product, and began.

Now. Rolling a roll with the seaweed on the outside is a simple enough matter. After all, the stuff you put inside can be mooshed into the rice thus holding it in place like a little plaster cast. Just lay out the stuff (crab, fish, veggies, what have you) in a line from edge to edge on the seaweed, smoosh it in there, and start rolling.

Really, anyone who's played with Pla-doh(tm) as a child is familiar with this sort of activity.

In fact, I daresay that I suppose rolling your own cigarettes could be helpful in this sort of thing, if you want a very, very tiny and skinny sushi roll, After all, the seaweed is a bit like paper, and the rice and fish, while not exactly like tobacco or your herb *du jour*, at least will stick together.

However, we were making an inside-out roll, where the rice is on the outside. This is a much more serious undertaking, as you can well imagine. Think of trying to roll a cigarette with the tobacco on the outside of the paper stuck together with some vinegar and sugar, and I think you'll see my point.

No, this was it.

The finale.

The last, great obstacle in my sushi extravaganza.

I paused for a moment, and made my decision.

It would be EASY.

And FUN.

Oh yes, yes it would, **by God**.

By.

God.

"Take a sheet of plastic wrap, and lay it flat over the sushi rolling mat," the Little Book of Sushi cheerfully advised me, "ensuring there are no wrinkles. Then place the rice side down upon the plastic so that it is evenly set centered on the mat."

The sticky rice would work in my favor, this time. I could sense it. I slapped my palm down on the rice-covered sushi, and lifted. Sure enough, it came away immediately stuck to my hand. I had Rob place the plastic over the rolling mat, and I turned to lay my concoction back down on the mat.

But something was wrong ... in hindsight, I should probably have lifted the sushi by an edge so I could flip it over. Lifting it up by the rice stuck to my palm would leave me no alternative but to lay it back down *seaweed-side down*!

I tried a few different turns, and angles, but to no avail. The rice which so lovingly clung to my hand was the rice that was *supposed* to be lovingly clinging to the plastic wrap.

How do I get myself into these things? I really should have paid more attention in Physics class, but, I mean, good Lord, it was at 7am!

"Um ... maybe you can just hold your hand so the seaweed side is up, slap it into your other hand, and then use *that* hand to put it so the rice side is down?"

I whipped around and stared at Rob.

The temperature in the room dropped by ten degrees, and all was silent.

Slowly, I turned back to the counter.

And did exactly what he had suggested.

Rob's not the only wise person in the kitchen, and, after all, what kind of Sushi Warrior would I be if I didn't listen to my trusty sidekick? Yeah, yeah. Shut up, you.)

With the rice side down on the plastic on the rolling mat on the counter in the kitchen in the house the Jack built – well actually, "that George built," but that's another story – I was now ready for the ingredients!

I laid out the strips of premium imitation crab-flavored seafood product, the thin slices of cucumber and avocado I had deftly carved from the original vegetables using Chef Tony's Miracle Blade III Perfection Series Rock 'n Chop(tm). (Dad watches a lot of infomercials. I'm probably lucky I wasn't cutting up the stuff with something made out of Coral Calcium and Sea Silver. But I digress.)

Rob watched over my shoulder, his eyes filled with doubt.

This was most likely because I had very painstakingly arranged the line of the ingredients exactly perpendicular (see, I did listen in Physics class!) to the way the mat was meant to roll. See, the mat is made up of these little bamboo sticks held together with string. Go one way, and they all roll up. Go at a 90-degree angle and ... well ... you get a lot of toothpicks and bamboo splinters.

Not my idea of low-fiber dining, know what I mean?

But that was okay: little thing like *that* wasn't going to stop me from this FUN task.

I reached out, and carefully slid a corner of the plastic wrap around so that the stuff was lined up in a manner consistent with rolling.

It was EASY.

(Take *that*, Little Book of Sushi!)

Holding the edge of the plastic somewhat away, I began to roll, tightly holding the mat with one hand, and keeping the contents compressed as well as I could with the other. The rice stuck the roll together as I went. The plastic kept it from sticking to the mat! All was going well.

It was good. Very good.

And if long, green, pieces of avocado were squooshing out either end like some bizarre excretion of a sea serpent, well.

That was ... just fine.

I said, *it was FINE*.

I got the roll rolled to the end, and removed the mat. The plastic wrap allowed the mat to fall away easily, joyously, as if it knew its labor was done.

I started to unwrap the plastic, when Rob stopped me.

"I think the sushi chefs at the bar just cut it up in the plastic, and then take the pieces out," he stated.

Well who am I to ignore Rob after his timely, and – dare I say? – brilliant salvaging of the unfortunate rice-covered-palm incident earlier.

Carefully taking Chef Tony's Miracle Yadda Yadda Whatever Filet & Boning Whatsis, I began in the middle of the roll, and made a tentative slice.

It worked.

By God, you can say what you want about infomercials, but Chef Tony was *there* for me, man. *There* in my time of need!

As I was saying, it sliced through the seaweed!

It sliced through the plastic!

I sliced through the crab and cucumber and ....

Damn. Only thing I can think of to rhyme with that is "spastic." Moving right along...

Several slices later, I had my roll. I slowly pulled the plastic off. It came off each piece slowly, tantalizingly, like a teasing vixen in a clingy silk teddy, taking it all off ... waiting ... for the tobiko and Sesame Seeds!

Yeah, baby. Sesame Seeds. Uh huh. You know I like that. Mm Hmm.

Oops...sorry. Don't know where that came from.

Using a spoon, I gingerly sprinkled toasted sesame seeds atop each piece. Then, using the tines of a fork, I gathered up the tiny eggs of tobiko, and placed a dab on each piece as well.

It looked beautiful. *Beautiful*! (Well, other than the fact that each piece was about three inches in diameter and weighed about as much as a Pro-Certified Hockey puck.)

It was time to taste ... the roll ...

Rob and I gazed soberly at each other. It was time, truly the time of reckoning! We had waited at least four hours for this moment.

We each picked up a piece, dipped it in the wasabi-flavored soy sauce, and raised them to our mouths.

I glanced at Rob, waiting for him to complete the tasting, as I considered his contributions to the night's endeavors. Though I've only briefly mentioned him in the context of his brilliant and sage advice in re the seaweed-glued-to-hand incident, he had, in fact, been vital to the entire sushi battle.

Rob is, after all, the one who found the tobiko.

And the unagi.

And the tuna.

The SUSHI GRADE tuna.

"Be sure when selecting fish that it is clearly labeled SUSHI GRADE," warned the Little Book of Sushi. So I know that's very important. Critical, even. And Rob, my dear, dear friend Rob, had found some.

Earlier that afternoon, flush from my triumph at the International Market, I got a phone call. It was Rob, on his cell phone, asking if the hubby and I wanted to get together and do anything, it being New Year's Eve and all. When I mentioned that I was planning to attempt sushi-making, his normally bored and disinterested voice took on a spark of life.

"Sushi?" he asked. "Did you get the fish already?"

Well, of course, I had gotten some Genuine Premium Crab-Flavored Seafood product, avocado, cucumber, gari (remember the gari?), seaweed, sesame seeds, roller mat thingies, wasabi powder, soy sauce, and stuff to make the rice with. That was good enough, right?

"You can NOT," he stated with certainty, "just make California rolls."

"And even if you do ... what about Tobiko?""

Hm.

He had a good point there. California Roll Deluxe with Tobiko was one of our favorites. I was going to just settle for the sesame seeds, but obviously, that was not okay.

At least, it was not okay with Rob.

I should probably mention that Rob is not only a very talented computer programmer, but also a gifted gourmet chef.

Rob watches the Food Network more than I do.

And he cooks. I mean, he has Real Cooking Implements. Me, I'm just as likely to cut up a turkey with an X-Acto knife I previously used in an art class if that's what's handy. I buy El-Cheapo brand cookie sheets off the rack in the grocery store for 75 cents. I'm happy with an omelet if it is mostly not-burned, mostly not-raw, and has a quarter ounce of salt on it. With Rob, it would probably not be acceptable unless it was called "Le Grande Omelette Du Montagne au Kierkegaard" and served with some kind of cheese that cost $2,000.00 a pound.

(My husband, though not quite at Rob's level of obsession with cookery, is also quite a talented chef in his own right. It's always interesting when the two of them are discussing the proper procedures for something like – oh, I don't know – blintzes. Makes me want to go fix a diesel engine or something. Vrooom! Vroom!)

So of course, as you can plainly imagine, now that Rob was involved, there would be no POSSIBLE way I could get away with rice, seaweed, and fake crab stuff.

"Where'd you get the rice?" he asked.

Rice.

Oh shit.

My heart skipped a beat in a brief moment of panic. I mean, I had rice. Everyone has rice! Look in any house in the United States, and you will find rice, salt, and potato flakes. (I think it's in the Constitution.) *Of course* I had rice. And I thought nothing of using the normal, American, medium-to-long-grained rice (or whatever the normal, Constitutional rice type is) for making sushi. Rice is rice, right?

Right?

But this was Rob on the phone.

Rob ... would never ... *never* ... accept normal everyday rice in sushi. It would be blasphemy, anathema! I knew, deep down in my heart, that a man who would make "Le Grande Omelette Du Montagne au Kierkegaard" as a simple afternoon snack would simply NOT stand for such whimsy.

"Hello? Are you still there? What kind of rice did you get?"

He sounded insistent. I had to answer him before he thought the cell phone was cutting out. And so, I did the only thing I could do. I attempted to bluff it out.

"Oh, I figured I'd just use normal rice, you know. 'Cause the vinegar/sugar solution goes over it anyway."

I held my ear slightly away from the phone, cringing a bit in anticipation of the response, and held my breath. Please, God, please, God, please, God, let him go for it just this once, this one little time, please, please, please, much love, Me, I prayed.

"*Are you HIGH*???"

(Dammit. Thanks a lot, God, we'll be talking more later, much love, Me.)

"*YOU CAN'T MAKE SUSHI WITH REGULAR RICE*!!!!!"

"Sure you can." (Oh, I was way too far into this to back out now.)

"*No!*"

"Come on, Rob, what's the difference?"

"The DIFFERENCE?" I wondered how far his eyes could roll up before they got stuck. Even over the cell phone, I could hear, yes, HEAR his eyes rolling up in disgust. Not a pleasant sound. "It. Is *not*. The *right*. *Kind*. Of *rice*," he explained slowly and deliberately, as though talking down a maniac from a hostage situation. He'd probably be pretty good at that too, come to think of it: "Put *down*. The *rice*. And *step*. *Away*. From the *sushi*." I'll have to remember to mention that to him the next time I see him, in case the whole programming and/or chef thing doesn't work out.

One thing was certain, I was not going to win the rice battle.

"Look," he said reasonably, "There's another oriental market on the way home from work. I'll just stop by there and pick up a few things. Maybe they'll have fish. And Tobiko. But we have to have the right kind of RICE or why even bother?"

I sighed. "Fine. Okay."

"Okay then. Call you later."

click

Rice, for God's sake.

That was okay, though. Because now, it was Rob's turn to meet the horrors of the International Market. No, not the same one that I had survived that day, but another one on the other side of town. I knew, however, that somehow the Dark Mistress of the International Market would know of our connection, and that Rob's fate had been sealed.

He would pay for his insistence. Oh yes. Yes he would.

I sat back and returned to work, grinning slightly in anticipation of Rob's next call.

And I knew he'd call.

Rob had recently gotten a cell phone. Under ordinary circumstances, getting a cell phone is no big deal. Heck, most people have 'em these days. Even my Mom, bless her heart, has a cell phone (although Dad has so far resisted the temptation). For most people, a cell phone is just an extra thing to carry around for occasional use. Get in a wreck? Use the cell phone. See a crime in progress? Use the cell phone. Late for a meeting because you're stuck in traffic? Cell phone. As Martha Stewart would say, "It's a Good Thing."

For some people, however, the cell phone becomes more, so much more, than just an emergency aid. For those who fall under the spell of the cell, it becomes an extension of themselves. A part of their very being. Another hand, or foot – vital to their very existence.

And they use the cell phone. Several times a day. At every opportunity. Every.

Opportunity.

"Hi, it's me: what time is it?"

"Um... three o'clock. Where are you?"

"At the gas station."

"What are you doing?"

"Getting gas. I don't have my watch."

"Oh. Okay. Bye."

"Bye."

click

"Hi, it's me. We're at Staples and they have that wireless router for 100 bucks plus rebate."

"Um ... okay. Thanks."

"Figured you'd want to know."

"Um ... yeah. Okay. Thanks. Bye."

"Bye."

click

"Hi, it's me. I'm stuck in traffic. Figured I'd say hi."

"Um ... hi."

"You and Charlie want to do anything tonight?"

"Um ... I'll have to check with him."

"Okay, gotta go."

"Bye."

click

Rob had a cell phone, and it was now integrated into his very soul.

So, like I said, I knew he'd be calling. The only question was when. I buckled back down to working on my current project. After a little while, I'd gotten to that zen-like state of programming where the code flows freely and true, hours pass in an instant, and the universe becomes a single point outlined by the clacking of the keyboard and the characters on the screen.

The phone rang, making me jump half out of my chair.

"Hey, it's me."

It was Rob.

"Hey."

"So, I'm down here at the international store, and I'm looking at rice, but I'm not sure which kind we need."

I thought about it for a second. "Hang on, let me check Google."

I did a quick search.

Got it.

"Short to medium-grain white rice," I informed him.

"Yeah, but what *kind*? There are a bunch of different brands here. We have to get the right *kind*."

Of course we did.

Another quick search, and I had a name. "Kokuho Rose or Nishiki. Those are recommended by most of the sushi sites."

"Are you sure? 'Cause I have Kokuho Rose here, but also Nishiki."

"Just get the Kokuho Rose, Rob."

"Well, I've heard of Kokuho Rose, but how do we know it's the right kind?"

I wondered if he could hear MY eyes rolling up into my head.

"Rob. The sushi-making sites say to get Kokuho Rose short-grained rice. They do not specify anything at all in particular besides 'short-grained' white rice. None of the sites say anything about any kind of special distinction for the rice. Just. Get. The. Rice."

"But what if ..."

"It will be fine."

"But ..."

"Rob, for God's sake, it will be fine."

"Oh all right."

He got the Kokuho Rose. Progress. Now it was time to get serious. We needed Tobiko. And fish. Real fish, not that imitation crab-flavored stuff. Now that Rob was involved, there was no way I could half-ass the sushi making with just a few simple California rolls. No way.

Rob wandered through the maze of the market, just as I had earlier, until reaching the freezers. I had ignored the freezers in my International Market adventure, after a quick glance told me that there were few labels, and those labels that did exist were not in characters I could read. For all I knew, they could just say "Brown frozen paper-wrapped package," "White frozen paper-wrapped package," "Slightly greasy paper-wrapped frozen package." I didn't want to mess with it.

Rob, however, was not yet bowed from the struggle to find a logical product placement in the International Market. Besides, he had me on the phone for moral support.

So we were going to do it. We were going to hit the freezers.

Many discussions, and comments, and despairing, "What the hell is this supposed to be?" comments later, there was a silence on the other end of the phone.

"Rob? You still there?"

"Oh my God," was the barely audible response.

"Rob? Hello?"

Suddenly, his voice was clear and strong: "We ... we have Unagi! I repeat, we have Unagi!"

"Unagi?"

I was incredulous. Rob had found unagi: my favorite, all-time, number one, sushi taste treat. A terrible thought occurred to me: could this be a joke?

But no. Rob wouldn't joke about something as important as this. Not about unagi. And not to me.

"You seriously found unagi?" I asked.

"Seriously! It's pre-cooked and everything. Frozen. We just slice it up, microwave it, and we've got caterpillar rolls and just ... unagi!"

I was amazed. Speechless. It seemed too good to be true.

"Now we just need some unagi sauce."

Uh oh.

The sauce.

Of course, you can't just have unagi without unagi sauce. That would be as bad as making sushi with the wrong kind of rice. We needed the sauce, and we needed it badly.

"So what's it called, the sauce?"

Rob's question brought me back to reality.

"Um ... what?"

"What's the unagi sauce called?"

"What ... what's it called?"

"Yes, what's it called? You don't just call it 'unagi sauce' or 'eel sauce' do you?"

I ... I didn't know. I had *no* idea what to call the unagi sauce in terms that would make sense in the International Market.

I ... did ... not ... *know*!

I could sense the unagi slipping away ... I had to find out what the sauce was called, so that Rob could look for it and find it. I had to!

I desperately wracked my brain for an answer – thinking, thinking.

It came to me suddenly, like an epiphany – a bolt of brilliance bursting from a formerly cloudy sky – I had Google. There was no need to panic. Though I may not have known the Secret Name of Unagi Sauce, no matter.

Google would know.

Google knows all, sees all, is all things good and true in this crazy, mixed-up world.

Google would, like the ATM card in the old commercials, fix everything.

I had to stall Rob, though. Just for a minute.

"Hang on, let me check something." My fingers flew frantically over the keys, trying for the perfect search phrase. "Unagi sauce," I typed in.

"Thick Unagi Sauce is a sauce brushed on cooked unagi to make them tasteful. To make the sauce, professional cooks use the stock in which unagis have been boiled," was the result from SushiMan.net.

Damn. I already *knew* that. The Little Book of Sushi even had a recipe for Unagi sauce. "The main ingredient in the special sauce used with UNAGI is actually UNAGI! Bones, skin and ALL!" The Little Book of Sushi, I was beginning to think, was entirely, ENTIRELY, too cheerful.

How about "buy unagi sauce?" Well, that gave me recipes. At least, I think they were recipes. Some of them, I wasn't quite sure of, such as the one from TastyWeb.nl, that said, in part, "Het gebruik van deze unagi sauzen wordt uitgelegd op de unagi recept pagina." I recognize "unagi," and "sauzen" could conceivably be some ancient cognate of our word "sauce," but since it looked like instructions on how to make it, it did not help us to buy it. Other pages suggested that we buy teriyaki sauce, add some sugar, and call it done.

I don't think I have to tell you what Rob would have said to the idea of using fake unagi sauce, now do I?

I thought not.

There had to be *something* that would tell me a name! Something ... but ... yes! There it was!

There it was!

Hidden away in the midst of a sushi page at RecipeCottage.com, I found it: "get a little extra bottle of unagi bbq sauce (called tare) ..." it said.

"You still there?" came Rob's voice over the line.

"Yeah, I was just trying to find out what that unagi sauce is called," I said calmly.

"What, just look it up on Google," was Rob's sage advice.

· · ·

I let him live. I'm nice that way, sometimes. Besides, he was on the other end of a cell phone connection, across town, and out of my immediate reach. "It's called Tare," I informed him.

"*Tare*! Oh yeah! Tare! Now I remember."

The immediate crisis was over. Rob returned to wandering the maze of the Other International Market, now on a quest for Tare. The almost sinister similarity to my earlier Trial of Gari was never more apparent, as the cell phone signal sputtered in and out with staticky hissings. First Gari, now Tare. But we would prevail. This time, I knew it.

We had, after all, found Unagi.

"Hey, you want me to see if there's any more fish here?" Rob asked.

"Sure, as long as you're there."

I didn't mind. I was, after all, safe at home with Google close at hand. If Rob wanted to further brave the Other International Market's freezers, hey: more power to him.

"Hey, I found tuna!"

There was silence for a moment, and then, in a voice filled with awe, "It ... it says 'sushi grade'."

"It *says* 'sushi grade'?" I was dumbfounded. "In English, just like that, on the package, it says, it actually says, 'sushi grade tuna'?"

"Yeah." His voice was soft, almost reverent.

Another pause, then, "What are the *odds* of *that* happening?" Rob's voice sounded like a kid on Christmas who has just received not only the Red Ryder BB Gun, but a set of life-sized target dummies, a child-sized Jaguar with a V-6 engine, and forty-seven pounds of candy.

What are the odds, indeed. Personally, I was beginning to think it was time for a drive down to a local casino to play a few rounds of MegaBucks, or maybe a drive over the border into California to grab a lottery ticket.

But that could be done later. We were still on a roll.

Rob: 2 Other International Market: 0

Life was good!

After a few more minutes of wandering around the shop (Rob), Googling for various brand names (me), and listening to the cell phone cut in and out (both of us, I imagine), Rob found what looked like Tobiko. Another brief setback ensued, when he discovered that there were two things which looked identical: Flying Fish Roe and Capelin Roe. The flying fish roe had added sugar. The Capelin roe had MSG. The flying fish roe was twice as expensive as the Capelin roe.

I had to go through forty-seven separate websites, all of which said that the two were interchangeable, before Rob would budge. I even got my husband in there with his words of wisdom: "Rob, get the stuff with the MSG. MSG is awesome. Makes stuff taste great.... yeah, side-effects, schmide-effects. MSG rules, bro."

I think that did it. When your fellow blintz baker recommends the Capelin roe, well, what can you do?

He picked it up. Now we had Tobiko! Well, maybe "Faux-biko," but hey, forty-seven websites can't be wrong.

Our run of good luck wasn't quite over either: just down a short way from the Tobiko were little bottles labeled "Tare."

"It says 'something something Tare'," Rob pointed out, "and it's right near the Tobiko and stuff."

"Well, does it say 'unagi' anywhere on it?" I asked.

"No, but it says tare. I mean, how many kinds of tare could there be?"

"Okay, just grab it," I told him.

He did.

"Anything else, while I'm here?" he asked.

"No, unless you can think of something."

"No, I don't think so. I should probably go, too. I've been wandering around this store for a half hour now on the cell phone the whole time, and they're starting to look at me funny."

Oh. Really. You don't say.

I tried not to comment. Really, and truly I tried. But I couldn't resist one last parting shot:

"Maybe it was the 'Agent Zeta: We have Unagi! I repeat: We have Unagi' that tipped 'em off," I said with a completely straight face.

Rob ignored my razor-sharp wit. "Okay, I'll be by in awhile."

"Okay, bye."

click

We were nearly there.

The trials we had faced had been many, and great. It all came down to this: this moment, this one action which would give us, once and for all, our answer.

Had we triumphed, or had we merely fought a holding action? Were we the victors in the fight against the Dark Forces of the International Market, StickyRice.com, and Chef Tony, or would it be merely a Pyrrhic victory wherein our beautiful (although giant sized and heavyweight) sushi pieces, while finished, would end up crawling back up our throats as punishment for our arrogance in attempting this heroic feat?

Now was the time: the time of the tasting!

Rob took a quick bite.

I mirrored him.

That is, we both tried to take a quick bite, but one of the things about sushi is, if you don't get everything quite right, and eat it quick enough, the seaweed takes on rather the consistency of a piece of old auto tire. Most likely, a tire off of something built in 1985. With a diesel engine. Vroom. Vroom. I briefly considered whether or not I wouldn't have been better off spending the evening in the garage with the power tools.

But no!

We. Could. Do. This.

Rob raised his eyebrows at me as if to seek reassurance. I nodded slightly, and buckled down to some serious chewing.

After this, after all this, no *way* a little seaweed was going to get in the way of our sushi quest.

Not after having come this far. No: we could not back down. So we did the only thing we could do: we chewed. Yes, we chewed, my friends, we chewed long and hard until, suddenly, the seaweed gave way and we had our mouthful.

A mouthful of sushi!

It was *glorious*! The rice, the seaweed, the avocado! The delicate salt of wasabi-laced soy sauce! And yes, the toasted sesame seeds and Tobiko topping it all with a bit of crunch and pop and smoky sesame taste! It was sushi! Sushi in our midst – created with our own hands!

Glorious.

It was glorious!

"Hmm," said Rob, and dipped his piece again for another go.

"Uh huh," I responded cheerfully, and did the same.

We chewed some more. And yet more. My jaw was beginning to feel the burn, as though it were getting a workout it had never expected. Sugarless bubblegum will give you a similar effect, as you may know, but this was no sugarless bubblegum! No indeed. This was the real thing.

But it was sushi! Our sushi! Our very own, hand-made, oriental taste treat formerly available only in the formal context of a Sushi Bar at great cost of both money and pain. (Damn Sushi Bars and their tortuous high-backed high stools!)

And if the rice no longer resembled rice at all but rather kindergarten white craft paste with the odd whitish lump, well then – what of it?

What ... of ... it?!

And if we had to use our teeth as grinding, tearing, cutting, shaving implements to bite through the seaweed, well then – what of that?

What of that, indeed.

All too soon, we were finished.

"Not bad," said Rob.

"Yeah," I replied. "Not bad at all."

Rob thought for a minute. "I don't think the rice is right."

"Yeah. Maybe we did too much stirring and smooshing."

"I don't think you're supposed to smoosh it," Rob pointed out. "I told you you were smashing it down too much."

"Maybe you're right." I was feeling generous, after all: we had just eaten homemade sushi! After over four hours, life was good.

"It's really pretty good," I said.

"Yeah," Rob agreed, "I mean, it is sushi!"

I grinned happily at him.

"But you know ..." he began...

"What?"

"Well..."

"What? What?"

"If someone served us this at an actual sushi bar ..."

Rob and I looked at each other for a long moment, and finished the sentence together:

"We would never, ever go there again."

"And they'd get NO tip," Rob added.

Rob always has to have the last word. But this time, well ... this time, I wasn't going to argue.

. . .

Epilogue

The next day, I had extra rice. Oh, it wasn't completely prepared for sushi, but it was cooked. When we had begun the rice-washing process, we talked a bit about how much rice to make. I told Rob that the Little Book of Sushi said that two cups of rice would equal eight rolls.

"Double it," was his immediate response.

Truth to tell, I could probably eat eight rolls of sushi myself if I didn't mind rolling around on the couch in pain for a few hours, so that sounded good to me.

The Little Book of Sushi, however, did not point out that the eight rolls you made (assuming you limited yourself to using all the rice and making only eight rolls) would be huge, gargantuan – much larger than anything you get in the sushi bar. The way our batch of sushi-vinegared rice turned out (not to mention the consistency of the seaweed), you could jump rope with one of those rolls.

This, when added to the fact that you can only cook about 2 cups of rice at a time in our rice cooker, left us with a big cake of cooked rice, which I had dumped out of the cooker, wrapped in plastic like a big (heavy, gluey) cake, and put into the fridge after finishing the sushi we could eat. I figured I could always heat it up and have rice with dinner.

Of course, I forgot about the rice, as I often do about leftovers. The cake sat in the fridge, hidden, tucked away in that space between the meats drawer and the vegetables drawer. There, it lay dormant – waiting. Until the third day.

On the third day, I was looking through the fridge and thinking that sushi sounded pretty good. I wasn't particularly looking forward to the whole rice-washing, cooking, steaming process, though. I mean, who has that kind of time? Honestly. Suddenly, I remembered the rice cake.

I wondered if it could possibly work. The Little Book of Sushi gave dire warnings and exhortations against refrigerating fully prepared sushi rice, but this was just rice. Just cooked rice. Maybe I could just heat it up in the microwave, make up some more vinegar and sugar sauce, and that would work.

I had nothing to lose. I stuck the plastic-covered cake of rice in the microwave, and set it to five minutes. Turning back to the stove, I began to gather the ingredients for the sushi rice sauce, and picked up the recipe to refresh my memory.

I looked at the recipe.

I looked at it again.

I blinked.

A horrible realization began to dawn on me. In the midst of our sushi-making extravaganza, we had misread the instructions! I distinctly remembered it being two tablespoons of sugar and two tablespoons of vinegar, but now, the recipe stated clearly to use FOUR tablespoons of vinegar and TWO of sugar.

We had not ... made ... the sauce ... correctly.

No *wonder* the rice had turned out like it did!

Worst of all, I was going to have to tell Rob. I was going to have to tell Rob, Gourmet Chef Rob, Real-Cooking-Implement-Owning Rob, that I had a list of three ingredients, and that I messed up one of them.

Three ingredients.

I wondered what kind of Deluxe Miracle Blade Chef Tony would recommend for committing seppuku?

Okay, it was all right. I could make the sauce correctly now. I'd think of something to tell Rob.

Maybe I just wouldn't tell him at all. It could just be our little secret, right? I could just pretend that it was the smooshing and stirring of the sauce into the rice that did it. Yeah. Yeah. That would work. I could get away with that. Yeah.

I made up a batch of the sauce, this time, following the recipe exactly.

The microwave dinged to let me know the rice was done. Total time: 5 minutes.

As I carefully pulled the hot, plastic-wrapped pile of rice out of the microwave, I had another flash. The books suggest that you spread the rice out in a large, flat-bottomed wooden bowl, and then pour the sauce over it. We had just stuck the rice in a plastic Tupperware bowl, hence the amount of stirring necessary. Although I didn't have a flat-bottomed wooden bowl, I did have a large wooden cutting board. Maybe if I spread out the rice on that, I wouldn't have to stir it up so much!

I spread out the microwaved rice on the cutting board. Total time: 20 seconds.

I poured the vinegar/sugar mixture over the rice on the cutting board. Total time: 15 seconds.

I flipped the rice around a bit to make sure the sauce covered it all. Total time: 30 seconds.

I looked at the result in awe and agony: It was perfect. The rice looked like rice, slightly shiny, but not gluey. I picked up a small handful. It stuck together without sticking to my hand. I ate some: it was delicious. I pulled out a piece of seaweed, and began placing the rice on it to make a roll. It was perfect.

It was EASY.

It was ... FUN.

Total time to sushi roll: about ten minutes.

Ten minutes.

Obviously, the evil sushi gods have an irksome sense of humor.

Oh, I told Rob all about it, of course. You see, along the way that second night, I discovered that Rob had purchased the wrong kind of sauce for the Unagi. "Tare," as it turns out, probably means "sauce" or something similar. Rob had picked up "Kabayaki no Tare" or "Barbecue Sauce" where what he needed to get was "Unagi no Tare" or "Unagi sauce." After buying the wrong kind of sauce, he couldn't exactly taunt me for making the sauce wrong, now could he? (Well, yes, actually, he could, but since there was mutual taunting going on, I decided to call it good.)

Now that I know the secret, I'm finding the time for more sushi making. I'm even experimenting a bit: I've tried making it without washing the rice at all, just sticking it into the rice cooker. That seemed to work out fine. Washing the rice just a little seems to work fine as well. I have really only one last challenge to face in the sushi arena, just one more hurdle before I will know myself to have fully triumphed over all the odds.

I will attempt making sushi with regular rice, the normal rice that is in all American cupboards. If I succeed, I will know, truly know, that I am the master!

Oh, but I don't think we need to mention that to Rob.

No, I don't think we need to mention that at all.

THE BEFORE TIME
K.A. Thompson

I can tell by the way he watches me in the mirror, his face slathered with shaving cream as he attempts to scrape away the whiskers and watch me dress at the same time, that he doesn't see the same person anymore. He doesn't care about the stray gray hairs, the way gravity is gradually taking its toll on me, the extra five or ten pounds. But he sees someone different. Someone who looks like me but isn't completely me. Someone else. And I know when he turns around, his hand towel sliding quickly over his chin, that what I see in his eyes will be pain and guilt, and he won't understand why.

"I have no frame of reference," he says, almost in a whisper, looking down at his clenched hands, his feet crossed at the ankles. The way he sits, with his back hunched slightly and head hung down, symbolic of his fear, is one of the few ways I can ever be certain of what emotion is surging through his veins. I know that if I could see his eyes, bright blue and liquid, they would be dark with feeling.

We have been "a couple" for fifteen years, long enough to read the signs, the almost imperceptible nuances that make up character. Ten of those years have been bonded by marriage, the five before we were high school sweethearts. Scott and Lisa. Lisa and Scott. Mr. and Ms. Perfect. The Couple Most Likely To... To what? Mutilate each other before the ten year reunion? Live in ecstatic bliss until doomsday? Shack up, have fifteen kids, grow our own vegetables and shun red meat and dairy products? No one ever said.

Ten married years, long enough to accumulate all the dust and dirt of adult baggage, memories of weddings and birthdays, a baby's first step, first word. Long enough to photograph thousands of happy moments, smiles frozen in perpetuum and plastered on page after page of plastic photo albums. Long enough to endure heartache, and changes made willingly an unwillingly. Long enough to have a sense of "before" and "after."

"God, no. No point of reference at all."

~

Christy is Scott's pride, one of his Reasons For Living. She squeals with delight at the sound of his car crunching gravel in the driveway, and races to the door as the front gate creaks open. It is a ritual that began as soon as she learned to walk; she hides around the corner and waits for the front door to swing open and for Daddy to step through, her little fingers creeping around the corner in search of the nearest shoelace, pulling it quickly and to her father's feigned chagrin. "Gotcha again, Daddy!" she squeals. Scott frowns pretentiously and swears to replace his well worn Reeboks with slip on deck shoes, but his day would never be complete without having at least one shoe carefully violated.

It is also the only ritual that remains. The others, the games they played with abandon and at ear splitting decibels are long gone, memories from the before time. Scott is terrified of chasing her through the house, threatening to tickle her, afraid that the squeals of laughter may become screams of terror in a later memory.

I lie awake most nights to watch him sleep, wishing that I could wipe away the worried frown, praying that a gentle caress might unknot his eyebrows, ease the pain, that is seeping around the edges. I never move, I lie there frozen, knowing that the touch won't come, not yet, not until all the demons have been exorcised from my own memories.

Not until I can fully understand why a half hour in hell has touched every corner of my life and turned the bright colors of my existence into a murky, watercolor gray.

Therapy was Scott's idea. It was one of the first things out of his mouth, after the police were gone and the doctors told him he could take me home, he quietly pleaded with me to find the best therapist as soon as possible. His quiet understanding was something I should have expected; it fell neatly into character.

At first he waited at home, staring at a blaring TV set, or blindly playing games with Christy. He would be out the door at the first sign I was home, waiting by the front gate, and the same question slipped from his lips each time: "Are you okay?"

Taking him with me was an impulse, an idea that suddenly seemed right. With a willing neighbor to watch Christy and a surge of courage pumped up from some deep well I was barely aware of, I urged him into those godawful leather hightop sneakers and out the front door. He watched me as I drove, his fingers scrunched around the shoulder harness of his seat belt, his back against the car door. "Are you trying to tell me I'm going crazy?" he said lightly as I maneuvered the car into a parking slot. "My mother always suspected it, you know. If you're looking for confirmation..."

His laughter dies off uncertainly, as if he wonders.

We make love on my terms, tentatively and infrequently. Most of the time it is quiet and mournful, Something That We Have To Do. His gentleness then touches me more than his body; he is afraid to touch me, afraid to do anything that might remind me of my half hour in hell. Most of the time it is easier to simply whisper "I love you," and turn out the light, hands barely touching under the covers. And when we do, when I summon the courage to make the first move, Scott's touch is careful and practiced.

He is afraid that I will scream and lash out at him.

I hate what I am doing to him. I hate the control.

"Should she be afraid of me?" he asks the therapist, the puzzlement on his face suggesting that the idea is fresh, a sudden revelation. "Am I some kind of threat to her?"

I want to protest; no, I have never been afraid of Scott. He is my safe haven, the one steady rock I can count on in my life. But the therapist raises an eyebrow, impressed with this lanky blonde's insight.

"Stereotyping is a natural human trait. Women tend to generalize men, toss them all into the same pot, so to speak."

He laughs lightly. "Bastard stew. Deep down we're all the same."

"Do you honestly think so?"

Scott leans forward, the fear all but gone. "I don't ever want to hurt her," he says emphatically.

"Do you think that you could?"

I have never given Scott any of the gruesome details. What he knows he knows from police reports and quick, agonizing discussions with doctors after the fact. He has never pressed me for any information that I haven't volunteered. I sometimes wonder if he's afraid to know.

He tapes talk shows; Oprah Winfrey and Maury Povich, sometimes Sally Jesse Raphael. Late at night, the times he can't sleep, he wades through the piles of videotapes in search of enlightenment. Oprah, he tells me, admits that she was molested as a child.

"I'm a grown woman, Scotty," I tell him, unsure of his point. "I'm not sure it's the same."

And I'm not. In the quiet moments of the early morning, just before the alarm is set to go off, I wonder which is worse: a knife held to your throat in a deserted parking lot, or a child's trust shattered by a relative. I'm not sure there should be a comparison at all. But I do know that Scott won't find his answers on videotape.

God knows, I watch those shows live.

Work prevents Scott from going to every therapy session; it's just as well, and he admits that I need the time by myself. I'm not so sure.

"I think more about what this is doing to Scott than what it's doing to me," I admit for the first time, though she can already see that much. "He blames himself, and for the life of me I can't understand why."

"He's frustrated. He probably thinks he should have been there. He reasons that if he had been, it wouldn't have happened."

"He doesn't treat me the same way," I complain.

"You're not the same person. Neither is he."

"I didn't want to change. I never wanted to change."

Scott holds me through the nightmares, the only time he dares to touch me first. His arms envelope the pain, and I wake to the sound of his whispers saying my name over and over. When he is certain that I'm awake, that the man I see before me is him and not some stranger, he retreats to his side of the bed, lifting himself up on one arm, gentle eyes searching my face.

For the first time, his retreat bothers me. I snuggle up with my neck in the crook of his neck, trying to push him onto his back. "It's not your fault," I murmur, hugging him tightly. "None of it is your fault."

Does he think I blame him? I wonder sometimes. He rushes about the house, picking up after Christy, making sure the dishes are done and the laundry put away, all as if he were trying to make up for something he did wrong, some wrong he desperately wants to right.

There is no reasonable way to blame Scott. He couldn't have been there; he never, under the most normal of circumstances, would have been there. Seven fifteen in the evening, the same as 14 out of every 28 days, coming off a 12 hour shift at the hospital; Scott never picked me up from work, I never would have wanted him to.

And I wonder, when I finally go back to work, will he be able to let me go off by myself?

Scott finally quits taping Oprah and Maury. He throws himself back into his work, planning the upcoming baseball season for his high school team. His talk revolves around a potential wonder, a freshman first baseman worth Scott's weight in gold. His only worry for the entire season is convincing the school to let this athletic prodigy on the field; no girl has ever before played varsity.

Scott only goes to the therapist with me every sixth session. More and more I think the doctor is discouraging him from being there, and what's worse is that Scott seems to understand and agree. I find myself looking forward to those sixth sessions, sitting together on the couch, his arm resting behind my shoulders.

His openness and honesty confounds and touches me. When asked if he could have anything he wanted, he replies simply, "For things to be the way they were."

I feel selfish for admitting that all I really want now is a new car.

"You need to tell him," she says firmly, unblinking. "Scott can't be expected to get a good handle on this when you evade the little details."

"Does he really need to know?"

"Doesn't he?"

I hate that, being answered with a question. How could knowing the gruesome facts help Scott? How could him knowing help me? He had enough pain to deal with anyway, he didn't need more.

"Because," she says quietly, "he has no idea what you went through. He has no idea how it could even happen."

"So he blames me?"

"Does he?"

Scott finds it necessary, crucial, that Christy attend a community center class on child molestation. She needs to know the difference between and good touch and a bad touch. She needs to know what to do.

You never know what to do, I think, unsure that her five year old mind is capable of digesting such heady information. I thought I knew what to do. You always think you know what to do.

Talking is easier at night. Not in bed, not in such intimate quarters, but on opposite ends of the sofa, the light off, room dark except for the soft glow of fluorescent aquarium lights. It is easier to tell him without seeing him, to explain about the feel of sharp metal poised just so, feeling the knife point with each pulse of blood surging through my carotid artery. It is easier to tell him why he can't touch my breasts, that some stranger found his perverse thrill in dogging his fingers sharply into my flesh, twisting the nipples angrily, my absolute befuddlement that this man who chose to violate me carefully— protecting himself with a condom—found it necessary to complete his debasement by urinating across my bare chest. It was easier to tell him how it felt to have my wrists tied painfully above my head, my hair caught under my right shoulder, twisting my head to one side. The sudden, searing pain of penetration.

It is always easier to talk through the dark.

"I'm afraid I'll do something to make it worse," he confesses, his hands twisted against each other. "To remind her."

I am finally brave enough to interrupt. "I'll tell you if you do, Scotty."

His head turns just a little; he hears me, though he doesn't want to look up from his hands.

"We can't go back to before," I go on. "We have to quit looking behind us."

"Can you?"

I don't know; with a life divided into sharp pieces of Before and After, I'm not sure I can keep my eyes forward to the after part and not look back. I'm not sure I can talk in the light.

I'm not sure that a half hour in hell can ever be named for what it really is.

September 27th, 1992.
Rob Matsushita

Montclair, New Jersey.

It must be morning.

Gotta be.

It feels like morning.

Walking the streets.

Alone.

The sun is much much too bright.

I rub my mouth, and my upper lip smells like vaginal fluid.

The smell does not make the headache go away.

I was pretty sure that none of this had happened. That I had made it up.

It's hot out, and yet I'm wearing a big black overcoat.

I like to wear my big black overcoat when I walk outside.

It used to make me feel cool but now I just doesn't.

I have little memory of how I got here, why I'm walking, and where I even am.

I look ahead.

Oh, yeah. The train station.

Not too far.

Less than nine hours ago, I turned 21.

Suddenly, I'm home, and my mom is in the kitchen. She has made coffee.

"How was the party?"

My mouth tastes vaguely of vomit.

Hm?

"Your big birthday party. You and your lowlife friends have fun?"

Ah, yes. My friends.

Yeah, 's alright.

"You want some coffee? I just made some."

Yeah.

I pull half a videotape out of my pocket.

Oh, *this* oughta be interesting.

I reach in my other pocket and pull out the other half of the videotape.

The tape has clearly been deliberately broken in half.

From deep within the other pocket, I pull the other half of the tape out.

"What the hell is that?" My mom asks.

A videotape.

"Who did that to it?"

I look at the tape for a long time.

Um.

I'm pretty sure I did.

Oh, yeah.

I remember last night, all right.

Sometime earlier.

The party hasn't really gotten started yet, but people have basically arrived.

This is my friend Steve's apartment. It's really his mom's. He tells me he's kicked her out for the night.

Where is she?

"I dunno. And I don't give a FUCK!"

You never know if Steve's kidding when he says stuff like that.

I know most of these people from work.

We all work at the same job.

Mary walks in and hands me a bottle of Jack Daniels.

Right behind her is Irene, another co-worker.

Mary says, "Happy birthday, Rob," smiling.

Let me tell you a little about Mary.

Mary is one of the managers at my job.

She is also Montclair, New Jersey's own doorknob.

Mary's a big flirt on the job, off the job, all over the place.

My first day working with Mary, her shirt was unbuttoned just a wee bit too low – and Mary has very large breasts – so I tell her she's got a button undone.

She's actually pissed off at me for mentioning it, accusing me of being offended. I tell her that I just thought it was an accident, but she's hearing none of it.

In high school, I used to say that the difference between and slut and a tease is that a tease is a slut who won't put out, and a slut is a tease who comes through.

Well, Mary is not a tease.

She becomes my manager.

By the time she's manager, she's flirted with, had sex with, blown, or otherwise been naughty with everyone at The Job.

Except me.

Now, I'm going to be clear on this. It's not so much that I wish she would flirt with me.

But does she have to flirt with everyone *but* me?

One day, at work, Mary mentions that I'll probably be getting a blowjob from her for my birthday.

Just like that.

The way a normal person would say "oh, by the way, I may be late on Rosh Hashana."

CUT TO Mary handing me the bottle of Jack again.

It's not as if I was really looking forward to the blowjob.

But I wasn't *not* looking forward to it, either.

At this point in my life, I am still twenty, and could count the number of women I have slept with on one hand. And still be able to eat with chopsticks.

But the second she hands me the bottle, I realize that Jack Daniels is what I'm getting in lieu of my birthday blowjob from Mary.

And the second I see Irene, I understand why.

Irene likes me.

Everyone wants Irene to dump her boyfriend and hook up with me.

And I can't stand Irene.

"Hi, Rob," Irene says, smiling. "Happy Birthday..."

Meanwhile, in the present...

I root through my videotapes and find one I don't like.

With a jeweler's screwdriver, I take it apart, replace it with the magnetic tape from the broken tape (which I have now spliced), and screw the whole mess together.

I put it in the rewinder until it pops.

I put it in the VCR.

I press play.

Oh, dear god.

Mary is interviewing me.

"So, how does it feel to be twenty-one?" She's clearly already somewhat in the bag.

Well, I'm not twenty-one yet.

I, clearly, am not drunk enough.

"But you're pretty much already twenty-one...so how do you feel?"

I dunno...I guess overwhelmed.

"What does that mean?"

It means overwhelmed...um...bewildered by it all.

"I think you should drink more."

She pushes the bottle of Jack in my hand closer to my mouth.

I drink.

And on the tape, I can see Irene smiling over my shoulder.

Irene, of course, also works at The Job.

I don't really like Irene. It's just a feeling I have.

When asked why, I can't come up with any answers, but I think it's because she insults me all the time.

They're playful insults – I don't actually think they're serious (stuff like "jerky-treat," "Doodie-head;" that kind of thing).

The thing is, sometimes I find that even more aggravating.

Because I know why she's doing it. It's because she likes me.

And again, everybody thinks our little mini-arguments are cute because they think I like her, too.

Which is what Lara, the other manager (who I really have a crush on) tells me, months earlier.

"Well, it's obvious you two like each other."

But I can't stand her. She's always annoying the crap out of me.

"Yeah, but isn't that what people always do when they like each other?"

This is not The Brady Bunch. I say what I mean. When I say I really don't like someone, I really don't.

"But I thought that you were just saying that." Lara is clearly stunned.

Look, if I like someone, I'm gonna say so, or I'm gonna say nothing. I'm not going to say the opposite.

"Oh," Lara says, months ago.

I finish taking my long-ass drink of the Jack.

I suddenly wonder where the hell Lara is. I was kind of hoping she'd show.

Never mind that her boyfriend is a huge straightedge skinhead-lookin' motherfucker.

I'm not sure how, but I've ended up on the couch, now.

Next to Irene.

And Mary decides that it's time to play "Truth Or Dare."

Or as we've now renamed it...

"Truth or Treat."

Truth Or Treat.

Truth Or Treat gets its name from an impromptu game of Truth Or Dare played at the apartment shared by Mary and Betty, one of the other employees of The Job.

That's the thing about The Job. It's populated mostly by people who lived in Montclair, New Jersey, graduated high school, and then, for reasons known but to God, decided to stay in New Jersey. All of our friends escaped to other places. Maybe not better places, but they weren't in Montclair and that was the big thing.

So, during the day, your life is about The Job, and at night, your social life is about people who worked at The Job.

Did you know "incestuous" isn't in the dictionary? If you don't believe me, you can fuck my sister.

Anyway, the Truth Or Dare game happens out of the blue at Mary's apartment—we'd gone over directly from The Job with Betty.

Mary's just out of the shower, so she's wearing a robe.

Now, I'm absolutely no fun at this game.

With me, it's "Truth," every time.

And I have no real secrets.

Well, no really good ones, anyway.

But Peter, the horndog of The Job, plays rough.

Lick the bottom of an ashtray.

French kiss the dog.

Flash your tits to the neighbors.

This sets a precedent.

Steve, also there, gets dared to pull out his dick (during which the other men are forced out of the room by both Steve and the women in the room) and two of the women (Betty and Irene, who's also there) get dared to make it hard for him.

From what we can hear from the other room, this doesn't take long.

But I keep saying "truth," so I don't get dared to do shit.

Mary jumps a step.

See, the way Truth Or Dare is supposed to work is you make people do things to each other or themselves.

But what Mary does next, well, is just plain dirty pool.

She says, "I dare Peter to lick me from toe to head."

There is that moment – and it's not as long as you'd think – where we all look at each other, trying to figure out if that's too far, or if Peter is really gonna do it.

That's a moment longer than it takes for Peter to start sucking on Mary's toes.

No one ever addresses what we're supposed to be doing while this is going on.

And, dammit, Peter keeps backtracking.

He sucks on her toes (good thing she just took a shower).

Works his way up her foot.

Kisses the back of her knees. You know the spot.

Then goes back to the calf again.

All this time, I'm thinking how I was only stopping in for one beer.

And again, since Mary's just gotten out of the shower, all she's wearing is the robe.

And Pete keeps going up.

Pete licks the inside of Mary's thigh.

Backtracks.

Slides his tongue along the inside of her other thigh.

We're thinking he's going to stop.

Even Peter seems to wonder how far this is going to go – if Mary will stop him, if anyone will stop him...

His face slides right between Mary's legs.

And there's no doubt as to what's happening. This is a small enough room that we can actually hear Mary's pubic hair rustle.

No one says anything as Pete slides his tongue up and down Mary's vaginal lips.

Up and down.

Up and down.

And then.

Definitely in.

Mary gasps.

Someone nervously giggles.

"Um, should someone else dare someone else?" Betty asks.

She is not met with an answer.

Pete reaches up and squeezes one of Mary's breasts, and his other hand is trying to push her legs farther apart.

Mary, in the meantime, watches Peter eat her out, holding up both sides of her robe so we can't really see anything.

And I'm thinking:

Well. *This* is a strange time to get shy.

So, I say to Steve, still trying to convince himself that this IS NOT HAPPENING.

Um. How 'bout those Knicks?

He says to me. "'Cause they can't get the smell out of the fish."

Because I hang out with Steve a lot, I know this is the answer to the question "Why don't they let women swim in the ocean?"

Hey, don't look at me.

It's Steve's joke.

Just then, Mary climaxes loudly.

"Good dare," she says, dreamily. "Gooooood dare." She's actually purring.

And so, Truth or Dare officially, in that moment, becomes Truth Or Treat.

And less than ten minutes later, Pete gives me a ride home.

But that was then.

At my 21st birthday party, most of the details of the Truth Or Treat game are unknown to me. I had finished almost half of the bottle of Jack on my own.

Luckily, and sadly, there was tape.

And there I am, on the couch, Mary straddling me, grinding her crotch into me forcing an erection out of my drunk, drunk, body as I sleepily reach up and grab her tits.

Although I am drunk, there is a part of me that isn't, and that's the part that decides to feel up Mary.

Mary's so drunk she doesn't even realize I'm doing it.

Peter is at this party as well, And he's flirting with everyone in sight.

He stops short of Irene.

Everyone knows about Irene.

Irene sits next to me on the couch as I complain that Peter's getting all the sexual attention, and it's my birthday, dammit.

This from the guy who just got a lap dance and can't remember why.

Mary responds to this by sticking her tongue in my mouth.

On the tape, I can see Irene forcing a laugh.

Later on.

People disburse.

I stand, yelling at the camera.

For Christ's Fucking Sake! I scream. I'm not even INTERESTING on my birthday!!!

"I can't wait for your mom to see this tape and see how FACED you are," Steve says. He's holding the camera.

I'm not faced! I scream, even though I clearly am. I'm just PISSED OFF!!!

How or why I'm in this mood is unclear.

When you're really drunk, sometimes it's unclear why you act a certain way. Are you doing it because you're drunk? Or are you doing it because "being drunk" is a great excuse to act any way you want?

Because I don't need THIS, I say, grabbing the bottle of Jack. And I don't need YOU! I don't need ANYONE. NOBODY LOVES ME! I'M A FREEEEEEAK!!!

And I chug the bottle.

Suddenly, no one else seems to be in the room—although I know Steve must be. He's still on camera. And I can hear him laughing.

I feel a pair of breasts touch my back.

A pair of hands encircle me.

One hand reaches down to my pants.

I'm saying all of this out loud.

Just as Mary feels my erection growing again...

She backs off and walks away.

Steve laughs like an asshole.

Story of my life, I say.

Only I'm more screaming it.

In the background, Mary looks at Irene, who has just entered—and seeing the whole thing. Mary mouths something to her.

And Irene leads me to the couch.

The old bait and switch, the sober me from the future thinks.

Mary pushes Steve into the other room, taking the camera with him.

On the tape, I see Irene and I on the couch together, getting farther and farther away.

Then the door slams on us.

On the couch.

Irene's hair is very long.

It's actually so long that I can see nothing else but her face.

And I can't even see that very well.

We've been like this for a very long time.

I'm pretty sure I'm still on Steve's couch.

I'm not sure how Irene is situated, but she's on the couch with me, and all I can see is her.

She's whispering things to me that I can't make out.

I can't really talk at this point.

Still, I'm not saying yes and I'm not saying no.

And that has been my undoing more times than I can think of.

She's saying something to me.

I have no idea what she's saying.

"Come on."

Oh, yeah. That's right.

While I'm wishing myself farther into the couch (and still not saying no, mind you) she's asking me what would be so wrong with going ahead and doing it?

"What would be so wrong?"

Her lips are so close to mine that I can feel them brush against mine as she keeps saying "Why can't you? What would be so wrong?"

SHUT UP, I think, as I impolitely mash my mouth into hers, granting us our first kiss together.

As drunk as I am, it seems like no time at all between us deciding to have sex and us ending up in Steve's room on his bed.

We begin with some minor-to-major fooling around – me fondling her breasts, sucking her nipples – all through this she's squealing – literally, squealing with glee (I didn't think anyone actually did that) –

as I realize more and more how much this whole thing is like a manifest destiny for her.

This truly pisses me off no fucking end.

Not only am I now having sex with a girl I don't really want to have sex with, but now she's acting like she won, or something.

Because me admitting that I'm wrong is such a big turn on for me, and all.

Speaking of, this leads to another problem.

By now, both of us have our clothes off, and she's fondling me...

...and I can't get it up at all.

I mean, at all.

And there is no worse feeling in the world.

I tell her, look, I'm really sorry, but I have had a lot of whiskey, and I'm not feeling that great—

She's already giggling.

—and...I'm having a little trouble here.

She lets out a big laugh.

I seriously consider smothering her to death with one of Steve's pillows.

I don't.

She eventually stops laughing and leans down.

Her hand, stroking lightly up and down, she takes me in her mouth. I'm still somewhat flaccid.

This makes me feel both better and worse.

I push her leg up, and kiss her panties, sucking the crotch into my mouth.

This is something that seems cool on The Playboy Channel (press 3, 5, and 7 and you're halfway to having it) but in real life...

Well, it's not.

I pull off her panties and she starts giggling again.

If she doesn't stop that giggling, I think, she's never going to be able to giggle again.

Strong words coming from the guy french-kissing her vagina, let me tell you.

After some of the sloppiest foreplay know to man or womankind, we kiss, and it is decided that we have to have some serious sex, now.

Um, I say.

"Come on," she says.

Um.

"Come on," she says, "fuuuuuck me..."

I never thought anyone actually said this, ever.

It doesn't turn me on in this context. It just puts the pressure on.

I think I have a condom.

"Oh, Rob, you don't need—"

No, I'm gonna get one.

Here's a switch. The woman tells then MAN she doesn't want him to wear one. Sorry to disappoint you, toots, but I'm drunk, but not fucking brain-dead.

I grab my pants, pull out my wallet (I know, I know, you're not supposed to keep it there) where I pull out the condom.

And look at it.

"What?" she says.

I look at the condom.

And the condom tells me a story.

The Condom.

It is a few months earlier.

I am at Pete's home and there are a few workers from The Job there.

I am in the bathroom, and I am urinating.

KNOCK-KNOCK.

What the fuck?

"Hey," I hear on the other side of the door.

Why does someone always want me while I'm in the goddamn bathroom?

Who is it?

"It's Fitz."

Fitz. He used to work at The Job, and quit, or was fired, I don't really know.

What do you want? I'm pissing.

"You got a rubber?"

I'm pissing.

"You got a rubber?"

Ask me when I'm no longer pissing.

"You bet."

I finish, and I open the door, condom already in my hand. Fitz is right there, waiting for it, like a junkie.

"Thanks, man, I owe you," he says, "I'm about to boff Mary."

Well, go now. Beat the crowds.

"Oh, she's such a hog," he says, chuckling. I'm chuckling, too. "We haven't even kissed. I am a pig. And I shall have my sow."

He runs off to a room, slams the door, and that is the extent of my involvement in that story.

But the next day, at The Job, Mary is the floor manager, and pulls me aside.

"Thank you so much for your help last night," she tells me, "Matt told me it was yours."

She presses a condom into my hand.

"That's to replace the other one."

Um. Thanks.

But later, at another "Truth Or Treat" game, Mary gets dared to put a condom on Peter. Guess which one she borrows?

I give her the condom that she gave me that replaced the one that I gave Fitz, and to a larger extent, Fitz gave Mary.

After an initial blowjob (Of course! How ELSE would Peter get hard?) Mary puts The Condom That Jack Built on Peter's semi-hard erection.

This time, later on, Peter replaces that condom.

And it's the condom I'm holding now.

The condom I'm going to fuck Irene with.

As I unwrap it, she's rubbing her fingers up and down my cock.

This actually doesn't feel as good as you'd think – it's actually kind of distracting and annoying, sees as she's doing it with no grace, no style, no lubricant, and apparently, thinks she's good at it.

She helps me on with the condom. Admittedly, this doesn't feel bad.

And I am in her.

She's squealing again, and that makes me angrier, which makes me pump her harder, which makes her squeal louder, which makes me kiss her hard just to shut her the fuck up, already...

There is a period of time where I think I'm no longer hard only to find out that I am. I know I'm not alone in this feeling.

And I'm in her again, her whispering, "yes, yes," again and again, me thinking of Lara, the other manager at The Job who I wish this was but she didn't even show up in the first place and I'm still pissed off over that shit...

Lara told me she'd come to my party.

Well, that's not true.

I told her I wanted her to come.

She told me she might, but...she'd see.

And she's not here.

I'd like to think it's because she knows that there was a good chance that she'd end up here, with me, but the truth is probably that her boyfriend told her not to.

During heated moments with him, Lara tells me, she's been known to call him "Rob."

Whereas Lara and I share no heated moments.

Irene whispers in my ear.

"I knew this would happen."

Oh, dear God.

"You kept saying it wouldn't, but I knew. I knew we'd end up together."

Jesus CHRIST, Irene! I'm drunk and this is a party! Even I don't count this as us being "together!"

I don't say this, of course.

I could have said no, and I didn't. She still has the moral high ground.

"But I knew."

I should probably also mention that Irene has a boyfriend.

One that's been punishing her by withholding sex from her.

I shit you not.

See what bang-up results THAT tactic gets you?

And I come inside Irene.

Well, I come inside the condom I'm wearing, anyway. That overfilled-waterballoon-feeling.

We dismount.

And already we know.

It wasn't very good.

I reach down to pull off the condom.

I don't find it.

I realize that Irene is sitting up.

Indelicately, I reach between her legs and yank out my condom.

And her head pops off and confetti flies out.

Okay, no, not really.

But no words go along with my yanking out the condom. Neither of us really find it funny.

I have no memory of what happened to the condom.

At this point, I've found some way to blame Steve for all of this.

And I'm just wiped out.

I can't move.

I can't talk.

I can barely breathe.

The Jack Daniels has caught up with me.

I also realize as Irene cuddles next to me that this will never work.

I realize why it is that I don't really like Irene much.

It's not her that I don't like.

It's this guy I seem to become in her presence.

It's like reverse chemistry. Being around her makes me angry for reasons I can't even pinpoint.

It's like love, but the opposite.

I don't say this out loud, or anything.

What saddens me is that Irene thinks that things have changed between us, and well, they have and they haven't.

We hear the sounds of people coming back into the living room, which is right next to Steve's bedroom.

"Think they'll come in?"

No, I think they know where we are, and they know what we've been doing. Only an *idiot* would—

And Steve opens the door, spilling light into the room.

"God, let some air in, you fucks," he says.

No one seems to notice us.

I'm too tired to yell.

Shut the door...

It's almost a whisper.

Sh-shut the fucking...shut the fucking door...

I will note that Irene isn't helping at *all*.

Would you shut the fucking door...

We can hear them out there, speculating on where we are? No one has thought to look in here, thank God for small favors.

Would you...

Would you shut the...

Shut...

SHUT THE FUCKING DOOOOOOOOR!!!

Everyone in the other room shuts up as Steve yells "Geez, hah! I didn't know there was anyone in there!"

SLAM!!!

And I can zonk.

"I wonder where everyone else was," Irene asks, as I fade away.

That was something I didn't find out until I watched the tape.

The Tape.

Various things that also appear on the videotape:

Steve saying from behind the camera: "Hey, someone hold the camera – I gotta take a squirt."

"Hey," says Larry, another friend of mine, "film it!"

"What," Steve says, "ME film ME taking a pee? From MY point of view?"

"Yeah."

"Okay."

He's gonna DO IT!!! You can hear me scream. This must be before I end up in Steve's bedroom with Irene.

Suddenly, we see a toilet bowl. Considering how drunk Steve must be at this point, and that he's got to work the camera, too, and that it's a CONSIDERABLY long pee, Steve's doing a great job.

"Welp," says Steve, after flushing, "I said I wasn't gonna get my penis on camera but I guess I LIED."

Jump cut.

Larry yelling at the camera to "get that shit off him!" without realizing that, until he said anything, the camera wasn't.

Jump cut.

People watching Ren and Stimpy as Steve gives Mary a backrub.

Faintly, in the background, Larry can be heard yelling at the camera to get off of him again. Something about if he's on camera he can never run for office.

Jump cut.

Irene on top of me as I lay on the couch. The way our heads are, it looks like we're kissing.

"No, no," Irene says, "My head was here, his was here."

Sure, Irene. And you're just lying on top of me to keep me warm.

Jump cut.

Me, obviously drunk and worn out.

Steve's on camera, again, asking how I feel. From his tone, he apparently thinks that me making out with Irene is a *good* thing.

I hold up a middle finger, and, as calmly as I can muster, suggest that he ram it up his ass.

Jump cut.

Irene and I are left on the couch together, the door slamming on us.

Ah.

Here's the stuff I wasn't there for.

And what happens here isn't all that exciting.

Mary, in Steve's bathroom, debating whether or not she's going to throw up.

Peter rubs a cold towel over her face.

"Oh," she coos, "that feels really good."

It's around here that Mary, drunk as can be, accidentally lets go that she used to be a prostitute.

Someone says something as a joke, and Mary says, matter of fact, and not kidding, "It was twenty for a blowjob. Fifty for a lay."

Is she telling the truth? Is she just trying to get attention? Is the answer to both of these questions "yes?"

The subject is quickly dropped when Mary sticks her face in the toilet.

She doesn't puke, but she does make the universally recognized "Puke Face."

The camera, bastard that it is, stays on her.

But, no, she doesn't puke.

"I'm not gonna puke," she says.

Then she pushes everyone out of the room except for Peter.

Jump cut.

Me, sometime after I have obviously had sex with Irene. My hair is disheveled, my shirt is mostly unbuttoned.

Larry points at the hair on my chest, telling me that he's jealous. I have never figured out why some men want hairy chests.

Someone else comes up (Virginia, another manager) and tells us she just caught Mary giving Peter a blowjob in the kitchen.

Fun Party Fact: If you give someone a blowjob at a party, *don't* do it where the beer is. You will be caught. And videotaped.

I wave the camera to follow me, like on Mr. Robinson's Neighborhood.

Then I just take the camera entirely.

Peter, standing, is mashing one of Mary's tits with his hand as we slide in.

His back is to us, and Mary's back is against the fridge as she pumps her face on his cock.

He lets go of her tit (how was he able to stand without hunching and still grab her by the tit?) and waves us away.

Mary responds by pushing Peter onto the table...

Giving us a much better look.

Yup, there's no getting around it.

Mary's really giving him a blowjob.

Peter doesn't want to be filmed, but, finally, he seems to figure he can't stop it from happening, either.

He gives the camera a big thumbs up.

And the picture goes dead.

The Big Awful.

Almost everyone has left the party.

It's Steve's apartment, so he stays.

Mary's too drunk to drive, so she pretends to stay, waits until she thinks we're all asleep, finds her keys that we didn't hide well enough, and drives home anyway.

Steve goes back to his room and passes out.

Irene and I sleep together on Steve's mother's bed.

Sleep, as you've probably already guessed, is not the operative word.

Which doesn't really make me happy.

In the quiet words of Mark Renton, I'm not sick yet, but it's in the post, that's for sure, and in the meantime, Irene wants to continue going into lovey-dovey mode.

Well, I used my only condom, so it ain't gonna happen, lady.

I don't say this of course. I'm too busy making out with her.

It's either this or talk to her.

I'm starting to feel pangs of sober, so I'm a little more there during this time in bed with Irene.

We pull each other's clothes off, sleepily, and she's already saying she wants me in her again.

Why is it that the only people who say this to me are people I never want to hear say it at all?

She's still telling me how she knew that we would be together from day one. This makes me a little more aggressive, which she's mistaking for passion.

Since there is more light in this room than in Steve's, I can actually see Irene.

She's actually very pretty.

One thing I focus on is that she does, actually, have really nice nipples.

A weird thing to focus on, I'll grant you, but I'm in a weird place and I'm taking weird souvenirs.

I suck one of her nipples into my mouth, running my tongue across it.

This drives her nuts.

Some women, I've noticed, don't care for this at all.

She keeps trying to get me to fuck her again, and I don't want to. Everything else is fine, but I'm not about to have unprotected sex. I know me, I know my luck, and I'm not taking any chances.

So I do a Sam Kinison.

You know what a Sam Kinison is.

That's when you lick her pussy for two fuckin' hours.

Sometimes you have to.

It's just something you have to do.

I was out of practice, and gosh darn it, I just like doing it.

Another thing Sam Kinison was right about, too.

The alphabet.

Licking the alphabet really does work.

With my tongue, I lick capital A through Z, then lowercase Z through A.

Then DEAR SANTA.

Then HELP ME.

Then SHUT THE FUCK UP.

Irene goes nuts.

I finish.

Okay, it wasn't quite two hours, but I finish anyway. There are only so many words I know.

I climb back up into her arms.

She kisses me right on the mouth.

If she doesn't mind, I don't mind.

"Thank you," she tells me, "Sweetie."

And she's wiped out.

I roll over and try to go to sleep.

She reaches around me, her arms around my stomach.

She starts to tell me how she really feels about me.

And squeezes.

And that's all she wrote.

I get up, I don't have to pull on my pants because they're already on, I run to the bathroom which is conveniently right there, I slam the door, I lift the lid on the toilet...

And there is a moment of indecision.

Because I'm not sure which orifice it's coming out of.

I got a fifty-fifty chance of getting this right.

I shove my face in the toilet, mouth wide open.

Nothing happens.

I'm wrong.

I flip around, hand already to my belt (why am I wearing a belt to bed, anyway?) yank down my pants, and land on the toilet bowl.

The seat, of course, was still up.

And up I go, lowering the lid just in time...

And I won't go into details.

Let's just say it was loud, nasty, long, and hurt.

I flush.

But my bathroom adventure isn't nearly over.

I notice that we're a little low on toilet paper here.

I also notice that it's time for me to start puking.

I no longer care that Irene can probably hear this whole thing.

And it's easier for me to puke this time.

All I have to do is think about what the bowl was last used for.

Again, I won't go into details.

What Bill Cosby says about the side of the bowl being nice and cool is true, too.

I look down between my legs.

My underwear is still around my ankles.

Only I realize something.

This isn't my underwear.

It's Steve's underwear.

After Irene and I fucked in his room, I must have grabbed a pair of his underwear by accident.

I realize that it must be Steve's underwear, because the pair I had originally been wearing didn't have as many track marks and holes.

I am a sad bastard.

Eventually, I crawl back into bed.

Irene seems to get that I don't want to be hugged.

Morning happens all of a sudden.

"Thanks, pal," Steve says, ruefully, "thanks for dropping that load in my bed. That was great."

I almost tell him Thanks for not keeping me from fucking Irene, but I realize she's still next to me.

This time, she is hugging me.

"Sweetie," she says.

This word is ruined for me.

Her cab arrives. She must have called it earlier on.

She kisses my cheek, ruins the word "sweetie" for me again, and leaves.

I get up, grab my coat, find the two pieces of videotape in the pockets...

The memory of pulling the tape out of my camcorder comes back to me. I broke the tape in half for reasons I wasn't even sure of then...

I walk outside.

To home.

The story, of course, does not end there.

Payday.

Still tired.

Still out of it.

I head to The Job to pick up my pay, even though it's still my birthday.

Really, who am I kidding – I just want to see what-all people have heard.

At the job, we have what the owner calls "Pay-Cashes." We just get our pay in cash, in envelopes.

Since we're all too young and stupid to think about things like taxes or fraud, we take the money.

I'm on my way in to take my money, when I see a co-worker friend of mine. Marie.

When I say "girl from New Jersey," Marie's the girl you picture: Big hair, tawk-like-dis, super-tanned. Oh, yeah. You know her.

Sweet girl, though. A friend.

She also used to date Peter.

I grab a water as she comes up.

"Heard about the party last night."

Oh, yeah? I say. I'm not sure if I'm wearing sunglasses or not.

What'd you hear?

"I heard that Irene pretty much raped you."

I wonder if that means Charles Bronson will hunt her down and execute her. Probably not.

Add that to the list of things I don't say.

Um, I say. You heard that already, huh? Hear anything else?

"Yeah," she says, "I heard you gave great head."

SPPPPPPPPPFFFFFFFHH!!!

My first real-life spit take.

The grapevine, it seems, has footnotes.

I'm gonna get my pay cash.

I walk into the office.

"How was the rest of the party?" Betty, the other manager asks. "I heard it was pretty wild."

What else did you hear?

"I heard you gave great head."

SPPPPPPPPPPPFFFFFFHH!!! How many people did she tell?!?

(I wasn't even drinking anything for that spit-take, either.)

Did she also tell you I puked for about an hour?

"She said you got sick – but she also said you were really great in bed."

How did – she said I was great?

"Oh, yeah. Two thumbs up."

Well, I guess there are worse rumors about me to be going around.

Mary enters – it's time for her shift.

And she enters with, "I keep hearing you gave great head!"

I leave with my money.

I head across the street to the diner that Lara works her second job at.

I order a coffee.

"Wild party, huh?"

God, she's fucking gorgeous.

Yeah. Pretty wild.

"Heard *you* had a good time."

Yeah. Pretty good.

"Heard Irenc had a pretty good time, too."

Did she tell you I gave good head?

"She said you gave *great* head."

Of course she did. Why wouldn't she?

All these women telling me I gave great head, and none of them are telling me in the context that I would prefer.

"I almost went," she tells me, "but I just didn't think...um..."

...It would go over well with your boyfriend?

"No, no, I figured you were going to sleep with Irene, so I kinda felt like I'd be out of place."

She hands me my black coffee, four sugars.

I sip the coffee.

Hey.

Wait a—

How did you know that I was going to sleep with Irene?

"Well..."

She doesn't finish the sentence.

You knew everyone was setting this up, right? "Well, yeah," she says like she's surprised I didn't. "You wanted to, right?"

I don't answer.

All the women in my world are conspiring together to make me sleep with women I don't like.

"Did you want to sleep with her or didn't you?"

I guess I did.

"Are you gonna talk to her?"

Not if I can avoid it.

I mean to add that to the list of things I don't say out loud, but it gets inched off the list by the phrase *I would have rather slept with you.*

"Oh," Lara says, and I have to mentally backtrack to see which of those I actually said out loud – God, what am I even doing out in the world?

"So, you didn't want to sleep with Irene?"

Not really.

"But you did anyway."

Yeah.

"You know, you could have said no."

Yeah.

"Why didn't you?"

Maybe I wanted to sleep with *somebody.*

Lara doesn't say anything. I must be the saddest looking man alive.

I will never have Lara. I know this now.

I owe you for the coffee.

"No, you don't. It's on the house."

Really?

"Really. Happy birthday, Rob."

Yes.

Happy birthday, Rob.

Lara.

I should probably explain that by now, Lara no longer works at The Job.

The Owner Of The Job, known from here on as Mr. P., has a habit of harassing some of the female employees.

Also giving them little bonuses, little raises here and there, in exchange for feeling them up from time to time and talking to them in a suggestive manner.

More than once, Lara would walk down the hall, a bit shaken, and ask me "Did you just hear any of what Mr. P. just said to me?"

And, of course, I couldn't. The way the air in the building works, my station is in the one area where you can't hear anything, even from ten feet away.

At a friend's house, Lara tells us how Mr. P. is with many (but not all) of the women who work there.

I ask Marie if he's ever done anything to her.

She tells me that he once held on to her arm and wouldn't let go, and that it freaked her out – "and, y'know, he's always said stuff," but he hasn't really done anything else.

But that mainly because she makes sure not to be alone with him, ever.

Most of the other women have quickly picked up on this – and so has Peter, putting himself in the room if it looks like a woman's going to be left alone with Mr. P.

The managers do not have this luxury, having to work one-on-one with him regularly.

Betty says that he never touches her. "But that's because I'm fat," she adds, because she knows we're all thinking it.

Mary's attitude, predictably, is sluttily pragmatic: "What's the big fucking deal? He touches my tits for, like, three seconds. He gives me fifty bucks for it. The way I see it, that's a good deal."

Lara does not share this world view, and it's starting to get to her.

Hearing all of this, I'm stunned.

Mainly because I'd never realized it until now.

Lara tells us she's gonna quit The Job.

I tell her that I just bought a wireless microphone.

She looks at me.

How long are you gonna stay with The Job?

"Two weeks."

Well, Lara, what if for those two weeks I set up my video camera in the office, and just sort of let it record anything that goes on in there?

And what if, say, I were to wire you for sound, set up to record whatever anyone says to you while you're in there?

"What would happen with those tapes?" she asks.

Whatever you want, is what I'd guess.

But hey.

We're just talking.

She seems unsure.

Everyone else in the room is really curious to see what's going to happen next.

If nothing happens, I say, then nothing happens. We wouldn't be entrapping anyone.

She looks into my eyes.

Trying to see if I'm kidding.

I'm not.

"Okay," Lara says. "Okay."

Lara wears a set of falsies the next day – she says that Mr. P. tends to strike when she's wearing them (which is why she doesn't much). This works out for me, seeing as I lost the windguard for the mike anyway.

I give her the mike and turn my back.

Within seconds she's got it slipped in – right inside her right falsie (Mr. P. makes his attack left-handed).

"Can you see it?"

She smiles an amused half-smile that she's asking me to look at her breasts.

Looks okay. Turn around.

She spins for me.

I clip the power-pack to the mike to the belt at the small of her back, then pull her shirt down over it.

I switch her on.

You're live, I say over her shoulder.

"Okay."

Walk outside. I want to see if I can still hear you.

I have a small tape recorder on my hip, with an earpiece under my shirt and in the ear you can't see from the angle I sit in my workspace. I deal directly with customers. They can see it, but if Mr. P. walked in, he wouldn't be able to. Plus, I practice getting it in and out of my ear.

I hear Lara talking to a couple of my co-workers.

"So, can Rob actually hear us now?"

"I don't know."

Lara looks over at me, through the window in my workspace.

I give her thumbs up.

"You can hear me?"

I nod.

She steps out of my sight.

"Roy," she says. I smile. This is a bit from the movie "The Grifters," and she knows it creeps me out. "Roy... What if I told you I wasn't really your mother? That we weren't related?"

Two customers come up. I'm trying not to laugh as Lara whispers in my ear: "You'd like that, wouldn't you? Sure you would. You don't need to tell me. Now, why would you like it, Roy?"

Man, you are *mean,* Lara.

She tells me that Mr. P. is coming. She comes into the office and sits down.

As I set up the camera, Mr. P. walks in. I hurriedly set up, trying not to make it look like I'm doing what I'm doing.

I've hit record on the camera and gotten out of the way as Mr. P. staggers out.

I can smell the booze on his breath from here.

"Did you get that?" Lara asks.

Did he—

"You didn't see it?"

No. I didn't have the recorder going, either.

I rewind the tape.

Lara and I watch on the camera's viewfinder.

On the tape, Mr. P. straightens up and walks out. As he walks out, the shifting of his body reveals Lara, slumped in her chair.

She looks at the camera, mugging, hands to face in "Home Alone" position, trying to joke trough it with a certain amount of dignity.

Shit, I say.

You can't see anything.

"Nope," she says.

The jokey-face at the end doesn't help, either.

"He did it really quick, too," Lara adds.

Yeah. I don't see how he gets anything out of it.

"It's a power thing," she says.

Soon after, Lara quits.

No one gets caught.

Everyone gets away with it.

Lara comes in to get her last pay-cash.

"I'm still working at the diner over there," she says.

We're standing just outside The Job.

Yeah, I say.

She looks at me.

And kisses my cheek.

What was that for?

"I felt like it," Lara says. "See ya."

She walks away, then turns to see if I'm checking out her ass.

And I am.

Coffee.

It's decided that Irene and I should meet up and spend some time alone.

I don't know who decides this, so don't ask.

Irene goes to visit me at my second job, a comic book store.

It's about closing time when she walks in, so I lock the door behind her and proceed to clean up.

After cleaning up, I see Irene sitting on the steps at the front of the store.

I sit down next to her.

From here on out, I have no idea what we talk about, because all that's going through my mind is how possible it is that I could have sex right now in this store.

Soon, I'm trying to hide an erection.

And Irene, bitch that she is, knows it. She's giggling.

I figure the only way to get rid of my hard-on is to focus on that giggling.

Focus on the reality of the situation.

Focus on what things would be like if we had sex again.

And zap.

It's gone.

Now, it may not make sense, but here is my conflict. I really want to have sex again, but I don't want to have sex with Irene.

For a lot of reasons.

Okay, two big ones.

One, I'm just not that attracted to her – and besides, although no one else seems to be able to see it, the idea of a relationship with Irene (which, make no mistake, is what sex with her again would mean) has disaster written all over it.

Two, and not enough has been made of this, she's *got* a boyfriend. Why doesn't she just break up with him? Why is she just trying to transfer over to me?

And let me tell you how much confidence *that* instills into the beginning of a relationship.

Okay, fuck *this*.

We go for coffee.

And, my life being my life, we go to (of fucking course) the same diner that Lara works.

Don't get excited, because nothing interesting happens.

We walk in, Lara says hi, we sit down, Lara keeps her distance, we have a cup of coffee, talk about pretty much everything else but having sex again, and that's really about it.

She has to work and I don't, so we go our separate ways.

As we leave, Lara gives me a look. She knows I'm not interested, and yet, to her, it looks like we're starting something.

About two days later, I get a little postcard from Irene in the mail.

Nothing big, just a little note that says hi.

Which is when I suddenly wonder:

Why can't I do the one night stand thing like everyone else?

How *do* other guys do it?

Peter can do it.

Steve can do it.

Pretty much everyone seems to be able to do it.

My last girlfriend, I was crazy about. She was funny, and pretty, and we really liked being together.

But she was moving to California, and as a result, she couldn't really give all of herself to me, and that was driving me nuts.

My girlfriend before that, we went out for a month before she told me that magic was gone and that we'd be better friends.

I didn't have any girlfriends before that.

So there are these women in my life that I care about, that I'd want to be with, who are more than comfortable for their relations with me to be transient at best.

Then there's the girl I lost my virginity to (she was somewhere in between the first girlfriend and second girlfriend), who was supposed to be a one night stand, and then kept calling my house again and again for the better part of a year.

And now here's Irene.

A drunken scrap at my twenty-first birthday party, and now she's sending me postcards.

I decide that this has gotta stop.

I decide that everyone else is just wrong about us.

I decide that I'm not getting into a relationship just because everyone else says I should.

This shit has to stop.

So, me being me, I just avoid Irene until the Halloween party.

The Halloween party.

Where there will be beer.

And food.

And fun.

Followed by screaming.

Followed by backstabbing.

To be followed by me punching a brick wall.

So, you know.

Costume optional.

Halloween.

Come one, come all.

Gather 'round, gather 'round.

Come and see the dancing freak.

My costume is that of a vampire.

It basically consists of my big black coat (again), black pants, black shirt, red tie, sunglasses, and fangs (two sets, upper and lower).

I had all of this stuff already.

So, basically, it's not so much a costume as it is an excuse to wear all this stuff at once.

Different people from The Job are here – most have brought their significant others.

Irene hasn't.

It seems likely that she wants to have another during-party hookup.

My mission: Stop that from happening.

I make an early decision *not* to drink, which I end up having no trouble at all sticking to, as the only thing to drink there is beer, and beer has always had kind of a bile taste to me. But that could just be a sense-memory thing.

At any rate, most of the usual cast is here.

Mary and Betty (it's their apartment).

Lester, another friend of mine.

Peter, who has brought his current steady girlfriend, Suzi.

And, of course, Irene, who's in full on flirt-mode with me.

I'll be honest.

Most of this party comes back to me in fragments.

I can only assume that, because I didn't drink at the party, I must have mentally blocked it.

One fragment:

People are dancing.

Irene, having just seen "Basic Instinct," slides up next to me and dances like Sharon Stone.

My gut cringes.

Another fragment:

Irene tries to put her arms around me.

I walk away from her.

She doesn't follow.

Another fragment:

In a room full of my friends, I suddenly have no one to talk to.

Irene giggles near me.

I move to the other room.

What the fuck am I still even doing here?

Another fragment:

I sit on a couch, surrounded by people.

Across from me is Suzi, Peter's girlfriend.

She's dressed in a tight black number, and I notice that she doesn't seem to have anyone to talk to, either.

On the TV nearby, someone puts on "Evil Dead 2: Dead By Dawn."

"Oh, cool," Suzi says.

You like Evil Dead?

"Oh, I love Evil Dead!"

I can't get over that this girl even knows what Evil Dead is.

Irene sits next to me.

How apropos.

Peter leans over, saying, "Oh, yeah, she's into all those horror movies."

Really? I say.

"Oh, yeah, I liked 'American Werewolf' a lot, but the big one for me is Sam Raimi."

Oh, you gotta love Raimi.

"Oh, yeah."

Irene puts her hand on my knee.

I decide to ignore it. I'm finally having a conversation I can get into, and I don't want to end it.

Am I hitting on Suzi? I choose not to think so, and if I was, Peter's sitting right there – he could easily say something. He actually seems amused that Suzi's so enthused about something – this is the first time she's been able to open up all night.

Although, you know, Suzi is really cute.

And there's nothing cooler than talking horror movies with a cute girl.

Well, I say, have you seen "Bad Ta—"

Irene slides her hand under my arm, making me jump. I give her annoyed, and go back to Suzi.

Have you seen "Bad Taste?"

"'Bad Taste?' What's that?" Suzi says.

It's this movie by Peter Jackson. If you like Sam Raimi, you should check out his—

Irene leans closer, her hand rubbing up and down my knee.

Finally, I take Irene's hand off my knee. This makes her giggle even more.

"What's his name?"

Peter Jackson. He's from New Zealand – he's great.

"This is so cool that someone else is into this!"

Oh, I love horror—

Irene wraps her arms around my stomach, and puts her head on my shoulder.

Would you excuse me for a moment?

I get up, leaving Irene there.

She follows me into the other room.

"What's wrong?" she asks.

I...

I let the sentence die.

"Do you have some sort of problem with me, now?"

I had a problem with you before!

"What's that supposed to mean?"

I'm having a conversation – my first of the night, mind you, and you're all over me like a...like a...

I totally blank on a good metaphor, which is fine, because she interrupts me anyway.

"I'm just playing around!"

And I don't like it! I've never liked it! Can't you—

I stop myself.

"What?"

Can't you take a hint?

She suddenly looks incredibly hurt.

I'm sorry, okay, I'm sorry, but you've got this whole thing built up so much that...

I suddenly realize that I'm still dressed like a vampire, and that I don't want to have this conversation looking like this. I take off my sunglasses.

"*I* built it up? Why can't you just tell me what you want?"

I take out my fangs.

I *did* tell you!

"No, you didn't!"

Oh, she's right, I didn't.

Okay...uh...well, I'm telling you, now.

"Telling me what?"

I take off my tie.

That I don't want us to be a couple, okay?!? That this is not going to work!

Irene, to her credit, holds her anger very tightly.

She's not going to cry, not in front of me, anyway. She doesn't want to give me the satisfaction.

Never mind that the idea of seeing her cry gives me no satisfaction whatsoever.

It was just a thing that happened, okay?

"Yeah," she says, no longer really listening.

Look, I say, I'm sorry you feel you're trapped in your other relationship with your boyfriend, but if you want out of that, just get out of it. You shouldn't use me—

This is a mistake.

Never offer advice during a breakup.

Of course, since there never really was a relationship, is this really a breakup?

"Then maybe you should have said *no*," she yells, and walks into Betty's bedroom.

Betty follows her in, and I hear the sounds of Irene being comforted by Betty and others who were just in there.

I hear the sounds of criticisms of me, in hushed female whispers.

I look back at the room where the party is.

I can't go back in there, now.

I look at the room where Irene is.

More crying.

I'm the most hated man at the party.

I made Irene cry.

My work here is done.

I walk out to the fire escape.

Mary's out there. She's heard the whole thing.

I light a cigarette.

I only started smoking because it was the only way to get a break at The Job.

Mary's already passing judgement.

I throw an angry look her way.

All of you wanted this to work. She wanted it to work. Everyone wanted it to work.

"Then why didn't it work?" Mary says, angrily.

Because *I* didn't want it to work. How I felt about it wasn't really taken into account.

Mary, for the first time since I've known her, is struck speechless.

"Then you should have said *no*," she says, stomping off, angrily.

Great, I think, walking down the escape.

Now you tell me.

I notice a brick wall as I get off the escape.

What's that, wall?

What did you say?

And I punch the wall.

Hard.

Let's try that again.

Punch.

There we go.

Punch.

How's that feel?

Punch!

My watch breaks off from the strain.

I look at my knuckles.

Not that bloody.

Oh.

Yeah.

Who's bad?

I look up at the party, and hear someone come out on the fire escape. I hear this someone discussing me, and asking whether or not I've left.

Yes.

Yes, I have.

And I walk home, alone.

The List.

All of the managers, Lara once told me, played favorites.

When Lara was the head manager at The Job, I was her favorite.

After she left, Mary became head manager, because she was Mr. P's favorite.

Who was Mary's favorite?

Everyone except me.

The Job became a little harder in a whole lot of ways.

At the time, I was trying to shoot a video project for a class (all through this, I'd been working on it). I'd made the mistake of getting virtually everyone from The Job involved in it.

Irene takes to making fun of the script, and Mary reschedules everyone to work on days I've scheduled to shoot (I had put my shooting schedule in the office).

The project goes from being a ninety minute horror/action movie to being a two-minute trailer for a horror/action movie that would never get made.

Someone, as a joke, puts up a checklist of stupid things that customers say.

Later on, this becomes the "Sick Of" list.

It's more of a personal statement.

Sick of:

1. Not being appreciated by the men in my life—Mary
2. Not being appreciated by the women in my life, who used to be so important—Mary.

Now, who knows where *this* comes from.

3. Being considered an over-doting, un-fun wife by all his leaching friends—Betty.

Betty's referring to her boyfriend – who also used to work at The Job.

4. Stupid people!!! –-Betty.

Chances are, she's talking about The Customers.

5. Allergies and reading the wrong schedule.

This from Daniel, one of the more laid-back guys at The Job. He and I trade mix tapes back and forth all the time.

6. Hypocrisy—Mary.
7. Abusive, misled customers! –-Betty.

From here on, most people stop signing their list entries.

8. Being scared shitless and not being able to figure out what the hell to do.
9. Constantly complaining about my (love) life, & somewhat enjoying it

Judging from the handwriting and the tone, this could be Mary.

10. Waiting for Satori and the #71 bus.

Daniel, trying to make our lives a little more surreal.

11. "Real life experiences."

Daniel tells me that he wrote this because he hated that this was supposed to be a railing-on-the-customers-thing, and now it's a bullshit-angst thing.

Can't say I disagree.

Can't say I didn't help it along, either.

12. "College Music."

Daniel again. He hates college music.

13. Daniel, who doesn't give a hoot about "college music." By the way, he's a big doodie.

Irene wrote this.

Underneath it, I have written:

Hey, I happen to *like* that doodie!!! (He's my favorite kind of doodie!)

Then, Tabitha, a friend of Marie's and ex-girlfriend of Peter, writes:

14. Trying to be happy, but not being allowed to.
15. Exchanging friends for boyfriends and vice-versa.

Then I write (in cursive so no one will know it's me):

16. This list. It's getting kinda ugly, don't you think?

Under this, Betty writes:

I think not! This is a useful tool of communication, kinda like Oprah!

Under this, I write:

I rest my case.

Everyone guesses it's me right away.

17. Wondering about my future & dreading what it may hold—Betty.
18. Ham on the posters!

No idea who wrote this or what it means.

Irene writes:

19. Having dreams about sex with Ross Perot then Dennis Miller walks in and I can't decide between old & more experienced and young & viral. Life is so full of choices!
20. Spamburgers and that potty training doll that comes with the flushing toilet.

Then, Mark joins the game. Mark is someone who doesn't work that often. He's a friend of Pete's. Pete's a little nervous around him, because Mark has a thing about getting into peoples' personal spaces.

Mark is very effeminate, but also refutes the idea that he's gay. We don't know if he's refusing to admit it for personal reasons (no one at The Job is going to judge at this point) or he just simply wants to will himself into being straight.

Anyway, he writes:

21. Everything & everyone.

Marie writes:

22. FRIENDS exchanging friendships for boyfriends.
23. Pain—Marie.
24. People who have nothing better to do than sit here & [the word "complain" is crossed out] **BITCH about their lives & situations (especially when they have no one to blame but themselves & deserve what they get. -- Mark.**

Under this is a series of entries written by Tabitha in a cursive script so thin it must have been written rushed and angrily:

25. Having people argue an issue for someone else. If that someone else has something to say, it should be said by that person to my face.
26. Not being able to read minds. (It would make my life a whole lot easier)
27. People who think I'm taking a boyfriend over a friendship, when in reality that person is the one pushing away a friendship.

Crossed out next to this one is: **(only it would never be said to my face, only to other**

She continues:

28. People openly discussing another's personal life without consent, then in turn that "other" is approached by people asking questions and viewing their own thoughts on something they only know one side of.
29. In reference to #24, why was 21 & 24 written then? Unless #24 is aimed at a specific person!!

Mark draws an arrow pointing to the word "was" in the above entry, with a note:

Tabitha writes English goodly.

Next to this, I write:

See #16.

Tabitha crosses out the "was," replaces it with a "were," and adds:

Sorry, Mark, I didn't mean to offend you.

Daniel writes:

30. Whiners.

In handwriting I cannot recognize is written:

31. Batman Reterns!
32. Stupidity and #6.

Irene writes:

33. People who misspell returns (i.e. #31)

Actually, it'd be "e.g.," but I don't write that.

Daniel writes:

34. The green person (he's Sigourney Weaver's dad)

Next to this I write:

What?

Irene continues:

35. The little man with the wooden leg that visits me in my bed at night. No! No! I will not give you the secret code of the Blue Iguanas! STOP HAUNTING ME!!!

36. Cop Watch, Cops, and any other stupid "real life" cop show. Who cares? Why not have a show about "real life" here at The Job!! Oh, joy!!

Under this, I write:

Yeah, but then I'd have to shoot everybody just to make it interesting, so cops would enter into it anyway.

Then, under this:

37. Friends dropping loads in my bed! You know who you are. -- Steve.

Irene writes:

38. Doodie heads that should be happy the "load" was cleaned up & he's (the doodie) not sleeping in it. So there weenie-breath.

Steve:

39. Being called a "doodie" and a "weenie-breath" in the same sentence.

Irene, under this:

If you look closely, there are *two* sentences involved.

She continues:

40. MONEY PROBLEMS & having my hormones all fucked up. 41. Eating disorders.

Me:

42. People telling me how I feel or felt. You're not me, so shut the fuck up.

Mary:

43. Trusting people who disappoint you!

Me:

44. Being disregarded and called defensive for being annoyed by it.

Steve:

45. Everything that annoys me but isn't on this list yet!
46. This Goddamn Christmas music, that I've only heard for the last 3 years.

Under this, I write:

(Tell me about it.)

Then:

47. Using birth control—Betty.

In huge magic marker I write:

48. Working on X-mas!

Which I had to do that year.

Someone else writes in magic marker:

49. Women!

Daniel writes:

50. Gravity.

Steve writes next to this:

(Gravity? How can you hate gravity? Gravity hold you to the ground so you don't go flying off into the cold void that surrounds this planet—Dr. Science)

Daniel then writes:

51. Infomercials.

Another worker writes:

52. Chicks...God Damn chicks!

Daniel:

53. 2541

To this day, I have no idea what "2541" means.

Maybe it's a marked-down "Les Miz" reference.

Daniel continues:

54. Scumbag rich kids trying to get over even though it's obvious that they've never even thought about getting a job and all their plentiful cash comes out of their slob parents' pockets...
55. Bitterness.

Irene writes:

56. People who use the word "chicks." We are WOMYN! Not chicks, tomatoes, foxes, bitches, witches, wenches, sluts, hoes, babes, or "Hey, Ladies!" Would you rather I called men pigs, dicks, pricks or penises? I thought not.

Under this, I write:

Chill out, chick.

Under this, she writes:

Yeah, okay, boy.

Under this I write:

That's "pig" to you.

Irene goes on:

57. Skinny/Rib-e-skeletal models everywhere! Jenny Craig saying "food has no power over you!" & every Tom, Dick, and Jack LaLaine telling me to get a Stairmaster – Fuck you! No wonder bulimia and other eating disorders are on the rise! Take a tip from Sir Mix-A-Lot! "Baby's Got Back!" Hooray for the Heiney!

Daniel:

58. Chicks with big butts.

Marie responds:

59. The fuckup who probably couldn't get a womyn at all, regardless of the size of her backside, so keep your god damn comments to your undersexed little self. JERK! --signed, The Job Womyn

Daniel:

60. The abuse I'm taking for writing #58, so here goes: I apologize sincerely from the bottom of my sneakers to all womyn were offended by my not so savory comment.

Underneath this, in big letters, and not in Daniel's handwriting, is written:

Daniel (the sexist pig)

Under this, I write:

That's "pyg."

Angered by someone feeling the need to identify Daniel directly, I continue:

60. The sexist, prejudiced, knee-jerk bullshit I gotta put up with. If you've got the right to tell me I should like big butts, I've got the right to say I don't. Got it? – The Job Myn.
61. Poor Daniel getting "outed" by a chyck.

My mistake here is the use of the term "outed." To me, this is a new term, and I think it means, simply, to reveal anything about someone without their permission.

Mary:

62. you have no respect 4 others because you have no respect for 4 yourself. it's obvious, to me, but then, maybe you're just blinded by your wit. get a hobby, all of you, the list is coming down soon.

Strong words from the person who put the list up in the first place.

I debate writing, **Oh, cheer up**, but think better of it.

Irene:

63. Yeah, okay, Andrew Dice Clay Jr. (60&61) I never said you should like big butts. I said Take A tip!

When Irene gets mad, she gets really semantic.

She continues.

Daniel brought the "outing" on himself – but unlike some people, he was joking – and I knew that. But sometimes it seems so hostile when you poke fun at the way we spell things. It seems cold.

And I'm not just saying this because we had a sloppy, drunken, one night stand and you didn't want to have a relationship afterwards, either.

And it wasn't poking fun at the way all women everywhere spell things.

It was just the spelling on *one* thing.

This isn't gonna make me popular, but I'm gonna step out here and say that I think that the "womyn" spelling is the dumbest, most pointless, and immature thing that I've ever heard of. It's the kind of thing that makes feminism look bad – it's the equivalent of "I'm gonna take my ball and go home."

It's going under the assumption that the word "woman" springs from the word "man," and that the word "woman" indicates that "without man, woman cannot exist."

"Woman," I believe (and if I'm wrong, please tell me – I am nothing if not willing to learn) comes from the word "womb," and both words come from the word "human."

And I don't think my opinion on this makes me misogynist, or anti-feminist.

It's just not *English.*

Don't start making up words on me and start telling me that I can't say the old ones!

Did you know that I had to be told that I couldn't refer to myself as an "oriental?"

Yeah.

A *white* chick had to tell me that.

An ex-girlfriend white chick.

I say I'm an Oriental, and she tells me, "Asian."

Gesundheit. What?

"It's Asian."

I didn't even know that was the preferred term until I started watching "In Living Color."

If we can't say "Oriental" anymore, what am I supposed to call those rugs?

Gook Mats?

Anyway, back to Irene's entry, where she's calling me "cold."

Is that what you want us to believe about you? Womyn aren't that bad you know. Sorry if you got trampled, but I've been hurt too – and I'm not bitter (not much).

Uh *huh*.

Anyway, I think we need to society's attitude towards women—

Oops.

—not just mens' attitudes toward them. "Can't we all just get along?"

I don't respond. What's the point?

Daniel:

64. Outed? Is that what that was? Look, people, I like you all but I don't need the aggravation of proving my hetness to my co-workers. Man, I'm glad this list is coming down.

And finally, Marie writes:

65. DAMN! That's all I have to say – DAMN!!!

I find the list in the trash can.

I take it out.

I notice as I pull it out, that Daniel has written something on the back of it.

It's common knowledge that the world is flat
And the meaning of life is printed
On Howard Johnson's paper placemats
It's 80 miles to the next bowling alley
And aren't you happy that we're living in a world
Of "real opportunities" and shiny Cadillacs.

I put the list in my bag and seriously contemplate quitting The Job.

The sign.

I hit the light on my watch.

It's around 11:30 pm.

Until I hit my watch light, there was no light in the boiler room, where I wait, in solid darkness.

I'm waiting to be the only person in the building.

I can hear the humming of the boiler.

I can hear that there are still some people here.

So I wait.

I pull out my walkman and listen to it as I sit there on the floor.

I think of my relationship with The Job.

To when I first started working here.

My first day of the job, I am introduced to Capp.

Capp is installing a light-up sign at one of the counters.

Stick-on letters on the sign spell: NEXT IN LINE.

Under this, an arrow, pointing directly under the sign, badly made from green electrical tape.

He flips a switch, and a tape loop plays in his voice:

"Will the next person in line please step to the end of the counter. Thank you for your business, and have a nice day."

The counter is less than ten feet long.

The sign and recorded message is clearly unnecessary.

But Capp seems very satisfied with his sign.

As Steve has pointed out, Capp has been at the job "longer than the existence of ice."

Capp collects autographed pictures of celebrities, and has them everywhere.

Capp also has a tendency to build things.

From his workstation, he has a monitor with a direct feed to the security cameras.

From time to time, we also find microphones hidden here and there, to listen to us. Whenever I can, I spray window cleaner into them.

It becomes a gag – if we need something from upstairs, we yell to the microphone how nice it would be if we had some paper towels, and boom, there Capp is, with paper towels.

Capp has the posture and gate of Lee Harvey Oswald.

Actual conversation between Capp and Daniel:

Capp: We out to the lake with my daughter.

Daniel: How is she?

Capp: She almost drowned.

What? I say, as Daniel tells me this story.

"She almost drowned," Daniel says. "She fell in."

What did Capp do?

"Nothing. He said, 'I can't swim, so what can I do?'"

So he just watched.

Eventually, she made it to shore.

Side one of my tape ends.

I get up, stretch, and listen.

The boiler is too loud to make anything out, really, so I go up the stairs.

It's still pitch dark, so I use my flashlight – but only for when I'm going up the stairs.

The building sounds like it could be empty.

I look at my watch.

Midnight.

I put an earpiece in my ear, and switch on my walkie-talkie.

Stanley? I say. Stanley?

Stanley's an old friend of mine.

He's the one who got me The Job.

When he was working there, the management was entirely different, and they had just had to lay off almost the entire staff.

Seems virtually everyone was ripping off The Job left and right.

Of course, so was Mr. P.

Earlier yesterday, I call Stanley up and tell him that I need his help – and that he's someone I can trust.

Stanley doesn't work at The Job any more. He quit long ago. But back when he quit, he'd grown to hate The Job more than I do, so I know he can appreciate what I'm about to suggest.

I tell him that what I'm about to suggest is slightly illegal, and if he doesn't want to hear any more he should tell me now.

He says, "Keep talking."

I'm walking through the storage room of The Job, still listening for people still at The Job and for Stanley to copy back.

"Rob," I hear Stanley say through the walkie-talkie.

Welcome to the party, pal, I tell him.

Stanley's job is to be both my lookout and getaway driver.

What I'm going to do will look pretty odd if anyone spots it, so it's Stanley's job to tell me if he can see me or the light from my flashlight from the outside.

He also has to tell me if he sees any cops around.

Where are you?

"I'm in the parking lot."

I tell him that Mr. P. drives a brown Oldsmobile, and read the plate number off a small note pad.

He tells me he doesn't see it.

I tell him that Pete might be working late, and that he drives a blue Dodge. I also tell him the plate number of that car, too.

Stanley suppresses a chuckle.

Hey, I tell him. I don't do things unless I know I can get away with them.

I walk out into the open.

I see the security cameras.

I know that they're not connected to anything except monitors, so I don't worry about it.

I don't have to wear gloves, because until two hours ago, I was an employee. There's no reason why my fingerprints wouldn't be all over the place.

The deciding factor in my quitting The Job had nothing to do with personal strife, or infighting with my co-workers, or even a desire to get a new life.

No, it was about money.

I had been working there for three years, and had never gotten a raise.

I had pulled extra hours when they needed me.

I had been honest.

Well, okay.

That's not totally true.

At one low point at The Job, I squirrel away some cash. I'm not proud of it, but things were so insane that I drop my standards of what I do and don't do and buy myself a new walkman with my stolen money. Because of Mr. P's own theft from the customers, my crime is easy to cover up.

That was after the first time I had asked for a raise.

They said they'd give it to me, and then I discovered that everyone at The Job was getting a raise, too – even the people who had just started there.

The reason?

Minimum wage had gone up. Everyone got a raise anyway.

About a year later, I'm in The Job's boiler room listening to my walkman bought with stolen money waiting for everyone in the building to leave.

But that's in the past. Right now, in the here and now, I decide to make my move.

I look around The Job.

Man, I think. I could do anything I wanted.

Right now.

I look at everything I could destroy.

Everything I could steal.

Everything I could set on fire.

And I'd probably get away with it.

No.

Best to stick with my plan.

So Betty tells me that Mr. P's not going to give me a raise.

"He just said that seniority's not a reason for a raise."

I point out that of the senior employees, I'm getting paid the least.

"It sucks, I know," she tells me.

It occurs to me that I'm really only one pair of tits away from being paid the same as everyone else.

The irony does not go unnoticed.

So the next week, I tell Mary that I'm putting in my two weeks.

"Okay," she says, cheerfully.

That's it.

"Okay." Like she's been looking forward to it.

Can't say I blame her.

I haven't been pleasant to be around, lately. I even tell Steve, who I've been best friends with since high school, that I've grown to hate everyone at The Job, even him.

What can you say to that?

"Thanks, pal," was all he said.

The Job starts to frustrate me.

I get in a big fight with Betty on the first night she has to handle the payroll.

Mary, one night, loses her temper with me about a schedule change.

All of this is starting to speak to why I didn't get that raise.

But when I decide to quit, this is a big decision for me.

This is all my friends.

My whole social life.

Pretty much, my whole world for the past three years.

I'm quitting all of this, and no one seems to care.

Two weeks later, and after midnight, I turn my backpack around so that I'm wearing it backwards. This is so I can reach my tools without having to set them down anywhere.

I pull a large stool off from on top of the counter, and get on top of it.

Can you see me? I ask Stanley.

"I can't see shit in there," he tells me.

Good.

I pull out a screwdriver and a pair of pliers.

I go to work.

The two weeks goes by pretty much without event.

My last day, I get a little testy with a couple of customers, and make it pretty clear I don't want to be fucked with.

This stops no one from fucking with me, but I stop caring. My whole day is spent focusing on when my day is over.

And, the work day ends.

And I head to the boiler room.

Hours later, I tell Stanley, get to the back door. I got it.

"You got it? Already?"

Yeah. It was easier than I thought. Get ready, I'm coming out hard.

I walk through the back room.

Months earlier, some of us had to clean up this back area.

I move some boxes and see this door back there.

It only has this slide-lock on it, and that's it. When no one's looking I check to see if it opens.

It not only opens, but it was apparently put here before they installed the security system, since I don't hear any alarms.

I close the door, slide the lock, and file this piece of information away.

Months later, I slide open the lock, slam the door behind me, and jump into Stanley's car.

"Did you get the thing?"

I show it to him. He laughs.

"Wanna go to the diner?"

Sure, I say.

I'm told, some years later, after I have already settled in in my little dorm room in Madison, that the conversation the next day went this way:

"Wow, I completely expected Rob to go nuts on his last day, but actually it was pretty uneventful," Lester says.

"Yeah," Steve says, leaning against the counter, "considering he always used to talk about burning the place down."

"Come on," Irene says, "What damage would he really do?"

And all three of them look at the ceiling, at a small hole with some wires sticking out of it.

It is a few months later, and I am at Chicago O'Hare airport, waiting for my connecting flight to Madison.

I've got at least an hour before I have to be anywhere, so I'm bored.

I reach in my bag and pull out my camera.

Then I pull out something else and hold it up.

I snap a picture.

It's a picture of the "Welcome To Chicago O'Hare Airport" sign, and next to it, I'm holding up another sign.

This sign says, "NEXT IN LINE," with a green arrow badly made from electrical tape, and has wires sticking out of it.

I put the sign away and wait for the plane.

The plane that takes me away.

To my new home.

Epilogue.

Some years later.

Betsy isn't my wife yet, but we've been going out for a while.

We decide to visit New Jersey and stay at my mom's house.

Not much big happens.

Some things, in no particular order:

...Everyone pressures me to move back to Montclair, including my
Uncle Lawrence (who has always reminded me of the Jack Nicholson
character in "Prizzi's Honor").

I tell him that I can't just leave Wisconsin. I have roots.

"Roots?" he says, looking at Betsy, "Whaddayoumean 'roots?'"

I shrug. Suddenly I'm fifteen again, and not in a good way.

And I'd warned Betsy that my relatives might pull this.

...Lester picks Betsy and I up in the morning, and we go to a diner.

On the way there, Lester tries, none-too-subtly, to get my goat by
bringing up that he's just recently slept with Teri, my first ex-
girlfriend.

He's been basically kind of throwing this shit in my face since he went
out with her, and this was years ago. Before we even started working
at The Job.

But this is the first time he's able to do it in front of Betsy.

Betsy, who can barely contain her laughter as I say to Lester:

You slept with Teri again? What are you, still in high school?

"Well, you know, I had to..."

Well, yeah, apparently. It just amazes me that you think it's cool. Jesus
Christ, man, get out of your parents' basement and MEET PEOPLE,
you 'stalgia-fuckin' dumbass.

Take that, asshole, I think, as Betsy smiles at me.

I'd warned her that Lester might pull this.

...We go to Steve's house, and meet up with him and his wife.

Steve turns to me and says "Smoke and throw?"

Although I haven't seen Steve in a few years, I instinctively know that this means "Shall we step outside and smoke cigarettes while throwing knives at a cardboard target?"

I say, Smoke and throw, baby.

Steve has a couple of throwing stars as well, and those are the only things I'm able to hit the target with.

He also has something that he calls "The Spike O' Doom," which is basically a foot and a half long industrial screw, and he's filed both ends down into sharp points.

Steve throws this thing with apparently no grace or style, but he always is able to hit dead center.

He runs, joyfully to the target, pulling out the Spike O' Doom, and measuring the penetration level with his thumb.

"Four inches! OOOOoooooOOOOOOOHH!!!"

Betsy laughs.

I'd warned her we might do this.

...We go to another diner.

There, we run into Marie and Tabitha.

Everyone is happy to see each other, and we all hug.

Everyone looks pretty much the same, although it's years later.

They tell me that they're both teachers, now.

Someone mentions that Peter got married.

No one knows what happened to Mary or Lara.

No one thinks to ask either.

Lara just up and disappeared, and Mary left under a cloud of pathos. Or something.

It's all very surreal.

The crew from The Job, out for one last diner hop.

And I'd warned Betsy that this might happen.

...my mom's cat, Vito "The Cat" Manelli, who's a huge Maine Coon cat, decides that Betsy is the only human that he likes.

Betsy's very allergic.

Vito likes to sit in her lap.

And Vito doesn't like to sit in anybody's lap.

And she'd warned me that Vito might do this.

Animals only seem to gravitate to the people who are allergic to them, because they're the only people not interested in petting them.

...As a result of Betsy getting downright sick from her allergies, the last night in New Jersey is spent at my mom's house, instead of us going out.

So we decide that it's time for a poker party.

And damn near everybody shows up.

Daniel shows up, and we catch up.

Steve's there again.

My cousin Takeo shows up. He lives down the street.

My mom is even joining in the game.

Every few minutes the doorbell rings, and it's friends of mine, from the old days.

See, I don't come out to New Jersey that often.

I'm not sure why.

Well, these days, it's more of a financial thing, but there's other reasons.

This time, when I'm out, I realize that the place isn't really my home.

In private, Betsy and I talk about it.

I tell her that I wouldn't want to live out here again. I'd fall into the same patterns and never get anything done.

"What patterns?"

Shit job, do nothing, go to the diner. That'd be all my life would be.

"So break the pattern."

But I wouldn't. I'd fall in and I'd stay in.

"Maybe that's not such a bad thing. Your friends seem to mean a lot to you. And you seem to mean a lot to them. Look at how many people showed up to poker night!"

Meanwhile, in the past, at poker night, the doorbell rings.

It's Irene.

She's dating Lester's brother now, I find out.

The night goes on without incident.

Irene meets Betsy.

Betsy already knows about Irene.

I didn't warn her about this, but she expected something like this sooner or later.

Betsy goes to bed (her allergies are finally taking their toll), and people go home. I offer to ride with Daniel as he takes Irene home.

We ride to Irene's apartment, which I find out is Steve's old apartment.

This is all very surreal, I say.

"Brings back memories," Irene says.

Yeah, I say.

"Fun memories," Irene says, "Like your birthday party."

About which, I say, the less said the better.

Daniel looks over.

Irene won't let it go. She's enjoying making me squirm.

Again.

One last time, as it were, for the road.

Okay, fine, I wasn't going to talk about this, I was going to let it go without mention, but okay, since you want to talk about it...

"It wasn't that big a deal."

I was just pissed at everyone else, at the time. And...

She's starting to giggle.

"It was fun," she says.

And I can't tell whether she's just bringing it up to put me on the spot or...

No, wait, I *can* tell she's just bringing it up to put me on the spot.

Mercifully, we reach Irene's apartment.

Well, good to see you again.

"Yeah," Irene says, "are you coming out here again anytime soon?"

I don't know, I say.

But what I think is, yeah, like I'm telling *you.*

"Well, goodbye," Irene says.

I hug her good bye.

I let go of the hug.

She doesn't.

She kisses my cheek, and whispers in my ear:

"It was *good.*"

I look at her as she lets me go.

Well, *yeah.*

She heads up to her apartment, giggling.

I get back into Daniel's van, and we talk music as he takes me home.

Jesus.

Good*night*, Irene.

THE END